Technician Units 8 & 9

MANAGING PERFORMANCE AND CONTROLLING RESOURCES

For assessments in December 2003
and June 2004

Assessment Kit

In this May 2003 first edition

- For assessments under the new standards
- The June and December 2002 Exams
- The AAT's Specimen Exams are included as 'mocks' to attempt under 'exam conditions'

FOR 2003 AND 2004 ASSESSMENTS

PROFESSIONAL EDUCATION

First edition May 2003

ISBN 0 7517 1141 1

British Library Cataloguing-in-Publication Data
A catalogue record for this book
is available from the British Library

Published by

BPP Professional Education
Aldine House, Aldine Place
London W12 8AW

www.bpp.com

Printed in Great Britain by WM Print
Frederick Street
Walsall
West Midlands
WS2 9NE

We are grateful to the Lead Body for Accounting for
permission to reproduce extracts from the Standards
of Competence for Accounting, and to the AAT for
permission to reproduce extracts from the mapping
and Guidance Notes.

Contents

Introduction

How to use this Assessment Kit– Unit 8 and Unit 9 Standards of competence – Exam Based Assessment technique – Assessment strategy

Introduction

How to use this Assessment Kit

Aims of this Assessment Kit

To provide the knowledge and practice to help you succeed in the assessments for Technician Unit 8 *Contributing to the Management of Performance and the Enhancement of Value* and Unit 9 *Contributing to the Planning and Control of Resources.*

To pass the assessment successfully you need a thorough understanding in all areas covered by the standards of competence.

To tie in with the other components of the BPP Effective Study Package to ensure you have the best possible chance of success.

Interactive Text

This covers all you need to know for the assessment for Unit 8 *Contributing to the Management of Performance and the Enhancement of Value* and Unit 9 *Contributing to the Planning and Control of Resources.* Numerous activities throughout the text help you practise what you have just learnt.

Assessment Kit

When you have understood and practised the material in the Interactive Text, you will have the knowledge and experience to tackle the Assessment Kit for Unit 8 *Contributing to the Management of Performance and the Enhancement of Value* and Unit 9 *Contributing to the Planning and Control of Resources*, It contains past exams including the June and December 2002 exams and the AAT's Specimen Exam.

Passcards

These short memorable notes, focused on key topics for Units 8 and 9, are designed to remind you of what the Interactive Text has taught you.

Recommended approach to this Assessment Kit

(a)   To achieve competence in Units 8 and 9 (and all the other units), you need to be able to do everything specified by the standards. Study the text very carefully and do not skip any of it.

(b)   Learning is an **active** process. Do **all** the activities as you work through the text so you can be sure you really understand what you have read.

(c)   After you have covered the material in the Interactive Text, work through the **Assessment Kit.**

(d)   Try the **Practice Activities**. These are linked into each chapter of the interactive text, and are designed to reinforce your learning and consolidate the practice that you have had doing the activities in the Interactive Text.

(e)   Next do the **Full Assessments**. They are designed to cover the areas you might see when you do an exam.

(f)   Finally, try the AAT's **Specimen Exam** under 'exam conditions'.

Remember this is a **practical** course.

(a)   Try to relate the material to your experience in the workplace or any other work experience you may have had.

(b)   Try to make as many links as you can to your study of the other Units at this level.

Lecturers' Resource Pack activities

At the back of this knit we have included a number of chapter linked activities without answers. We have also included one full assessment for each of Units 8 and 9 without answers. The answers for this section are in the BPP Lecturers' Resource Pack for these Units.

v

Units 8 and 9 Standards of competence

The structure of the Standards for Unit 8 and Unit 9

The Units commence with statements of the **knowledge and understanding** which underpin competence in the Units' elements.

The Units of Competence are then divided into **elements of competence** describing activities which the individual should be able to perform.

Each element includes:

    (a)   A set of **performance criteria.** This defines what constitutes competent performance.

    (b)   A **range statement.** This defines the situations, contexts, methods etc in which competence should be displayed.

The elements of competence for Unit 8 *Contributing to the Management of Performance and the Enhancement of Value* and Unit 9 *Contributing to the Planning and Control of Resources* are set out below. Knowledge and understanding required for each unit are listed first, followed by the performance criteria and range statements for each element. Performance criteria are cross-referenced below to chapters in this Units 8 and 9 *Managing Performance and Controlling Resources* Interactive Text.

Unit 8: Contributing to the Management of Performance and the Enhancement of Value

Unit commentary

This unit is about collecting, analysing and interpreting information of help to managers in controlling costs and improving the performance of operations. There are two elements.

The first element focuses on the identification and analysis of costs that may be of help to managers. You will have to monitor and analyse costs against trends, standards and organisational needs, and explain any difference between actual and planned or expected costs. In addition, you will have to demonstrate your understanding of forecasting techniques as an aid to cost analysis and control.

The second element is concerned with monitoring the performance of an organisation or parts of an organisation and making recommendations that will enhance the organisation's value. In this element you have to identify and calculate performance indicators, monitor the performance of part or all of the organisation and make proposals that will enhance the value of the organisation.

You will have to obtain information from a variety of internal and external sources and monitor costs, performance indicators and movements in prices over an appropriate timescale. You will also be required to use the information to prepare and present management reports. As well as being familiar with manually developing information, you will also need to know how computer spreadsheets can assist you in preparing cost and performance information.

Knowledge and understanding

The business environment

1   External sources of information on costs and prices: government statistics, trade associations, financial press, quotations, price lists (Elements 8.1 and 8.2)

2   General economic environment (Elements 8.1 and 8.2)

Accounting techniques

3   Basic statistical methods: index numbers; sampling techniques; time series analysis (moving averages, linear regression and seasonal trends) (Element 8.1)

4   Use of relevant computer packages (Elements 8.1 and 8.2)

5   Methods of presenting information in graphical, diagrammatic and tabular form (Element 8.1)

6   Performance indicators: efficiency, effectiveness, productivity; balanced scorecard, benchmarking; unit costs; control ratios (efficiency, capacity and activity), scenario planning ('what-if' analysis) (Element 8.2)

7   Standard costing (Element 8.1)

Accounting principles and theory

8   Marginal and absorption costing: cost recording, cost reporting, cost behaviour (Elements 8.1 and 8.2)

9   Cost management: life cycle costing; target costing (including value engineering); activity based costing; principles of Total Quality Management (including cost of quality) (Element 8.2)

10   The use and limitation of published statistics (Element 8.1)

11   Effect of accounting controls on behaviour of managers and other employees (Elements 8.1 and 8.2)

The organisation

12   How the accounting systems of an organisation are affected by its organisational structure, its administrative systems and procedures and the nature of its business transactions (Elements 8.1 and 8.2)

13   The organisation's external environment and specific external costs (Element 8.1)

14   The contribution of functional specialists in an organisation (e.g. marketing, design, engineering, quality control, etc.) to cost reduction and value enhancement (Element 8.2)

Element 8.1   Collect, analyse and disseminate information about costs

Performance criteria

A   Identify valid, relevant **information** from internal and external sources

B   Monitor and analyse on a regular basis current and forecast trends in prices and market conditions

C   Compare trends with previous experience and identify potential implications

D   Compare standard costs with actual costs and analyse any **variances**

E   Analyse the effect of organisational accounting policies on reported costs

F   Consult relevant staff in the organisation about the analysis of trends and variances

G   Present reports to management that **summarise data**, present information using appropriate **methods** and highlight significant trends

Range statement

Information:
- Movements in prices charged by suppliers, competitors, and providers of services
- General price changes

Methods of summarising data:
- Time series (moving averages, linear regression, seasonal variations)
- Index numbers and sampling

Methods of presenting information in reports:
- Written analysis and explanation
- Tables
- Diagrams

Variance analysis:
- Material price and usage variances
- Labour rate and efficiency variances
- Fixed overhead expenditure, volume, capacity and efficiency variances
- Subdivision of variances

The build up of costs:
- Absorption costing
- Marginal costing
- Activity-based costing

Element 8.2   Monitor performance and make recommendations to enhance value

Performance criteria

A   Analyse routine cost reports, compare them with other sources of information and identify any implications

B   Prepare and monitor relevant **performance indicators**, interpret the results, identify potential improvements and estimate the value of potential improvements

C   Consult relevant specialists and assist in identifying ways to reduce costs and enhance value

D   Prepare exception reports to identify matters which require further investigation

E   Make specific **recommendations** to management in a clear and appropriate form

Range statement

Performance indicators to measure:
- Financial, customer, internal business, and learning and growth perspectives
- Efficiency, effectiveness and productivity
- Unit costs; resource utilisation
- Profitability
- Quality of service
- Cost of quality

Recommendations:
- Efficiencies
- Modifications to work processes
- Benchmarking

Unit 9 Contributing to the Planning and Control of Resources

Unit commentary

This unit focuses on the planning and control of resources in an organisation. There are three elements.

In the first element, you have to develop forecasts of demand, turnover, resources to be consumed and their cost.

The second element requires you to use forecasts to prepare draft budgets for income and expenditure. This may involve you changing your initial budget to take account of revised information about factors that limit the operations of the organisation.

The final element relates to part of the control function in organisations. You will be required to compare the actual performance of all or part of an organisation against what was planned to happen and advise managers of possible reasons for any difference.

You will need to ensure all relevant data has been included in your budgets and that all relevant staff have been consulted. In addition, you will need to ensure that transactions have been accurately recorded and appropriate accounting methods have been used for both the planning and monitoring of budgets. As well as being familiar with manually developing forecasts and budgets, you will also need to know how computer spreadsheets can help you in their development.

Knowledge and understanding

The business environment

1 External sources of information on costs, prices, demand and availability of resources (Elements 9.1, 9.2 and 9.3)

2 General economic environment (Elements 9.1, 9.2 and 9.3)

Accounting techniques

3 Basic statistical methods: time series (moving averages, linear regression and seasonal variations), sampling techniques; index numbers (Element 9.1)

4 Use of relevant computer packages (Elements 9.1, 9.2 and 9.3)

5 Development of production, resource and revenue budgets from forecast sales data

6 Co-ordination of the budget system (Elements 9.2 and 9.3)

7 The effect of capacity constraints, other production constraints and sales constraints on budgets; limiting (key or budget) factor (Elements 9.2 and 9.3)

8 Budgets for control: flexible budgets, marginal costing

9 The effect of budgetary systems on the behaviour and motivation of managers and other employees (Element 9.2)

10 Analysing the significance of budget variances and possible responses required by managers (Element 9.3)

11 Presentation of budget data in a form that satisfies the differing needs of budget holders

Accounting principles and theory

12 Marginal and absorption costing: cost recording, cost reporting, cost behaviour (Elements 9.2 and 9.3)

13 Uses of budgetary control: planning, co-ordinating, authorising, cost control (Elements 9.1, 9.2 and 9.3)

14 Relationship between budgets, forecasts and planning and product-life cycles (Elements 9.1, 9.2 and 9.3)

15 Different types of budgets: budgets for income and expenditure; resource budgets (production, material, labour and other resource budgets); capital budgets (Elements 9.2 and 9.3)

The organisation

16 How the accounting systems of an organisation are affected by its organisational structure, its administrative systems and procedures and the nature of its business transactions (Elements 9.1, 9.2 and 9.3)

17 The structure of the organisation and its responsibility centres and an understanding of the inter-relationships between departments and functions is required (Elements 9.1, 9.2 and 9.3)

18 Responsibility centres: expense centres; profit centres; investment centres (Element 9.3)

Element 9.1   Prepare forecasts of income and expenditure

Performance criteria

A   Identify relevant **data** for projecting **forecasts** from internal and external sources

B   Communicate with relevant individuals and give them the opportunity to raise queries and to clarify forecasts

C   Prepare forecasts in a clear format with explanations of assumptions, **projections** and adjustments

D   Review and revise the validity of forecasts in the light of any significant anticipated changes

Range statement

Data:
- Accounting information
- Wage and salary information
- Information about suppliers and availability of inputs
- Information about customers and markets
- General economic information

Forecasts:
- Income
- Expenditure

Projections:
- Trends
- Seasonal variations
- Market research

Element 9.2   Prepare draft budget proposals

Performance criteria

A   Present to management draft **budget** proposals in a clear and appropriate format and on schedule

B   Verify that draft budget proposals are consistent with organisational objectives and include all relevant **data** and assumptions

C   Break down budgets into periods appropriate to the organisation

D   Communicate with budget holders in a manner which maintains goodwill and ensure budget proposals are agreed with budget holders

Range statement

Types of budgets:
- Budgets for income and expenditure
- Resource budgets (production budget, material budget, labour budget ,fixed overhead budget)
- Capital budgets

Data:
- Accounting information
- Wage and salary information
- Market information
- General economic information
- Strategic plans

Element 9.3   Monitor the performance of responsibility centres against budgets

Performance criteria

A   Check and reconcile **budget** figures on an ongoing basis

B   Correctly code and allocate actual cost and revenue data to **responsibility centres**

C   Clearly and correctly identify **variances** and prepare relevant reports for management

D   Discuss with budget holders and other managers any significant variances and help managers take remedial action

Range statement

Types of budgets:
Budget for income and expenditure
Resource budget
Fixed and flexible budgets

Responsibility centres:
Expense centres
Profit centres

Variances:
Actual
Potential

Exam Based Assessment technique

Completing exam based assessments successfully at this level is half about having the knowledge and half about doing yourself full justice on the day. You must have the right **technique.**

The day of the exam based assessment

1   Set at least one **alarm** (or get an alarm call) for a morning exam.

2   Have **something to eat** but beware of eating too much; you may feel sleepy if your system us digesting a large meal.

3   Allow plenty of **time to get to where you are sitting the exam**; have your route worked out in advance and listen to news bulletins to check for potential travel problems.

4   **Don't forget** pens, pencils, rulers and erasers.

5   Put **new batteries** into your calculator and take a spare set (or a spare calculator).

6   **Avoid discussion** about the exam assessment with other candidates outside the venue.

Technique in the Exam Based Assessment

1   **Read the instructions (the 'rubric') on the front of the assessment carefully**.

Check that the format hasn't changed. It is surprising how often assessors' reports remark on the number of candidates who do not attempt all the tasks.

2   **Read the paper twice**

Read through the paper twice – don't forget that you are given 15 minutes' reading time. Check carefully that you have got the right end of the stick before putting pen to paper. Use your 15 minutes reading time wisely. **From June 2003**, reading time can only be used for **reading**. You cannot make notes of use a calculator during those 15 minutes.

3   **Check the time allocation for each section of the exam**

Time allocations are given for each section of the exam. When the time for the section is up you should go on to the next exam.

4   **Read the task carefully and plan your answer**

Read through the task again very carefully when you come to answer it. Plan your answer to ensure that you **keep to the point**. Two minutes of planning plus eight minutes of writing is virtually certain to produce a better answer than ten minutes of writing. Planning will also help you answer the assessment efficiently, for example by identifying workings that can be used for more than one task.

5   **Produce relevant answers**

Particularly with written answers, make sure you **answer what has been set**, and not what you would have preferred to have been set. Do not, for example, answer a question of **why** something is done with an explanation of **how** it is done.

6   **Work your way steadily through the exam**

Don't get bogged down in one task. If you are having problems with something, the chances arfe that everyone else is too.

7   **Produce an answer in the correct format**

The assessor will state **in the requirements** the format which should be used, for example in a report or a memo.

8   **Do what the assessor wants**

You should ask yourself what the assessor is expecting in an answer; many tasks will demand a combination of technical knowledge and business common sense. Be careful if you are required to give a decision or make a recommendation; you cannot just list the criteria you will use, but you will also have tpo say whether those criteria have been fulfilled.

9   **Lay out your numerical computations and use working correctly**

Make sure the layout is in a style the assessor likes.

Show all your **workings** clearly and explain what they mean. Cross reference then to your answer. This will help the assessor to follow your method (this is of particular importance where there may be several possible answers)

10   **Present a tidy paper**

You are a professional, and it should show in the **presentation of your work**. You should make sure that you write legibly, label diagrams clearly and lay out your work neatly.

11   **Stay until the end of the exam**

Use any spare time **checking and rechecking** your script. Check that you have answered all the requirements of the task and that you have clearly labelled your work. Consider also whether your answer appears reasonable ion the light of the information given in the question.

12   **Don't worry if you feel you have performed badly in the exam**

It more than likely that other candidates will have found the assessment difficult too. As soon as you get up to leave the venue, **forget** that assessment and think about the next – or, if it is the last one, celebrate!

13   **Don't discuss an exam with the other candidates**

This is particularly the case if you **still have other exams to sit**. Even if you have finished, you should put it out of your mind until the day of the results. Forget about the exams and relax.

Assessment strategy

Unit 8 and Unit 9 are assessed by **exam based testing** only.

An exam-based assessment is a means of collecting evidence that you have the **essential knowledge and understanding** which underpins competence. It is also a means of collecting evidence across the **range of contexts** for the standards, and of your ability to transfer skills, knowledge and understanding to different situations. Thus, although exam-based assessments contain practical tests linked to the performance criteria, they also focus on the underpinning knowledge and understanding. You should in addition expect each exam-based assessment to contain tasks taken from across a broad range of the standards.

Because exam-based assessments aim to cover the breadth of Units 8 and 9, an area of competence may be **assessed in one way in one assessment** and a **different way in a later one**. This has two main implications.

- There is little point in memorising the answers to previous assessment tasks.
- You need to be able to apply your knowledge and understanding in a variety of different situations.

Tasks will assess your ability to **apply basic management accounting techniques** in simple organisational situations and to **make recommendations** to management in a clear and appropriate form.

Unit 8 Contributing to the Management of Performance and the Enhancement of Value

Unit 8 will be assessed using an unseen examination that is set and marked by the AAT. The examination will be divided into two sections. It will last for three hours (plus 15 minutes' reading time) and will test a broad range of the performance criteria from the Standards.

Normally, there will be two tasks in each section and candidates have to reach a minimum standard in each section to be assessed as competent in the whole unit. Sometimes, however, there may be more than two tasks per section. This does not mean more work. Extra tasks will only be asked where they make the tasks clearer or where it reduces the amount of data to be considered before answering.

Each task will normally be a mini case study. The candidate will be given a realistic workplace-type problem and asked to solve it. Sometimes the techniques to apply will be obvious – as when candidates are asked to calculate standard costing variances. At other times, candidates may have to identify the technique or knowledge and understanding for themselves.

The two sections will **not** be the same as the two elements because some performance criteria can either be:

- logically assessed in either section; or
- assessed together because they are closely connected.

Generally, the first section will be concerned with the management of costs, the second with the wider aspects of management of performance and enhancement of value. An indicative guide to how the knowledge and understanding of Unit 8 relates to the two sections is shown below. Candidates must, however, remember that this is indicative only. It is neither exhaustive nor exclusive.

Section 1

- Standard costing

Section 2

- Performance indicators: efficiency, effectiveness, productivity; balanced scorecard, benchmarking; unit costs; control ratios (efficiency, capacity and activity), scenario planning ('what-if' analysis)

Either section

- External sources of information on costs and prices: government statistics, trade associations, financial press, quotations, price lists.

- General economic environment.

- Basic statistical methods: index numbers; sampling techniques; time series analysis (moving averages, linear regression and seasonal trends).

- Use of relevant computer packages.

- Methods of presenting information in graphical, diagrammatic and tabular form.

- Marginal and absorption costing: cost recording, cost reporting, cost behaviour.

- Cost management: life cycle costing; target costing (including value engineering); activity based costing; principles of Total Quality Management (including cost of quality).

- The use and limitation of published statistics.

- Effect of accounting controls on behaviour of managers and other employees.

- How the accounting systems of an organisation are affected by its organisational structure, its administrative systems and procedures and the nature of its business transactions.

- The organisation's external environment and specific external costs.

- The contribution of functional specialists in an organisation (e.g. marketing, design, engineering, quality control, etc.) to cost reduction and value enhancement.

Unit 9 Contributing to the Planning and Control of Resources

Unit 9 will be assessed using an unseen examination that is set and marked by the AAT. The examination will be divided into two sections. It will last for three hours (plus 15 minutes' reading time) and will test a broad range of the performance criteria from the Standards.

Normally, there will be two tasks in each section and candidates have to reach a minimum standard in each section to be assessed as competent in the whole unit. Sometimes, however, there may be more than two tasks per section. This does not mean more work. Extra tasks will only be asked where they make the tasks clearer or where it reduces the amount of data to be considered before answering a task.

Each task will normally be a mini case study. The candidate will be given a realistic workplace-type problem and asked to solve it. Sometimes the techniques to apply will be obvious – as when candidates are asked to prepare a flexible budgeting statement . At other times, the candidate may have to identify the technique or knowledge and understanding themselves.

The two sections will **not** directly relate to the three elements because some performance criteria can either be:

- logically assessed in either section; or
- assessed together because they are closely connected.

Generally, the first section will be concerned with planning budgets, the second with the control of resources. A guide to how the knowledge and understanding of Unit 9 relates to the two sections is shown below. Candidates must, however, remember that this is indicative only. It is neither exhaustive nor exclusive.

Section 1

- Relationships between budgets, forecasts and planning and product-life cycles.
- Basic statistical methods: time series (moving averages, linear regression and seasonal variations), sampling techniques; index numbers.
- Development of production, resource and revenue budgets from forecast sales data.
- Co-ordination of the budget system.
- The effect of capacity constraints, other production constraints and sales constraints on budgets; limiting (key or budget) factor.
- Different types of budgets: budgets for income and expenditure ; resource budgets (production, material, labour and other resource budgets); capital budgets.

Section 2

- Budgets for control: flexible budgets, marginal costing.
- Analysing the significance of budget variances and possible responses required by managers.
- The effect of budgetary systems on the behaviour and motivation of managers and other employees.
- Responsibility centres: expense centres; profit centres; investment centres.

Either section

- External sources of information on costs, prices, demand and availability of resources.
- General economic environment.
- Use of relevant computer packages.
- Presentation of budget data in a form that satisfies the differing needs of budget holders.
- Marginal and absorption costing: cost recording, cost reporting, cost behaviour.
- Uses of budgetary control: planning, co-ordinating, authorising, cost control.
- How the accounting systems of an organisation are affected by its organisational structure, its administrative systems and procedures and the nature of its business transactions.
- The structure of the organisation and its responsibility centres and an understanding of the inter-relationships between departments and functions.

Practice
Activities

Practice activities are short activities directly related to the actual content of Parts A to E of the BPP Interactive Text for Units 8 and 9.

PROFESSIONAL EDUCATION

chapters 1 and 2

Introduction/Behaviour, recording and reporting of costs

Activity checklist

This checklist shows which activities cover the performance criteria, range statements and knowledge and understanding points dealt with in Chapters 1 and 2 of the BPP *Managing Costs and Controlling Resources* Interactive Text.

Performance criteria		Activities
8.1.E	Analyse the effect of organisational accounting policies on reported costs	2, 3, 38, 39
8.2.B	Prepare and monitor relevant performance indicators, interpret the results and identify potential improvements and estimate the value of potential improvements	1

Range statement		
8.1	The build up of costs: absorption costing; marginal costing	2, 3, 38, 39
8.2	Performance indicators to measure: efficiency, effectiveness and productivity	1

Knowledge and understanding

Unit 8 Accounting principles and theory

6	Performance indicators: efficiency, effectiveness; productivity	1
8	Marginal and absorption costing: cost recording, cost reporting, cost behaviour	2, 3, 38, 39

Unit 9 Accounting principles and theory

12	Marginal and absorption costing: cost recording, cost reporting, cost behaviour	2, 3, 38, 39

1 Productivity, efficiency, effectiveness

Match the terms, definitions and measures below.

Terms
Productivity
Efficiency
Effectiveness

Definitions
The relationship between output and an organisation's objectives
The relationship between output (quantity produced) and input (resources put in)
The relationship between the value generated by output and input

Measures
Output per employee
Output per £ of fixed assets
Sales volume compared with budgeted market share (units)
Profit margin
Number of hospital patients treated within six months of going on a waiting list

2 Absorption costing and marginal costing

To help decision making during budget preparation, your supervisor has prepared the following estimates of sales revenue and cost behaviour for a one-year period, relating to one of your organisation's products.

Activity	60%	100%
Sales and production (thousands of units)	36	60
	£'000	£'000
Sales	432	720
Production costs		
Variable and fixed	366	510
Sales, distribution and administration costs		
Variable and fixed	126	150

The normal level of activity for the current year is 60,000 units, and fixed costs are incurred evenly throughout the year.

There were no stocks of the product at the start of the quarter, in which 16,500 units were made and 13,500 units were sold. Actual fixed costs were the same as budgeted.

Tasks

(a)   Calculate the following using absorption costing.

(i)   The amount of fixed production costs absorbed by the product
(ii)   The over/under absorption of fixed product costs
(iii)   The profit for the quarter

(b)   Calculate the net profit or loss for the quarter using marginal costing.

You may assume that sales revenue and variable costs per unit are as budgeted.

3 Absorption costing and marginal costing again

(a)   A company absorbs overheads on a machine hour basis. Actual machine hours were 22,435, actual overheads were £496,500 and there was over absorption of overheads of £64,375.

Task

Calculate the overhead absorption rate to the nearest £.

(b)   When opening stocks were 8,500 litres and closing stocks were 6,750 litres, a firm had a profit of £27,400 using marginal costing.

Task

Assuming the fixed overhead absorption rate was £2 per litre, calculate the profit using absorption costing.

(c)   Actual overheads were £496,980 and actual machine hours were 16,566. Budgeted overheads were £475,200.

Task

Based on the data above and assuming that the budgeted overhead absorption rate was £32 per hour, calculate the budgeted number of machine hours (to the nearest hour).

> The behaviour, recording and reporting of costs is also covered in activities 38 and 39.

chapter 3

Collecting data

Activity checklist

This checklist shows which activities cover the performance criteria, range statements and knowledge and understanding points dealt with in Chapter 3 of the BPP *Managing Costs and Controlling Resources* Interactive Text.

Performance criteria		Activities
8.1A	Identify valid, relevant information from internal and external sources	4, 5, 10
9.1A	Identify relevant data for projecting forecasts from internal and external sources	4, 5, 10
Range statement		
8.1	Methods of summarising data: sampling	4, 10, 28
9.1	Data: accounting information; wage and salary information; information about suppliers and availability of inputs; information about customers and markets; general economic information	5, 10
Knowledge and understanding		
Unit 8 Accounting techniques		
3	Basic statistical methods: sampling techniques	4, 10, 28
Unit 9 The business environment		
1	External sources of information on costs, prices, demand and availability of resources	4, 5, 10
Unit 9 Accounting techniques		
3	Basic statistical methods: sampling techniques	4, 10, 28

4 Data collection (35 mins)

The adult population of your organisation's Northern sales territory is 500,000. The territory is divided into a number of regions as follows.

Region	Adult population '000
Northia	90
Wester	10
Southam	140
Eastis	40
Midshire	120
Centrasia	100

In order to provide sales forecasting information, it has been decided to carry out a survey based on a 2% sample of the Northern sales territory's population.

Tasks

(a)   Describe how the sampling should be organised if the following methods are to be employed.

   (i)   Simple random
   (ii)   Cluster
   (iii)   Stratified
   (iv)   Systematic

(b)   Discuss which of these methods would be likely to give the most representative sample and why. Your answer should include discussion of the disadvantages of the other methods.

5 Surveys (30 mins)

One of the ways of conducting surveys is by the use of questionnaires.

Task

Discuss the advantages and disadvantages of conducting surveys by questionnaire using each of the following methods.

(a)   Personal interview
(b)   Telephone
(c)   Postal

Data collection is also covered in activities 10 and 28.

---

chapter 4

Analysing data

Activity checklist

This checklist shows which activities cover the performance criteria, range statement s and knowledge and understanding points dealt with in Chapter 4 of the BPP *Managing Costs and Controlling Resources* Interactive Text.

Performance criteria	Activities
8.1G Present reports to management that summarise data, present information using appropriate methods and highlight significant trends	8, 10, 13, 16, 48

Range statement	
8.1 Methods of summarising data: index numbers	6, 13, 16-19, 26, 42, 43
8.1 Methods of presenting information in reports: written analysis and explanation; tables; diagrams	8, 10, 13, 16, 48

Knowledge and understanding

Unit 8 Accounting techniques

3 Basic statistical methods: index numbers	6, 13, 16-19, 26, 42, 43
5 Methods of presenting information in graphical, diagrammatic and tabular form	8, 10, 13

Unit 9 Accounting techniques

3 Basic statistical methods: index numbers	6, 13, 16-19, 26, 42, 43

6 Using index numbers

(a)   AB Ltd set the standard cost of material C at £3.50 per litre when an index of material prices stood at 115. The index now stands at 145.

Task

Calculate the updated standard cost.

(b)   Culver Ltd decides to buy a machine from a French company for 100,000 FF, when the rate of exchange is 10FF. Payment for the machine occurs when the exchange rate is 11.2 FF.

Task

Calculate the difference between the planned cost and actual cost of the machine.

> Index numbers are also covered in activities 13, 16, 17, 18, 19, 26, 42 and 43.

chapter 5

Forecasting

Activity checklist

This checklist shows which activities cover the performance criteria, range statements and knowledge and understanding points dealt with in Chapter 5 of the BPP *Managing Costs and Controlling Resources* Interactive Text.

Performance criteria		Activities
8.1B	Monitor and analyse on a regular basis current and forecast trends in prices and market conditions	7
8.1C	Compare trends with previous experience and identify potential implications	10
8.1F	Consult relevant staff in the organisation about the analysis of trends and variances	10
9.1B	Communicate with relevant individuals and give them the opportunity to raise queries and to clarify forecasts	11, 33
9.1C	Prepare forecasts in a clear format with explanations of assumptions, projections and adjustments	15, 17
9.1D	Review and revise the validity of forecasts in the light of any significant anticipated changes	11
Range statement		
8.1	Methods of summarising data: time series (moving averages, linear regression, seasonal variations)	7-11, 14, 15, 17, 27, 33, 37
9.1	Forecasts: income; expenditure	8, 11, 15, 17, 27, 33
9.1	Projections: trends; seasonal variations; market research	7, 9, 10, 14, 17

		Activities
Knowledge and understanding		
Unit 8 Accounting techniques		
3	Basic statistical methods: time series analysis (moving averages, linear regression and seasonal trends)	7-11, 14, 15, 17, 27, 33, 37
Unit 9 Accounting techniques		
3	Basic statistical methods: time series (moving averages, linear regression and seasonal variations)	7-11, 14, 15, 17, 27, 33, 37

7 Blue Diamond Recovery (40 mins)

Blue Diamond Recovery plc is a motor accident and breakdown recovery organisation. Its membership is rising steadily. Members pay an annual fee of £50. When notified of a breakdown or an accident Blue Diamond Recovery will call out a local garage to the motorist. If the fault cannot be fixed immediately the car is taken to the garage for repair and the motorist is given a hire vehicle to complete the journey.

You are employed as a forecaster in the budgeting section of the company's management accounting department.

Each call-out involves taking the call from the motorist and then alerting a garage and/or the emergency services. It has been established that the number of call-outs has a close relationship to membership numbers, as one would expect. There is, however, a two-month gap between an increase in membership and the increase in call-outs. So, for instance, a 10% rise in membership in February will give rise to a 10% rise in call-outs from April onwards. The call-out pattern is also seasonal. It takes the following form.

	Jan	Feb	Mar	Apr	May	June	July	Aug	Sept	Oct	Nov	Dec
Seasonal variations as a percentage of trend	–	–10	+20	–10	–10	–10	–	+20-	–	–10	–10	+20

You have been asked by Belinda Casey, Blue Diamond Recovery's management accountant, to prepare a forecast of call-outs which can used for setting budgets in the next calendar year. She has provided the following additional information.

- The last three months' membership figures are as follows.

October	200,000
November	220,000
December	240,000

- There were 9,600 call-outs in December.

- If seasonal variations are eliminated, call-outs in a month average 4% of the membership numbers recorded in the month two months earlier.

- The company expects its membership to increase by 20,000 per month during January, February and March. A marketing campaign is planned for the period April to October. It is expected that membership for the period April to the following January will increase by 40,000 per month.

Task

Produce a table which covers the month just ended, December, and each of the next THIRTEEN months, January to January. Your table should contain the following.

(a)   Figures showing Blue Diamond Recovery plc's expected membership in each month
(b)   The forecast number of call-outs if there are NO seasonal variations
(c)   The forecast number of call-outs after adjustment for seasonal variations

8 Forecasting

The following data show the sales of the product sold by your company in the period 20X6-X8.

Year	Quarter 1 £'000	Quarter 2 £'000	Quarter 3 £'000	Quarter 4 £'000
20X6	86	42	57	112
20X7	81	39	55	107
20X8	77	35	52	99

Tasks

(a)   Plot the data and comment on them.

(b)   By means of a moving average find the trend.

(c)   The seasonal adjustments are as follows.

Quarter 1	Quarter 2	Quarter 3	Quarter 4
+9	−32	−16	+39

Give the sales for 20X8 seasonally adjusted.

(d)   Forecast sales for each quarter of 20X9 using a 'rule-of-thumb' approach and comment on the likely accuracy of your forecasts.

9 Time series analysis

You have collected the following data on your company's quarterly sales in recent years.

	Quarter			
	1 Units	2 Units	3 Units	4 Units
20X2	200	110	320	240
20X3	214	118	334	260
20X4	220	124	340	278

As part of the sales budget preparation you have been asked to analyse this data.

Tasks

(a)   Calculate a moving average of quarterly sales.
(b)   Calculate the average seasonal variations.

10 Eskafeld Industrial Museum (40 mins)

Eskafeld Industrial Museum opened ten years ago and soon became a market leader with many working exhibits. In the early years there was a rapid growth in the number of visitors. However, with no further investment in new exhibits, this growth has not been maintained in recent years.

Two years ago, John Derbyshire was appointed as the museum's chief executive. His initial task was to increase the number of visitors to the museum and, following his appointment, he has made several improvements to make the museum more successful.

Another of John's tasks is to provide effective financial management. This year, the museum's Board of Management has asked him to take full responsibility for producing the 20X9 budget. One of his first tasks is to prepare estimates of the number of visitors next year. John had previously played only a limited role in budget preparation and so he turns to you, an accounting technician, for advice.

He provides you with the following information.

- Previous budgets had assumed a 10% growth in attendance but this has been inaccurate.
- Very little is known about the visitors to the museum.
- The museum keeps details of the number of visitors by quarter but this has never been analysed.
- The number of visitors per quarter for the last two years is as follows.

Year	Quarter	Number of visitors
20X7	1	5,800
	2	9,000
	3	6,000
	4	14,400
20X8	1	6,600
	2	9,800
	3	6,800
	4 (Estimate)	15,200

Tasks

(a)   Calculate the **Centred Four-Point Moving Average Trend** figures and the seasonal variations.

(b)   Construct a graph showing the actual trend line, the extrapolated trend line and actual number of visitors, by quarter, for presentation to the Board of Management.

(c)   Estimate the forecast number of visitors for each quarter of 20X9, assuming that there is the same trend and seasonal variations for 20X8.

(d)   Prepare notes on forecasting for John Derbyshire. Your notes should:

   (i)   identify two ways to improve the forecasting of visitor numbers and highlight any limitations to your proposals;

   (ii)   explain why telephone sampling might be preferable to using postal questionnaires;

   (iii) explain how the concept of the product life cycle could be applied to the museum.

11 Star Fuels (50 mins)

Star Fuels is a multinational oil company selling oil for industrial and domestic purposes through a network of distributors. Distributors purchase fuel oil from Star Fuels and then sell it on to their own customers.

A regular complaint of the distributors is that they either have to pay for the fuel on delivery to their storage tanks or be charged interest on a daily basis on the amount owed. This problem could be reduced if the distributors were able to forecast their demands more accurately.

You are employed as the Assistant Management Accountant to Northern Fuel Distributors Ltd, a major distributor of Star Fuels's fuel oils. You recently attended a meeting with Mary Lamberton, a member of Star Fuels's central staff. At the meeting, she demonstrated a statistical software package used for estimating demand for fuel oil. The user enters sales volumes per period and the package then calculates the least-squares regression equation for the data. This is in the form $y = a + bx$ where x is the time period, y is the forecast and a and b are terms derived from the original data. Following further inputs by the user, the package can also estimate seasonal variations. Two forms of seasonal variation are calculated: the first calculates the seasonal variance as an absolute amount, the second as a percentage.

One week after the meeting, your copy of the software arrives at the head office of Northern Fuel Distributors Ltd and you immediately set about testing its capability. Purely for the purpose of testing, you assume seasonal variations occur quarterly. You enter this assumption along with the sales turnover figures for fuel oil for the last 20 quarters. Within moments, the software outputs the following information.

Regression line $\qquad\qquad y = £2,000,000 + £40,000x$

Seasonal variations

Quarter	A	B	C	D
Amount	+£350,000	+£250,000	−£400,000	−£200,000
Percentage	+15%	+10%	−15%	−10%

Quarter A refers to the first quarter of annual data, B to the second quarter, C to the third and D to the fourth. The pattern then repeats itself. In terms of the specific data you input, seasonal variation A refers to quarter 17, B to quarter 18, C to quarter 19 and D to quarter 20.

Actual sales turnover for quarters 17 to 20 was as follows.

Quarter	17	18	19	20
Sales turnover	£3,079,500	£3,002,400	£2,346,500	£2,490,200

Tasks

(a)   Making use of the formula derived by the software package, calculate the forecast sales turnover for quarters 17 to 20 using:

  (i)   the absolute seasonal variations;
  (ii)   the percentage seasonal variations.

(b)   (i)   From your answers to Task (a), determine which method of calculating seasonal variations gives the best estimate of actual sales turnover.

  (ii)   Having identified the preferred method, use that method to forecast the sales turnover for quarters 21 to 24.

(c)   Write a memorandum to your Managing Director. The memorandum should do the following.

    (i)   Explain what is meant by seasonal variations and seasonally adjusted data. Illustrate your explanation with examples relevant to Northern Fuel Distributors.

    (ii)   Suggest why your chosen method of seasonal adjustment might be more accurate.

    (iii)   Show how an understanding of seasonal variations and seasonally adjusted data can help Northern Fuel Distributors be more efficient.

    (iv)   Identify TWO weaknesses within your approach to forecasting undertaken in Tasks (a) and (b).

Forecasting is also covered in activities 14, 15, 17, 27, 33 and 37.

chapters 6 and 7

Variances

Activity checklist

This checklist shows which activities cover the performance criteria, range statements and knowledge and understanding points dealt with in Chapters 6 and 7 of the BPP *Managing Costs and Controlling Resources* Interactive Text.

Performance criteria	Activities
8.1D Compare standard costs with actual costs and analyse any variances	12-21

Range statement

8.1 Variance analysis: material price and usage variances; labour rate and efficiency variances; fixed overhead expenditure, volume, capacity and efficiency variances; subdivision of variances	12-21

Knowledge and understanding

Unit 8 Accounting techniques

7 Standard costing	12 -21

Unit 8 Accounting principles and theory

8 Marginal and absorption costing	2, 3, 15, 16

12 Standard costing

You are assistant management accountant at PQ Limited, an organisation which has two production departments – machining and assembly. Two of its main products are the Major and the Minor, the standard data for which are as follows.

	Per unit	
	Major	*Minor*
Direct materials:		
Material @ £15 per kg	2.2 kgs	1.4 kgs
Direct labour:		
Machining department @ £6 per hour	4.8 hrs	2.9 hrs
Assembly department @ £5 per hour	3.6 hrs	3.1 hrs
Machining time	3.5 hrs	0.9 hrs

The overhead rates for the period are as follows.

Machining department	*Assembly department*
£16.00 per machine hour	£9.50 per labour hour

Tasks

(a) Calculate the standard production cost for each product.

(b) During the period, actual results for labour were as follows.

		Major	*Minor*
Production		650 units	842 units
Direct labour:			
Machining department		2,990 hrs	2,480 hrs
	costing	£18,239	£15,132
Assembly department		2,310 hrs	2,595 hrs
	costing	£11,700	£12,975

Calculate the direct labour total variance and the rate and efficiency variances for each product and each department.

(c) Explain briefly what information the above variances provide for management.

13 Gransden Ltd (35 mins)

Gransden Ltd makes and retails a variety of furniture products. One year ago, the directors realised that their traditional financial accounting system was not providing sufficient information for the managers. As a result, they established a management accounting department headed by William Jones. He quickly established standard costing throughout the organisation as well as introducing performance reports for each division in the company. Both techniques have been effective and, as a result, you were recently appointed as the Assistant Management Accountant to the company.

Some managers, however, are still having difficulty understanding the meaning of the standard costing reports prepared each month. One manager, Helen Dale, particularly feels that the report for May was misleading. Her department manufactures high quality wooden display cabinets. She wrote to William Jones about the report, and an extract from the letter is reproduced below.

'In May, my department produced 5,000 cabinets, 500 more than required in my budget. According to your own figures, each cabinet requires five metres of wood at a standard price of £100 per metre, a total cost of £2,500,000 metres. For some reason, you show the result of this as being an overall adverse variance of £200,000, which you then break down into price and usage, despite my department only using 22,500 metres of wood in May.

Also, only yesterday, I read that the Retail Prices Index stood at 168 compared with an index of 160 when the standards were agreed. This shows inflation at 8% and so the £200,000 overspend on standard cost is entirely due to price inflation, which is out of my control. Your standard costing is not therefore particularly helpful to me as a manager.'

Tasks

William Jones plans to discuss with Helen the issues raised in her letter. Before doing so, however, he has asked you to do the following.

(a) (i)   Determine the material price and usage variances within the overall adverse variances.
     (ii) Check the accuracy of the index of inflation calculated by Helen Dale.

(b) Prepare a diagram or graph showing the standard cost, the variances and the extent of inflation within the price variance which may help Helen understand the overall variance.

(c) Identify THREE difficulties which might be experienced in interpreting the price variance, including the inflation element.

14 Priory Ltd (80 mins)

(a) You are employed as the assistant management accountant to Priory Ltd. Priory Ltd manufactures a single product, the Addid, an ingredient used in food processing. The basic raw material in Addid production is material A. The average unit prices for material A in each control period last year, and the seasonal variations based on several years' observations, are reproduced below.

	Control period 1	Control period 2	Control period 3	Control period 4
Average unit price of A	£90	£105	£80	£75
Seasonal variations	+£10	+£20	−£10	−£20

Tasks

(i)   Calculate the seasonally adjusted unit price of material A for each of the four control periods of last year.

(ii) Assuming a similar pattern of price movements in the future, forecast the likely purchase price for the four control periods of the current year.

(b) Priory Ltd operates a standard absorption costing system. Standards are established at the beginning of each year. Each week the management accounting section prepares a statement for the production director reconciling the actual cost of production with its standard cost. Standard costing data for week 7 of control period 2 in the current year is given below.

Standard costing and budget data for week 7 of control period 2			
	Quantity	Unit price	Cost per unit
Material (litres)	21	£110	£2,310
Labour (hours)	7	£7	£49
Fixed overheads (hours)	7	£42	£294
Standard unit cost			£2,653
	Budgeted units	Standard cost per unit	Standard cost of production
Budgeted production for week 7	1,150	£2,653	£3,050,950

During week 7, production of Addid totalled 950 units and the actual costs for that week were:

Inputs	Units	Total cost
Materials (litres)	18,200	£2,003,100
Labour (hours)	7,100	£41,200
Fixed overheads (hours)	7,100	£420,000

Using this data, a colleague has already calculated the fixed overhead variances. These were as follows.

Fixed overhead expenditure variance	£81,900 adverse
Efficiency variance	£18,900 adverse
Capacity variance	£39,900 adverse

Tasks

Your colleague asks you to do the following.

(i) Calculate the following variances.

    (1) Material price
    (2) Material usage
    (3) Labour rate
    (4) Labour efficiency

(ii) Prepare a statement reconciling the actual cost of production with the standard cost of actual production.

(c) The production director of Priory Ltd is concerned that the material price variance may not accurately reflect the efficiency of the company's purchasing department.

Tasks

You have been asked by your finance director to write a **brief** memorandum to the production director. Your note should:

(i) explain what variances are attempting to measure*;
(ii) list THREE general ways production variances arise other than through errors*;
(iii) identify THREE general reasons why there might be errors in reporting variances*;
(iv) use your solution to the task in (a) to suggest why the production director's concern might be justified.

*Note. In parts (i), (ii) and (iii) of this task, you should restrict your comments to variances in general and not address issues arising from particular types of variances.

15 Debussy Ltd (70 mins)

You have recently accepted an appointment as the accountant to Debussy Limited, a small family firm manufacturing a specialised fertiliser. The fertiliser is produced using expensive ovens which need to be kept at a constant temperature at all times, even when not being used. Because of this, the power which provides the heating does not vary with changes in production output and so its costs are viewed as being fixed.

The managing director, Claude Debussy, is concerned that the existing accounting system is not providing adequate information for him to run the business. By way of example, he shows you the accounts for the year ended 30 November 20X8. An extract from those accounts showing budgeted and actual results is reproduced below.

Extract from the Profit and Loss Account of Debussy Ltd for the year ended 30 November 20X8												
Units produced (tonnes)	Annual Budget 12,000			Annual Results 13,000			Quarter 4 Budget 3,000			Quarter 4 Results 2,400		
	£	£		£	£		£	£		£	£	
Material		144,000			188,500			36,000			35,280	
Labour		192,000			227,500			48,000			42,240	
Fixed overheads:												
Lease of machinery	60,000			60,000			15,000			15,000		
Rent	40,000			40,000			10,000			10,000		
Rates	56,000			64,000			14,000			16,000		
Insurance	48,000			52,000			12,000			13,000		
Power	120,000			140,000			30,000			36,000		
		324,000			356,000			81,000			90,000	
Total expenses		660,000			72,000			165,000			167,520	

Claude Debussy draws your attention to the high level of fixed overheads and how these are absorbed using labour hours.

'I do not fully understand the fixed overhead figures for the fourth quarter' he explained. 'The way they are presented in the accounts does not help me to plan and control the business. It is no good blaming the production workers for the increase in fixed overheads as we have been paying them £8 per hour – the same amount as agreed in the budget – and they have never worked any overtime.'

Claude Debussy turns to you for advice. He is particularly interested in understanding why the fixed overheads have increased in the fourth quarter despite production falling. He is also interested in knowing how many labour hours were planned to be worked and how many hours were actually worked in that quarter.

Tasks

(a)   For the fourth quarter, calculate the following information for Claude Debussy.

   (i)   The labour hours budgeted to be worked
   (ii)   The labour hours actually worked
   (iii)   The budgeted hours per tonne of fertiliser
   (iv)   The actual hours per tonne of fertiliser

(b)   Calculate the following variances for the fourth quarter.

   (**Note.** You should base your calculations on the TOTAL amount of fixed overheads and NOT the individual **elements**.)

(i)   The fixed overhead expenditure variance (sometimes known as the price variance)
(ii)   The fixed overhead volume variance
(iii) The fixed overhead capacity variance
(iv)   The fixed overhead efficiency variance (sometimes known as the usage variance)

(c) Claude Debussy is unfamiliar with standard costing, although he believes the actual fixed overheads for the year are higher than budgeted because more tonnes of fertiliser have been produced. He would like to use standard costing to control fixed overheads, but is uncertain what is meant by the fixed overhead variances you have prepared.

Write a memo to Claude Debussy. Your memo should:

(i)   **briefly** comment on his explanation for the increase in fixed overheads for the year;
(ii)   for each of the following three variances, give ONE possible reason why they might have occurred:

   (1)   the fixed overhead expenditure (or price) variance;
   (2)   the fixed overhead capacity variance;
   (3)   the fixed overhead efficiency (or usage) variance.

(d) On receiving your memo, Claude Debussy tells you that the annual budgeted fixed overheads have, in the past, simply been apportioned equally over the four quarters. However, the expenditure on power varies between quarters in a regular way depending on the outside temperature. The seasonal variations, based on many years' experience, are as follows:

	1st Quarter	2nd Quarter	3rd Quarter	4th Quarter
Seasonal variations for power costs	+5%	−10%	−20%	+25%

Claude Debussy believes that it would be more meaningful if the budgeted expenditure on power reflected these seasonal variations, but he is uncertain how this would affect the variances calculated in task (b).

Prepare notes for Claude Debussy. Your notes should:

(i)   use the seasonal variations to calculate the revised power budget for the four quarters of the year to 30 November 20X8;

(ii)   **briefly** discuss whether or not the revised power budget for the fourth quarter should be used for calculating the fixed overhead expenditure (or price) and volume variances for that quarter.

16 Hampstead Plc (70 mins)

(a) You are employed as the assistant management accountant in the group accountant's office of Hampstead plc. Hampstead recently acquired Finchley Ltd, a small company making a specialist product called the Alpha. Standard marginal costing is used by all the companies within the group and, from 1 August 20X8, Finchley Ltd will also be required to use standard marginal costing in its management reports. Part of your job is to manage the implementation of standard marginal costing at Finchley Ltd.

John Wade, the managing director of Finchley, is not clear how the change will help him as a manager. He has always found Finchley's existing absorption costing system sufficient. By way of example, he shows you a summary of his management accounts for the three months to 31 May 20X8. These are reproduced below.

Statement of budgeted and actual cost of Alpha production – 3 months ended 31 May 20X8					
	Actual		Budget		Variance
Alpha production (units)	10,000		12,000		
	Inputs	£	Inputs	£	£
Materials	32,000 metres	377,600	36,000 metres	432,000	54,400
Labour	70,000 hours	422,800	72,000 hours	450,000	27,200
Fixed overhead absorbed		330,000		396,000	66,000
Fixed overhead unabsorbed		75,000		0	(75,000)
		1,205,400		1,278,000	72,600

John Wade is not convinced that standard marginal costing will help him to manage Finchley. 'My current system tells me all I need to know,' he said. 'As you can see, we are £72,600 below budget which is really excellent given that we lost production as a result of a serious machine breakdown.'

To help John Wade understand the benefits of standard marginal costing, you agree to prepare a statement for the three months ended 31 May 20X8 reconciling the standard cost of production to the actual cost of production.

Tasks

(i)   Use the budget data to determine the following.

    (1)   The standard marginal cost per Alpha

    (2)   The standard cost of actual Alpha production for the three months to 31 May 20X8

(ii)   Calculate the following variances.

    (1)   Material price variance

    (2)   Material usage variance

    (3)   Labour rate variance

    (4)   Labour efficiency variance

    (5)   Fixed overhead expenditure variance

(iii)   Write a *short* memo to John Wade. You memo should:

    (1)   include a statement reconciling the actual cost of production to the standard cost of production;

    (2)   give TWO reasons why your variances might differ from those in his original management accounting statement despite using the same basic data;

    (3)·   **briefly** discuss ONE further reason why your reconciliation statement provides improved management information.

(b)   On receiving your memo, John Wade informs you that the machine breakdown resulted in the workforce having to be paid for 12,000 hours even though no production took place, and that an index of material prices stood at 466.70 when the budget was prepared but at 420.03 when the material was purchased.

Task

Using this new information, prepare a revised statement reconciling the standard cost of production to the actual cost of production. Your statement should subdivide both the labour variances into those parts arising from the machine breakdown and those parts arising from normal production, and the material price variance into that part due to the change in the index and that part arising for other reasons.

(c)   Barnet Ltd is another small company owned by Hampstead plc. Barnet operates a job costing system making a specialist, expensive piece of hospital equipment.

Existing system

Currently, employees are assigned to individual jobs and materials are requisitioned from stores as needed. The standard and actual costs of labour and materials are recorded for each job. These job costs are totalled to produce the marginal cost of production. Fixed production costs – including the cost of storekeeping and inspection of deliveries and finished equipment – are then added to determine the standard and actual cost of production. Any costs of remedial work are included in the materials and labour for each job.

Proposed system

Carol Johnson, the chief executive of Barnet, has recently been to a seminar on modern manufacturing techniques. As a result, she is considering introducing Just-in-Time stock deliveries and Total Quality Management. Barnet would offer suppliers a long-term contract at a fixed price but suppliers would have to guarantee the quality of their materials.

In addition, she proposes that the workforce is organised as a single team with flexible work practices. This would mean employees helping each other as necessary, with no employee being allocated a particular job. If a job was delayed, the workforce would work overtime without payment in order for the job to be completed on time. In exchange, employees would be guaranteed a fixed weekly wage and time off when production was slack to make up for any overtime incurred.

Cost of quality

Carol has asked to meet you to discuss the implications of her proposals on the existing accounting system. She is particularly concerned to monitor the **cost of quality**. This is defined as the total of all costs incurred in preventing defects plus those costs involved in remedying defects once they have occurred. It is a single figure measuring all the explicit costs of quality – that is, those costs collected within the accounting system.

Task

In preparation for the meeting, produce **brief** notes. Your notes should:

(i)   identify FOUR general headings (or classifications) which make up the **cost of quality**;

(ii)   give ONE example of a type of cost likely to be found within each category;

(iii)   assuming Carol Johnson's proposals are accepted, state, with reasons, whether or not:

(1)   a standard marginal costing system would still be of help to the managers;
(2)   it would still be meaningful to collect costs by each individual job;

(iv)   identify one cost saving in Carol Johnson's proposals which would not be recorded in the existing costing system.

17 Original Holidays Ltd (70 mins)

(a)   You are employed as an Accounting Technician by Original Holidays Limited. Original Holidays commenced business one year ago as a tour operator specialising in arranging holidays to the small island of Zed. Recent newspaper reports have stated that the cost of hotel bedrooms per night in Zed has been increasing over the last twelve moths due to its government refusing to allow further hotels to be built despite increasing demand from tourists.

The managing director of Original Holidays, Jane Armstrong, is concerned that this will affect the profitability of the company's operations to the island. She asked Colin Ware, the financial accountant, to provide data showing the nightly cost of a bedroom charged to Original Holidays over the last four quarters. Colin's response is reproduced below.

Memo				
To:	Jane Armstrong			
From:	Colin Ware			
Date:	5 January 20X8			
Subject:	**Nightly cost per bedroom**			

Thank you for your recent enquiry concerning the cost per night of a bedroom in Zed. I have analysed the amounts paid per quarter over the last twelve months and divided that amount by the number of bedrooms hired per night. The nightly cost per bedroom is as follows:

	Quarter 1	*Quarter 2*	*Quarter 3*	*Quarter 4*
Cost per night	£102.400	£137.760	£134.480	£68.921

(**Note**. All figures in pounds to 3 decimal places.)

On receiving the memo, Jane notices that the cost to Original Holidays per bedroom per night has actually been falling over the last three quarters and has asked for your help in reconciling this with the newspaper reports. You obtain the following information.

Over several years, there has been a consistent seasonal variation in the cost of bedrooms per night. According to the marketing manager, these are:

	Quarter 1	*Quarter 2*	*Quarter 3*	*Quarter 4*
Seasonal variation as percentage of trend	−20%	+5%	+40%	−25%

A financial newspaper provides you with the following exchange rates between the UK pound and the Zed franc:

	Quarter 1	*Quarter 2*	*Quarter 3*	*Quarter 4*
	2,000 francs	2,000 francs	2,800 francs	3,000 francs

Tasks

(i)   Using the quarterly exchange rates given, identify the actual nightly cost per bedroom in Zed francs for each quarter.

(ii) Using the information provided by the marketing manager, identify the trend in costs in Zed francs for each quarter.

(iii) Identify the quarterly percentage increase in the cost of a bedroom per night in Zed francs and express this as an annual percentage to 2 decimal places.

(iv) Forecast the cost in British pounds of a bedroom per night for the first quarter of next year using the exchange rate for the fourth quarter.

(b) On receiving your analysis of the cost per bedroom per night, Jane Armstrong expresses concern that the company's existing reporting system does not provide sufficient information to monitor operations. She shows you a copy of the operating statement for the third quarter prepared using the existing system. The statement excludes marketing, administrative and other head-office overheads and is reproduced below

Original Holidays Operating Statement for the 3rd Quarter – 20X7		
	Budget	*Actual*
Number of holidays	6,000	7,800
	£	£
Turnover	1,800,000	2,262,000
Accommodation	840,000	1,048,944
Air transport	720,000	792,000
Operating profit	240,000	421,056

Jane has shared her concerns with Colin Ware, the financial accountant. He has suggested that a standard costing report, reconciling standard cost to actual cost, would provide more meaningful information for management. To demonstrate to Jane Armstrong the improved quality of a standard costing system of reporting, Colin asks you to reanalyse the operating statement for the third quarter. To help you, he provides you with the following information:

• The accommodation is a variable cost. Its usage variance is nil.

• Air transport is a fixed cost and relates to the company's own 105-seat aircraft.

• The budget provided for 80 return flights in the quarter with each flight carrying 75 tourists. This volume was used to calculate the fixed overhead absorption rate when costing individual holidays.

• Due to operational difficulties, the aircraft only undertook 78 return flights, carrying a total of 7,800 passengers in quarter 3.

Tasks

(i) Using the budgeted data, calculate the standard absorption cost per holiday.
(ii) Using your answer to part (i), calculate the standard absorption cost of 7,800 holidays.
(iii) Calculate the following variances.

(1) Material price variance for the accommodation
(2) Fixed overhead expenditure variance for the air transport
(3) Fixed overhead capacity variance for the air transport
(4) Fixed overhead efficiency variance for the air transport

(iv) Prepare a statement reconciling the budgeted (or standard) absorption cost to the actual cost.
(v) Identify the single most important reason for the difference between budgeted and actual cost.

(c)   Write a memo to Jane Armstrong **briefly** explaining what the following variances attempt to measure and giving ONE possible reason why each variance might have occurred.

(i)   The fixed overhead expenditure variance
(ii)   The fixed overhead capacity variance
(iii)   The fixed overhead efficiency variance

18 Pronto Ltd (95 mins)

(a)   Pronto Ltd was recently established in the UK to assemble cars. All parts are sent directly to the UK in the form of a kit by Pronto's owner from its headquarters in a country called Erehwon.

The contract between Pronto and its owner is a fixed price contract per kit and the contract specifies zero faults in all of the parts. This fixed price was used to establish the standard cost per kit. Despite this, the managing director of Pronto, Richard Jones, is concerned to receive the following statement from the management accounting department where you are employed as an accounting technician.

	September 20X8	October 20X8	November 20X8
Kits delivered	2,000	2,100	2,050
Actual cost invoiced	£12,059,535	£11,385,495	£10,848,600
Unit cost per kit to nearest £	£6,030	£5,422	£5,292

Richard Jones cannot understand why, with a fixed price contract and guaranteed quality, the unit cost should vary over the three months. He provides you with the following information.

- The contract's cost was fixed in Erehwon dollars of $54,243 per kit.

- There has been no change in the agreed cost of the parts and no other costs incurred.

On further investigation you discover that the exchange rate between the UK pound and the Erehwon dollar was as follows.

At time of contract	September 20X8	October 20X8	November 20X8
$9.80	$9.00	$10.00	$10.25

Task

Prepare a memo to Richard Jones. Your memo should include the following.

(i)   A calculation of:

(1)   the UK cost per kit at the time the contract was agreed;
(2)   the UK cost of the kits delivered using the exchange rates given for each of the three months;
(3)   the price variance due to exchange rate differences for each of the three months;
(4)   any usage variance in each of the three months, assuming no other reason for the price variance;

(ii)   A **brief** discussion about whether price variances due to exchange rate differences should be excluded from any standard costing report prepared for the production manager of Pronto Ltd.

(b) Pronto uses a highly mechanised and computerised moving assembly line known as a track to build the cars. Although individual employees are assigned to particular parts of the track, they work in teams. If the production of cars slows below the speed of the track, teams help each other to maintain the speed of the track and the production of cars. Because of this approach, labour is viewed as a fixed cost and machine hours (the hours that the track is in use) are used to charge overheads to production.

For the week ended 28 November 20X8, the management accounting department has prepared a statement of budgeted and actual fixed overhead for Richard Jones. This is reproduced below.

Pronto Ltd: Budgeted and actual fixed overheads – week ended 28 November 20X8		
	Budget	Actual
Car production	560	500
Machine (or track) hours of production	140	126
Fixed overheads:	£	£
Rent and rates	16,000	16,000
Maintenance and depreciation	10,000	13,000
Power	75,000	71,000
Labour	739,000	742,000
Total	840,000	842,000

Richard Jones finds that the statement is not particularly helpful as it does not give him sufficient information to manage the company. He asks for your help.

Tasks

In preparation for a meeting with Richard Jones, do the following.

(i) Calculate the following.

(1) Budgeted overheads per machine (or track) hour
(2) Budgeted number of cars produced per machine (or track) hour
(3) Standard hours of actual production

(ii) Calculate the following variances using the information identified in (i).

(1) Fixed overhead expenditure variance
(2) Fixed overhead volume variance
(3) Fixed overhead efficiency variance
(4) Fixed overhead capacity variance

(iii) Prepare a statement for the week ended 28 November 20X8 reconciling the fixed overheads incurred to the fixed overheads absorbed in production.

19 Malton Ltd (120 mins)

(a) Malton Ltd operates a standard marginal costing system. As the recently appointed management accountant to Malton's Eastern division, you have responsibility for the preparation of that division's monthly cost reports. The standard cost report uses variances to reconcile the actual marginal cost of production to its standard cost.

The Eastern division is managed by Richard Hill. The division only makes one product, the Beta. Budgeted Beta production for May 20X8 was 8,000 units although actual production was 9,500 units.

In order to prepare the standard cost report for May, you have asked a member of your staff to obtain standard and actual cost details for the month of May. This information is reproduced below.

| | Unit standard cost | | | | Actual details for May | |
	Quantity	Unit price	Cost per Beta		Quantity	Total cost
			£			£
Material	8 litres	£20	160	Material	78,000 litres	1,599,000
Labour	4 hours	£6	24	Labour	39,000 hours	249,600
Standard marginal cost			184	Total cost		1,848,600

Tasks

(i) Calculate the following.

    (1) The material price variance
    (2) The material usage variance
    (3) The labour rate variance
    (4) The labour efficiency variance

(ii) Prepare a standard costing statement reconciling the actual marginal cost of production with the standard marginal cost of production.

(b) After Richard Hill has received your standard costing statement, you visit him to discuss the variances and their implications. Richard, however, raises a number of queries with you. He makes the following points.

- An index measuring material prices stood at 247.2 for May but at 240.0 when the standard for the material price was set.

- The Eastern division is budgeted to run at its normal capacity of 8,000 units of production per month but during May it had to manufacture an additional 1,500 Betas to meet a special order agreed at short notice by Malton's sales director.

- Because of the short notice, the normal supplier of the raw material was unable to meet the extra demand and so additional materials had to be acquired from another supplier at a price per litre of £22.

- This extra material was not up to the normal specification, resulting in 20% of the special purchase being scrapped prior to being issued to production.

- The work force could only produce the special order on time by working overtime on the 1,500 Betas at 50% premium.

Tasks

(i) Calculate the amounts within the material price variance, the material usage variance and the labour rate variance which arise from producing the special order.

(ii) (1) Estimate the revised standard price for materials based on the change in the material price index.

(2) For the 8,000 units of normal production, use your answer in (ii)(1) above to estimate how much of the price variance calculated in task (a) is caused by the general change in prices.

(iii) Using your answers to parts (i) and (ii) of this task, prepare a revised standard costing statement. The revised statement should subdivide the variances prepared in task (a) into those elements controllable by Richard Hill and those elements caused by factors outside his divisional control.

(iv) Write a **brief** note to Richard Hill justifying your treatment of the elements you believe are outside his control and suggesting what action should be taken by the company.

20 Travel Holdings Plc (100 mins)

(a) You are employed as a management accountant in the head office of Travel Holdings plc. Travel Holdings owns a number of transport businesses. One of them is Travel Ferries Ltd. Travel Ferries operates ferries which carry passengers and vehicles across a large river. Each year, standard costs are used to develop the budget for Travel Ferries Ltd. The latest budgeted and actual operating results are reproduced below.

Travel Ferries Ltd				
Budgeted and actual operating results for the year to 30 November 20X0				
Operating data		*Budget*		*Actual*
Number of ferry crossings		6,480		5,760
Operating hours of ferries		7,776		7,488
Cost data		£		£
Fuel	1,244,160 litres	497,664	1,232,800 litres	567,088
Labour	93,312 hours	466,560	89,856 hours	471,744
Fixed overheads		466,560		472,440
Cost of operations	STD cost —	1,430,784		1,511,272

(handwritten notes: "Per 1 Crossing STD cost 220·80"; "466,560 / 6480"; "466,560 / 6480 = £72")

Other accounting information

- Fuel and labour are variable costs.
- Fixed overheads are absorbed on the basis of budgeted **operating hours**.

One of your duties is to prepare costing information and a standard costing reconciliation statement for the chief executive of Travel Holdings.

Tasks

(i) Calculate the following information.

(1) The standard price of fuel per litre
(2) The standard litres of fuel for 5,760 ferry crossings
(3) The standard labour rate per hour
(4) The standard labour hours for 5,760 ferry crossings

(5)   The standard fixed overhead cost per budgeted operating hour

(6)   The standard operating hours for 5,760 crossings

(7)   The standard fixed overhead cost absorbed by the actual 5,760 ferry crossings

(ii)   Using the data provided in the operating results and your answers to part (i), calculate the following variances.

(1)   The material price variance for the fuel

(2)   The material usage variance for the fuel

(3)   The labour rate variance

(4)   The labour efficiency variance

(5)   The fixed overhead expenditure variance

(6)   The fixed overhead volume variance

(7)   The fixed overhead capacity variance

(8)   The fixed overhead efficiency variance

(iii)   Prepare a statement reconciling the actual cost of operations to the standard cost of operations for the year to 30 November 20X0.

(b)   On receiving your reconciliation statement, the chief executive is concerned about the large number of adverse variances. She is particularly concerned about the excessive cost of fuel used during the year. A colleague gives you the following information.

- The actual market price of fuel per litre during the year was 20 percent higher than the standard price.

- Fuel used directly varies with the number of operating hours.

- The difference between the standard and actual operating hours for the 5,760 ferry crossings arose entirely because of weather conditions.

Tasks

Write a memo to the chief executive. Your memo should do the following.

(i)   Subdivide the material price variance into two parts.

(1)   That part arising from the standard price being different from the actual market price of fuel

(2)   The part due to other reasons

(ii)   Identify ONE variance which is not controllable and give ONE reason why the variance is not controllable.

(iii)   Identify TWO variances which are controllable and which should be investigated. For each variance, give ONE reason why it is controllable.

21 Bare Foot Hotel complex (120 mins)   12/99

(a)   You are the assistant management accountant at the Bare Foot Hotel complex on the tropical island of St Nicolas. The hotel complex is a luxury development. All meals and entertainment are included in the price of the holidays and guests only have to pay for drinks.

The Bare Foot complex aims to create a relaxing atmosphere. Because of this, meals are available throughout the day and guests can eat as many times as they wish.

The draft performance report for the hotel for the seven days ended 27 November 20X1 is reproduced below.

Bare Foot Hotel Complex
Draft performance report for seven days ended 27 November 20X1

	Notes	Budget		Actual	
Guests		540		648	
		$	$	$	$
Variable costs					
Meal costs	1	34,020		49,896	
Catering staff costs	2,3	3,780		5,280	
Total variable costs		37,800		55,176	
Fixed overhead costs					
Salaries of other staff		5,840		6,000	
Local taxes		4,500		4,200	
Light, heat and power		2,500		2,600	
Depreciation of buildings and equipment		5,000		4,000	
Entertainment		20,500		21,000	
Total fixed overheads			38,340		37,800
Total cost of providing for guests			76,140		92,976

Notes

1   Budgeted cost of meals: number of guests × 3 meals per day × 7 days × $3 per meal
2   Budged cost of catering staff: each member of the catering staff is to prepare and serve 12 meals per hour. Cost = (number of guests × 3 meals per day × 7 days ÷ 12 meals per hour) × $4 per hour.
3   Actual hours worked by catering staff = 1,200 hours

Other notes
The amount of food per meal has been kept under strict portion control. Since preparing the draft performance report, however, it has been discovered that guests have eaten, on average, four meals per day.

You report to Alice Groves, the general manager of the hotel, who feels that the format of the draft performance report could be improved to provide her with more meaningful management information. She suggests that the budgeted and actual data given in the existing draft performance report is rearranged in the form of a standard costing report.

Tasks

(i)   Use the budget data, the actual data and the notes to the performance report to calculate the following for the seven days ended 27 November 20X1.

  (1)   The actual number of meals served

  (2)   The standard number of meals which should have been served for the actual number of guests

  (3)   The actual hourly rate paid to catering staff

  (4)   The standard hours allowed for catering staff to serve three meals per day for the actual number of guests

  (5)   The standard fixed overhead per guest

  (6)   The total standard cost for the actual number of guests

(ii)   Use the data given in the task and your answers to part (a)(i) to calculate the following variances for the seven days ended 27 November 20X1.

(1)   The material price variance for meals served

(2)   The material usage variance for meals served

(3)   The labour rate variance for catering staff

(4)   The labour efficiency variance for catering staff, based on a standard of three meals served per guest per day

(5)   The fixed overhead expenditure variance

(6)   The fixed overhead volume variance on the assumption that the fixed overhead absorption rate is based on the budgeted number of guests per seven days

(iii)   Prepare a statement reconciling the standard cost for the actual number of guests to the actual cost for the actual number of guests for the seven days ended 27 November 20X1.

(b)   On receiving your reconciliation statement, Alice Groves asks the following questions.

•   How much of the labour efficiency variance is due to guests taking, on average, four meals per day rather than the three provided for in the budget and how much is due to other reasons?

•   Would it be feasible to subdivide the fixed overhead volume variance into a capacity and efficiency variance?

Task

Write a memo to Alice Groves. Your memo should do the following.

(i)   Divide the labour efficiency variance into that part due to guests taking more meals than planned and that part due to other efficiency reasons.

(ii)   Explain the meaning of the fixed overhead capacity and efficiency variances.

(iii)   **Briefly** discuss whether or not it is feasible to calculate the fixed overhead capacity and efficiency variances for the Bare Foot Hotel complex.

chapters 8 and 9

Budgets

Activity checklist

This checklist shows which activities cover the performance criteria, range statements and knowledge and understanding points dealt with in Chapters 8 and 9 of the BPP *Managing Costs and Controlling Resources* Interactive Text.

Performance criteria		Activities
9.2A	Present to management draft budget proposals in a clear and appropriate format and on schedule	22, 23, 27, 28
9.2B	Verify that draft budget proposals are consistent with organisational objectives and include all relevant data and assumptions	25
9.2C	Break down budgets into periods appropriate to the organisation	24
9.2D	Communicate with budget holders in a manner which maintains goodwill and ensure budget proposals are agreed with budget holders	24, 26

Range statement		
9.2	Data: market information; general economic information; strategic plans	26
9.2	Types of budgets: budgets for income and expenditure; resource budgets (production budget, material budget, labour budget, fixed overhead budget); capital budgets	22-28
9.2	Data: accounting information; wage and salary information; market information	22-28

	Activities
Knowledge and understanding	
Unit 9 The business environment	
1 External sources of information on costs, prices, demand and availability of resources	26
Unit 9 Accounting techniques	
5 Development of production, resource and revenue budgets from forecast sales data	22-28
7 The effect of capacity constraints, other production constraints and sales constraints on budgets; limiting (key or budget) factor	23, 24, 25, 27
Unit 9 Accounting principles and theory	
14 Relationship between budgets, forecasts and planning and product-life cycles	10
15 Different types of budgets: budgets for income and expenditure; resource budgets (production, material, labour and other resource budgets); capital budgets	22-28

22 Budget preparation

You are assistant management accountant for an ice cream manufacturer and you are in the process of preparing budgets for the next few months. The following draft figures are available.

Sales forecast

June	6,000 cases
July	7,500 cases
August	8,500 cases
September	7,000 cases
October	6,500 cases

A case has a standard cost of £15 and a standard selling price of £25.

Each case uses 2½ kgs of ingredients and it is policy to have stocks of ingredients at the end of each month to cover 50% of next month's production. There are 5,800 kgs in stock on 1 June.

There are 750 cases of finished ice cream in stock on 1 June and it is policy to have stocks at the end of each month to cover 10% of the next month's sales.

Tasks

(a) Prepare a production budget (in cases) for the months of June, July, August and September.
(b) Prepare an ingredients purchase budget (in kgs) for the months of June, July and August.
(c) Calculate the budgeted gross profit for the quarter June to August.
(d) Describe briefly what advantages there would be for the firm if it adopted a system of flexible budgeting.

23 Product Q (60 mins)

Product Q is a product which is manufactured and sold by Alfred Limited. In the process of preparing budgetary plans for next year the following information has been made available to you.

- Forecast sales units of product Q for the year = 18,135 units

- Closing stocks of finished units of product Q at the end of next year will be increased by 15% from their opening level of 1,200 units.

- All units are subject to a quality control check. The budget plans are to allow for 1% of all units checked to be rejected and scrapped at the end of the process. All closing stocks will have passed this quality control check.

- Five direct labour hours are to be worked for each unit of product Q processed, including those which are scrapped after the quality control check. Of the total hours to be paid for, 7.5% are budgeted to be idle time.

- The standard hourly rate of pay for direct employees is £6 per hour.

- Material M is used in the manufacture of product Q. One finished unit of product Q contains 9 kg of M but there is a wastage of 10% of input of material M due to evaporation and spillage during the process.

- By the end of next year stocks of material M are to be increased by 12% from their opening level of 8,000 kg. During the year a loss of 1,000 kg is expected due to deterioration of the material in store.

Tasks

(a)   Prepare the following budgets for the forthcoming year.

   (i)   Production budget for product Q, in units
   (ii)   Direct labour budget for product Q, in hours and in £
   (iii)   Material usage budget for material M, in kg
   (iv)   Material purchases budget for material M, in kg

(b)   The supplier of material M has warned that available supplies will be below the amount indicated in your budget for task (a) part (iv) above.

   Explain the implications of this shortage and suggest four possible actions which could be taken to overcome the problem. For each suggestion identify any problems which may arise.

24 Arden Engineering Ltd (60 mins)

(a)   Arden Engineering Ltd makes a single product and, for planning purposes, the company breaks its annual budget into 13 four-weekly periods. From information provided by the marketing director, total sales for the year will be 3,296,500 units. This is broken down as follows.

Period	1	2	3	4	Each subsequent period
Units sales	190,000	228,000	266,000	304,000	256,500

   A similar pattern and volume of sales is expected next year. Because of the technical nature of the product, manufacturing has to take place one period prior to sale. In addition, there is a five per cent wastage which is only discovered on completion. This wastage has no monetary value.

Manufacturing labour is employed by the week and the wages cost per four-week period totals £270,000. The production director believes it is possible to manufacture up to 290,000 gross units per period although, because of wastage, good production will be below this figure. Any increase beyond the gross production of 290,000 units will involve paying overtime at a rate equivalent to £1.50 per extra unit produced. The material component of each unit costs £3.50. The only other production cost relates to fixed overheads. For the forthcoming year these are estimated at £6,940,000. Fixed overheads are charged to production on the basis of the gross number of units produced.

Task

For the first three periods of the forthcoming year, prepare the production budget, in a form suitable for consideration by the production director, on the assumption that all production takes place one period before it is sold. Your budget should show the total units to be produced per period, the production cost per period and the unit cost per period.

(b)   The production director is concerned that the budget involves overtime payments and suggests this is not necessary.

Two proposals are put forward: that part of the production is sourced from outside suppliers at a unit cost of £5.95 or that production is brought forward to periods when there is surplus capacity.

If production is brought forward, this will involve financing and other costs equivalent to 50p per unit per four-week period.

Task

Evaluate the two proposals given above and show, with supporting workings, the revised production schedule in units and the savings possible from your preferred proposal.

25 Amber Ltd (75 mins)

(a)   Amber Ltd is a subsidiary of Colour plc and makes a single product, the Delta. Budgets are prepared by dividing the accounting year into 13 periods, each of four weeks. Amber's policy is to avoid overtime payments wherever possible and this was one of the assumptions built into the preparation of Amber's budget for this year. However, some overtime payments have been necessary.

Helen Roy, Amber's finance director, has recently carried out an investigation and discovered why overtime has been paid. She found that the labour hours available over each four-week period were more than sufficient to meet the four-weekly production targets. However, **within** any four-week period, production levels could vary considerably. As a result, in some weeks, overtime had to be paid.

You are employed in the management accounting section of Colour plc as an assistant to Helen Roy. Although Helen did not have the next period's **production** volumes analysed by individual week, she was able to explain the problem by showing you the forecast **sales** of Deltas over each of the next four weeks. These are reproduced below.

Week	1	2	3	4
Forecast **sales** of Deltas (units)	23,520	27,440	28,420	32,340

Helen Roy also gives the following information.

- Amber's maximum production capacity per week before overtime and rejections is 30,400 Deltas.

- For technical reasons, production has to take place at least one week before it is sold.

- At present, all production takes place exactly one week before it is sold.

- Sales cannot be delayed to a subsequent week.

- The weekly fixed costs of wages before overtime is £21,280.

- Overtime is equivalent to £2 per unit produced in excess of 30,400 Deltas.

- The cost of material per Delta is £5.

- There is a 2% rejection rate in the manufacture of Deltas. Rejected Deltas are only discovered on completion and have no monetary value.

- Budgeted fixed production overheads for the year are estimated to be £3,792,825. These are absorbed on the basis of an estimated annual production before rejections of 1,685,700 Deltas.

Task

Helen Roy asks you to prepare Amber's WEEKLY production budgets for weeks 1 to 3 on the current basis that all production takes place exactly one week before it is sold. The budget should identify the following.

(i)   The number of Deltas to be produced in each of the three weeks
(ii)   The cost of any overtime paid
(iii)   The cost of production for each of the three weeks, including fixed production overheads

(b)   You give Helen Roy Amber's production budget for the next three weeks. She now tells you that it may be possible to save at least some of the overtime payments by manufacturing some Deltas in advance of the normal production schedule. However, any Deltas made earlier than one week before being sold will incur financing costs of 20p per Delta per week.

Task

Helen Roy asks you to calculate the following.

(i)   The number of Deltas to be produced in each of the three weeks if the overall costs are to be minimised

(ii)   The net savings if your revised production plan in (i) is accepted

26 Pickerings Canning Company (60 mins)

(a)   The Pickerings Canning Company produces a range of canned savoury and sweet products. The company prepares its budgets annually. The cost accountant has recently left and you, as the assistant cost accountant, have been requested to take over the responsibility of budget preparation. The managers of the company need the information quickly but they realise that the full budget will take too long to prepare. Because of this, a short-term budget for the month of September is requested. Before leaving, the cost accountant provided you with the following information.

- The only product which will be produced during the month is Apple Pie Filling and 80,000 cans per month are required by customers.

- The apples are purchased whole and there is approximately 50% waste in production.

- The net amount of apple in 1,000 cans is 100 kg.

- At the final stage of the production process 5% of the cans are damaged and they are sold to employees.

- The labour required to produce 1,000 cans is 6 hours.

- Each employee works 38 hours per week.

- The employees are currently in dispute with the company and there is 10% absenteeism. This problem is likely to continue for the foreseeable future.

- The employees are paid £4 per hour.

- The buyer at the company has provided prices for the apples but these are estimates mainly based on the actual figures for last year.

    ○   The basic price of apples is budgeted at £200 per tonne for August.

    ○   An internal index of apple prices for last year for the same period was:

    August 20X7   120
    September 20X7   125

Tasks

For the month of September 20X8:

(i)   prepare a materials purchases budget (at basic price);

(ii)   prepare a labour budget in terms of numbers of employees;

(iii)   assuming the rate of price increase is the same this year as last year, recalculate the cost of materials purchased.

(b)   The budget has been discussed with the production manager and he is concerned about two issues, namely:

(i)   how useful are the materials price indices supplied by the buyer for budgeting the costs of materials?

(ii)   given that the wages costs are significant, what information should be supplied daily, weekly and monthly to control this area?

Tasks

Prepare a memo for the production manager. Your memo should:

(i)   address the issues of concern;
(ii)   suggest and justify an alternative method for predicting materials prices.

27 Northern Products Ltd (60 mins)   12/99

(a)   You have recently been promoted to the post of management accountant with Northern Products Ltd, a company formed four years ago. The company has always used budgets to help plan its production of two products, the Exe and the Wye. Both products use the same material and labour but in different proportions.

You have been asked to prepare the budget for quarter 1, the twelve weeks ending 24 March 20X0. In previous budgets, the closing stocks of both raw materials and finished products were the same as opening stocks. You questioned whether or not this was the most efficient policy for the company.

As a result, you have carried out an investigation into the stock levels required to meet the maximum likely sales demand for finished goods and production demand for raw materials. You conclude that closing stocks of finished goods should be expressed in terms of days sales for the next quarter and closing stocks of raw materials in terms of days production for the next quarter.

Your findings are included in the data below, which also shows data provided by the sales and production directors of Northern Products Ltd.

Product data	Exe	Wye
• Budgeted sales in units, quarter 1	930 units	1,320 units
• Budgeted sales in units, quarter 2	930 units	1,320 units
• Budgeted material per unit (litres)	6 litres	9 litres
• Budgeted labour hours per unit	12 hours	7 hours
• Opening units of finished stock	172 units	257 units
• Closing units of finished stock (days sales next quarter)	8 days	9 days
• Failure rate of finished production*	2%	3%
• Finance and other costs of keeping a unit in stock per quarter	£4.00	£5.00

*Failed products are only discovered on completion of production and have no residual value.

Other accounting data	
• Weeks in accounting period	12 weeks
• Days per week for production and sales	5 days
• Hours per week	35 hours
• Number of employees	46 employees
• Budgeted labour rate per hour	£6.00
• Overtime premium for hours worked in excess of 35 hours per week	30%
• Budgeted cost of material per litre	£15.00
• Opening raw material stocks (litres)	1,878 litres
• Closing raw material stocks (days production next quarter)	5 days
• Financing and other costs of keeping a litre of raw material in stock per quarter	£1.00

Tasks

(i)   Calculate the following information for **quarter 1**, the twelve weeks ending 24 March 20X0.

   (1)   The number of production days
   (2)   The closing finished stock for Exe and Wye in units
   (3)   The labour hours available before overtime has to be paid

(ii)　Prepare the following budgets for quarter 1, the twelve weeks ending 24 March 20X0.

　　　(1)　The production budget in units for Exe and Wye, including any faulty production
　　　(2)　The material purchases budget in litres and value
　　　(3)　The production labour budget in hours and value, including any overtime payments

(iii)　Calculate the savings arising from the change in the required stock levels for the twelve weeks ending 24 March 20X0.

(b)　On completing the budget for quarter 1, the production director of Northern Products Ltd tells you that the company is likely to introduce a third product, the Zed, in the near future. Because of this, he suggests that future budgets should be prepared using a spreadsheet. He explains that the use of spreadsheets to prepare budgets not only saves time but also provides flexibility by allowing the results of changes in the budget to be readily shown. The sales director is not convinced.

The production director suggests you demonstrate the advantages of budgets prepared on spreadsheets by using a template of a spreadsheet and sales data for the planned third product.

He gives you the following sales data he has received from the sales director.

- Estimated annual volume for Zed is 20,000 units.
- Planned unit selling price is £90.00.
- Seasonal variations are as follows.

Quarter	Seasonal variation percentage change
1	+20%
2	+ 30%
3	− 10%
4	− 40%

Tasks

(i)　Calculate the budgeted volume of Zed for each quarter.

(ii)　Using the information provided by the sales director and a copy of the suggested spreadsheet template reproduced below, express the data provided by the sales director as formulae which would enable revised sales budgets to be calculated with the minimum of effort if sales price and annual volume were to change. (You may amend the template if desired to suit any spreadsheet with which you are familiar.)

	A	B	C	D	E	F
1		Unit selling price	£90			
2		Annual volume	20,000			
3		Seasonal variations	20%	30%	− 10%	− 40%
4			Quarter 1	Quarter 2	Quarter 3	Quarter 4
5		Seasonal variations (units)				
6		Quarterly volume				
7		Quarterly turnover				

28 Sandwell Ltd (80 mins)   6/01

(a)   Sandwell Ltd makes a single product, the Gamma. You are Sandwell's management accountant and you are responsible for preparing its operating budgets. The accounting year is divided into 13, four-week periods. There are five days in each week.

The sales director of Sandwell has recently completed the following forecast sales volume for the next five periods.

Sales forecast five periods to 18 November 20X1					
Period number	1	2	3	4	5
Four weeks ending	29 Jul	26 Aug	23 Sep	21 Oct	18 Nov
Number of Gammas	19,400	21,340	23,280	22,310	22,310

The production director provides you with the following information.

- On completion of production, 3% of the Gammas are found to be faulty and have to be scrapped. The faulty Gammas have no scrap value.

- Opening stocks: period 1, four weeks ending 29 July

    - Finished stock 3,880 Gammas
    - Raw materials 16,500 litres

- Closing stocks at the end of each period

    - Finished stock must equal 4 days' sales volume of Gammas in the next period.
    - Raw materials must equal 5 days' gross production in the next period.

- Each Gamma requires three litres of material costing £8 per litre.

- Each Gamma requires 0.5 hours of labour.

- Sandwell employs 70 production workers who each work a 40 hour week. Each employee is paid a guaranteed wage of £240 per week.

- The cost of any overtime is £9 per hour.

Tasks

Prepare the following budgets for the production director.

(i)   Gross production budget in Gammas (including faulty production) for each of the first four periods
(ii)   Material purchases budget in litres for each of the first three periods
(iii)   Cost of the material purchases for each of the first three periods
(iv)   Labour budget in hours for each of the first three periods including any overtime required in each period
(v)   Cost of the labour budget for each of the first three periods, including the cost of any overtime

(b)   After receiving your budgets, Sandwell's production director raises the following points.

- Overtime payments should only be made if absolutely necessary.

- The faulty Gammas are thought to be caused by poor work practices by some of the production workers although this is not known for certain.

- The 70 production workers work independently of one another in making Gammas.

Task

Write a memo to the production director. In your memo, you should do the following.

(i) Explain and quantify the value of any possible overtime savings.

(ii) Suggest ONE extra cost which might be necessary to achieve the overtime savings.

(iii) Identify TWO advantages of sampling as a way of discovering reasons for the faulty Gammas.

(iv) Briefly explain the difference between true (or simple) random sampling, systematic sampling and stratified sampling.

(v) State which form of sampling Sandwell should use.

chapters 10 and 11

Budgetary control and further aspects of budgeting

This checklist shows which activities cover the performance criteria, range statements and knowledge and understanding points dealt with in Chapters 10 and 11 of the BPP *Managing Costs and Controlling Resources* Interactive Text.

Performance criteria		Activities
9.2D	Communicate with budget holders in a manner which maintains goodwill and ensure budget proposals are agreed with budget holders	31, 32
9.3A	Check and reconcile budget figures on an ongoing basis	38, 39
9.3B	Correctly code and allocate actual cost and revenue data to responsibility centres	34, 35
9.3C	Clearly and correctly identify variances and prepare relevant reports for management	29, 33, 36
9.3D	Discuss with budget holders and other managers any significant variances and help managers take remedial action	35, 37

Range statement

9.3	Types of budgets: budget for income and expenditure; resource budget; fixed and flexible budgets	22, 29, 31-39
9.3	Responsibility centres: expense centres; profit centres	34, 36
9.3	Variances: actual; potential	29, 31-39

Knowledge and understanding		Activities
Unit 8 Accounting principles and theory		
11	Effect of accounting controls on behaviour of managers and other employees	31, 32, 35
Unit 9 Accounting techniques		
4	Use of relevant computer packages	27, 30
8	Budgets for control: flexible budgets, marginal costing	29, 31-39
9	The effect of budgetary systems on the behaviour and motivation of managers and other employees	31, 32, 35
10	Analysing the significance of budget variances and possible responses required by managers	33, 36, 37
11	Presentation of budget data in a form that satisfies the differing needs of budget holders	32, 34, 36, 37
Unit 9 Accounting principles and theory		
12	Marginal and absorption costing: cost recording, cost reporting, cost behaviour	32, 38, 39
13	Uses of budgetary control: planning, co-ordinating, authorising, cost control	32, 33
Unit 9 The organisation		
17	The structure of the organisation and its responsibility centres and an understanding of the inter-relationships between departments and functions is required	34, 36
18	Responsibility centres: expense centres; profit centres; investment centres	34, 36

29 Flexed budgets

Extracts from the budgets of Dexter Ltd, the company where you work as accounts assistant, are given below.

	Period 1	Period 2	Period 3	Period 4	Period 5
		Sales and stock budgets (units)			
Opening stock	4,000	2,500	3,300	2,500	3,000
Sales	15,000	20,000	16,500	21,000	18,000

		Cost budgets	
	Period 1	Period 2	Period 3
	£'000	£'000	£'000
Direct labour	270.0	444.0	314.0
Direct materials	108.0	166.4	125.6
Production overhead (excluding depreciation)	117.5	154.0	128.5
Depreciation	40.0	40.0	40.0
Administration overhead	92.0	106.6	96.4
Selling overhead	60.0	65.0	61.5

The following information is also available.

- Production above 18,000 units incurs a bonus in addition to normal wage rates.

- Any variable costs contained in selling overhead are assumed to vary with sales. All other variable costs are assumed to vary with production.

Tasks

(a)   Calculate the budgeted production for periods 1 to 4.

(b)   Prepare a suitable cost budget for period 4.

(c)   In period 4 the stock and sales budgets were achieved and the following actual costs recorded.

	£'000
Direct labour	458
Direct material	176
Production overhead	181
Depreciation	40
Administration overhead	128
Selling overhead	62
	1,045

Show the budget variances from actual.

30 Spreadsheets (35 mins)

A company is considering its budget for next year and estimates that it will sell 300 units of product J during August and 600 units during September.

Each unit of product J requires eight hours of labour, the labour rate being £8 per hour.

It is company policy to hold stocks of finished goods at the end of each month equal to 50% of the following month's sales demand.

At the end of the production process the products are tested: it is usual for 10% of those tested to be faulty. It is not possible to rectify these faulty units.

Explain clearly, using the data above, how you would construct a spreadsheet to produce the labour requirements budget for August 20X9. Include a specimen cell layout diagram containing formulae which would be the basis for the spreadsheet.

31 World History Museum (60 mins)

The World History Museum has an education department which specialises in running courses in various subjects. The courses are run on premises which the museum rents for the purpose and they are presented by freelance expert speakers. Each course is of standard type and format and can therefore be treated alike for budgetary control purposes.

The museum currently uses fixed budgets to control expenditure. The following data show the actual costs of the education department for the month of April compared with the budgeted figures.

Education department – April

	Actual	Budget	Variance
Number of courses run	5	6	(1)
	£	£	£
Expenditure			
Speakers' fees	2,500	3,180	680
Hire of premises	1,500	1,500	
Depreciation of equipment	200	180	(20)
Stationery	530	600	70
Catering	1,500	1,750	250
Insurance	700	820	120
Administration	1,650	1,620	(30)
	8,580	9,650	1,070

You have recently started work as the assistant management accountant for the museum. During a discussion with Chris Brooks, the general manager, she expresses to you some doubt about the usefulness of the above statement in providing control information for the education department manager.

Chris is interested in the possibility of using flexible budgets to control the activities of the education department. You therefore spend some time analysing the behaviour patterns of the costs incurred in the education department. Your findings can be summarised as follows.

- Depreciation of equipment is a fixed cost.

- Administration is a fixed cost.

- The budget figures for the catering costs and insurance costs include a fixed element as follows.

    Catering £250
    Insurance £100

    The remaining elements of the catering and insurance costs follow linear variable patterns.

- All other costs follow linear variable patterns.

Tasks

(a) Use the above information to produce a budgetary control statement for April, based on a flexible budget for the actual number of courses run.

(b) Calculate the revised variances based on your flexible budget.

(c) Chris Brooks's interest in the control aspects of budgeting has been sparked by her attendance on a course entitled 'Budgetary control for managers'. She has shown you the following extract from the course notes she was given.

    'A system of participative budgeting involves managers in the process of setting their own budgets. Participative systems are likely to be more successful in planning and controlling the activities of an organisation.'

    Write a brief memo to Chris Brooks which explains the advantages and disadvantages of participative budgeting as part of the budgetary planning and control process.

32 Parmod plc (72 mins)

(a)   Six months ago, Parmod plc established a new subsidiary, Trygon Ltd. Trygon was formed to assemble and sell computers direct to the public. Its annual budget was drawn up by Mike Barratt, Parmod's Finance Director. Trygon's plant was capable of producing 150,000 computers per year although the budget for the first year was only 80% of this amount. Factory overheads – defined as all factory fixed costs other than labour – were to be charged to finished stocks **at all times** on the basis of this 80% activity, irrespective of actual activity.

Trygon had entered into an agreement with the employees whereby their wages were guaranteed, provided the employees made themselves available to produce 120,000 computers per year. Because of this agreement, the labour element in finished stocks was always to be based on a production level of 120,000 computers. If output exceeded the 120,000 units, additional overtime equivalent to £70 per computer would be paid. Managers were also to be given a bonus of £15 per computer produced in excess of 120,000 units in the year.

At the beginning of the year, Mike had given all the managers a financial statement showing the annual budget (based on 80% activity) and the effect of operation at only half the planned activity. This is reproduced below.

Trygon Ltd budgeted profit for the year to 31 December 20X8

	Annual budget £	40% £
Direct materials	24,000,000	12,000,000
Direct labour	7,200,000	7,200,000
Light, heat and power	4,000,000	2,200,000
Production management salaries	1,500,000	1,500,000
Factory rent, rates and insurance	9,400,000	9,400,000
Depreciation of factory machinery	5,500,000	5,500,000
National advertising	20,000,000	20,000,000
Marketing and administration	2,300,000	2,300,000
Delivery costs	2,400,000	1,200,000
Total costs	76,300,000	61,300,000
Sales revenue	84,000,000	42,000,000
Operating profit/(loss)	7,700,000	(19,300,000)

In preparing the financial statement, Mike Barratt had made the following assumptions.

- Unit selling prices were the same over the different activity levels.

- No quantity discounts or other similar efficiencies had been assumed for purchases.

- Production fixed overheads comprised the depreciation of the machinery, the rent, rates and insurance, the production management salaries (other than any possible bonus) and part of the cost of light, heat and power.

Six months after Mike Barratt had issued the statement, you are called to a meeting of the directors of Trygon Ltd. Anne Darcy, the managing director, tells you that production and sales for the year are likely to be 112,500 computers.

Task

You are the Management Accountant to Trygon. Anne Darcy asks you to prepare a flexible budget for the year using the data given by Mike Barratt and assuming 112,500 computers are produced and sold. She also asks you to identify the budgeted profit.

(b)   On receiving your flexible budget, Anne Darcy reminds her fellow directors that Trygon plans a major marketing campaign at the beginning of the next financial year and this will require a building up of stocks in preparation for the campaign. The production director, Alan Williams, believes it is feasible to increase production close to capacity without increasing any of the fixed costs. As a result, the Board agrees to budget for sales of 112,500 units by the year end but to produce at 95% capacity.

A discussion then followed about the role of budgeting in Trygon Ltd. 'I do not know why we should take up all this time discussing budgets' said Anne Darcy. 'They are not my figures. I had no say in their preparation. Let Mike Barratt take responsibility for them – after all, it was his budget – and let us get on with the job of building up a business.'

'I agree,' Alan Williams said. 'I wish Mike would make up his mind what we are supposed to be doing. Are we just concerned with making short-term profits or are we supposed to be building up a quality product? Just what are our objectives when budgeting? Besides, you can prove anything with figures. Just look at the budget prepared by the Management Accountant compared with the annual budget prepared by Mike Barratt.'

Anne Darcy then turns to you. 'We need to resolve these issues. Will you please write a short report to the Board members giving us your advice.'

Task

In response to Anne Darcy's request, you are asked to write a short report drawing on the information given above. The report should do the following.

(i)   Recalculate the flexible budget based on production at 95% capacity assuming fixed overheads in finished stock are based on 80% activity.

(ii)   Explain why the revised flexible budget may differ from the one prepared in task (a).

(iii)   Answer the issues raised by Alan Williams regarding the two different budget statements, the uncertainty about budgetary objectives and the manipulation of budget data.

(iv)   Briefly discuss whether or not Anne Darcy should have been responsible for preparing the original budget.

33 Happy Holidays Ltd (90 mins)

(a)   Happy Holidays Ltd sells holidays to Xanadu through newspaper advertisements. Tourists are flown each week of the holiday season to Xanadu, where they take a 10 day touring holiday. In 20X8, Happy Holidays began to use the least-squares regression formula to help forecast the demand for its holidays.

You are employed by Happy Holidays as an accounting technician in the financial controller's department. A colleague of yours has recently used the least-squares regression formula on a spreadsheet to estimate the demand for holidays per year. The resulting formula was $y = 640 + 40x$, where y is the annual demand and x is the year. The data started with the number of holidays sold in 20X1 and was identified in the formula as year 1.

In each subsequent year the value of x increases by 1 so, for example, 20X6 was year 6. To obtain the **weekly** demand the result is divided by 25, the number of weeks Happy Holidays operates in Xanadu.

Tasks

(i)   Use the least-squares regression formula developed by your colleague to estimate the weekly demand for holidays in Xanadu for 20X9.

(ii)   In preparation for a budget meeting with the financial controller, draft a *brief* note. Your note should identify THREE weaknesses of the least-squares regression formula in forecasting the weekly demand of holidays in Xanadu.

(b)   The budget and actual costs for holidays to Xanadu for the 10 days ended 27 November 20X8 is reproduced below.

Happy Holidays Ltd Cost Statement			
10 days ended 27 November 20X8			
	Fixed budget	*Actual*	*Variances*
	£	£	£
Aircraft seats	18,000	18,600	600 A
Coach hire	5,000	4,700	300 F
Hotel rooms	14,000	14,200	200 A
Meals	4,800	4,600	200 F
Tour guide	1,800	1,700	100 F
Advertising	2,000	1,800	200 F
Total costs	45,600	45,600	0
Key: A = adverse, F = favourable			

The financial controller gives you the following additional information.

Cost and volume information

- Each holiday lasts 10 days.

- Meals and hotel rooms are provided for each of the 10 days.

- The airline charges £450 per return flight per passenger for each holiday but the airline will only sell seats at this reduced price if Happy Holidays purchases seats in blocks of 20.

- The costs of coach hire, the tour guide and advertising are fixed costs.

- The cost of meals was budgeted at £12 per tourist per day.

- The cost of a single room was budgeted at £60 per day.

- The cost of a double room was budgeted at £70 per day.

- 38 tourists travelled on the holiday requiring 17 double rooms and 4 single rooms.

Sales information

- The price of a holiday is £250 more if using a single room.

Task

Write a memo to the financial controller. Your memo should:

(i)   take account of the cost and volume information to prepare a revised cost statement using flexible budgeting and identifying any variances;

(ii) state and justify which of the two cost statements is more useful for management control of costs;

(iii) identify THREE factors to be taken into account in deciding whether or not to investigate individual variances.

34 Professor Pauline Heath (70 mins)

It is 1 March and Professor Pauline Heath has just taken up her new appointment as the head of the postgraduate business department in a new university. Due to unfilled vacancies throughout the current academic year, the department has had to rely on part-time academic staff. The cost of part-time staff who are self-employed is coded to account number 321, while those who are taxed under the pay-as-you-earn system are charged to account code 002. Both types of staff enter their claims within ten days of each month-end and these then appear in the management reports of the subsequent month. There are also unfilled clerical and administrative staff vacancies.

The university has a residential conference centre which the department makes use of from time to time. Sometimes this is because the department's allocated rooms are all in use and sometimes because the department teaches at weekends. The charge for the use of the centre is coded to account 673. An alternative to using the conference centre is to hire outside facilities at local hotels in which case the expenditure is coded to account 341.

The main forms of income are tuition fees and a higher education grant from the government. The extent of this grant is known before the commencement of the academic year and is payable in two parts, one third at the end of December and the balance at the end of April.

One of Professor Heath's first tasks was to check the enrolments for the current year. The financial and academic year commenced 1 September and is subdivided into three terms, each lasting four months. The Autumn term commenced 1 September and the Spring term 1 January. All courses commence at the beginning of the Autumn term, the MBA and MSc courses lasting three terms and the diploma course two terms.

The departmental administrator has presented Professor Heath with the enrolment data for the current academic year. Whilst absorbing this information, she also receives the latest management accounts for the department. Both sets of information are reproduced below.

Professor Heath is experiencing difficulties in understanding the latest management report. She has written a memo to the university's finance director expressing her anxieties about the presentation of the report and its detailed contents.

Enrolment data – current academic year	Fee £	Enrolments	Income £
MBA – three terms	3,500	160	560,000
MSc – three terms	3,200	80	256,000
Diploma Course – two terms	1,200	100	120,000
			936,000

Department of postgraduate business studies
Monthly management report – February

Code	Account heading	Annual budget	6 months to 28 February			Budget remaining
			Actual	Budget	Variance	
	Expenses					
001	Full-time academic	600,000	230,000	300,000	70,000	370,000
002	Part-time academic	84,000	48,000	42,000	–6,000	36,000
003	Clerical and administrative	84,000	36,000	42,000	6,000	48,000
218	Teaching and learning material	30,000	0	15,000	15,000	30,000
321	Teaching and research fees	20,000	19,000	10,000	–9,000	1,000
331	Agency staff (clerical and administrative)	300	2,400	150	–2,250	–2,100
341	External room hire	1,000	400	500	100	600
434	Course advertising (Press)	26,000	600	13,000	12,400	25,400
455	Postage and telephone recharge	8,000	1,200	4,000	2,800	6,800
673	Internal room hire	24,000	14,000	12,000	–2,000	10,000
679	Central services recharge	340,000	170,000	170,000	0	170,000
680	Rental light and heat recharge	260,000	130,000	130,000	0	130,000
		1,477,300	651,600	738,650	87,050	825,700
	Income					
802	Tuition fees	900,000	936,000	900,000	–36,000	–36,000
890	Higher education grant	750,000	250,000	250,000	0	500,000
		1,650,000	1,186,000	1,150,000	–36,000	464,000
	Net surplus/deficit	172,700	534,400	411,350	–123,050	–361,700

Tasks

(a) (i) Rearrange the account headings in a more meaningful form for managers. This should include columnar headings for any financial data you feel is appropriate but you DO NOT need to include any figures.

(ii) Briefly justify your proposals.

(b) In her memo, Professor Heath states that the current form of report does not help her manage her department. Identify the strengths and weaknesses apparent in the current system, other than the presentational ones covered in Task (a), and make and justify outline proposals which will help her manage the department.

(c) Referring to the detailed financial data under the heading of INCOME above, reproduce the actual income to date in a form consistent with accounting principles.

All working should be shown.

35 Rivermede Ltd (45 mins)   6/99

(a) Rivermede Ltd makes a single product called the Fasta. Last year, Steven Jones, the managing director of Rivermede Ltd, attended a course on budgetary control. As a result, he agreed to revise the way budgets were prepared in the company. Rather than imposing targets for managers, he encouraged participation by senior managers in the preparation of budgets.

An initial budget was prepared but Mike Fisher, the sales director, felt that the budgeted sales volume was set too high. He explained that setting too high a budgeted sales volume would mean that his sales staff would be de-motivated because they would not be able to achieve the sales volume. Steven Jones agreed to use the revised sales volume suggested by Mike Fisher.

Both the initial and revised budgets are reproduced below complete with the actual results for the year ended 31 May 20X5.

Rivermede Ltd – budgeted and actual costs for the year ended 31 May 20X5				
	Original budget	Revised budget	Actual results	Variances from revised budget
Fasta production and sales (units)	24,000	20,000	22,000	2,000 (F)
	£	£	£	£
Variable costs				
Material	216,000	180,000	206,800	26,800 (A)
Labour	288,000	240,000	255,200	15,200 (A)
Semi-variable costs				
Heat, light and power	31,000	27,000	33,400	6,400 (A)
Fixed costs				
Rent, rates and depreciation	40,000	40,000	38,000	2,000 (F)
	575,000	487,000	533,400	46,400 (A)

Assumptions in the two budgets

1   No change in input prices
2   No change in the quantity of variable inputs per Fasta

As the management accountant at Rivermede Ltd, one of your tasks is to check that invoices have been properly coded. On checking the actual invoices for heat, light and power for the year to 31 May 20X5, you find that one invoice for £7,520 had been incorrectly coded. The invoice should have been coded to materials.

Tasks

(i)   Using the information in the original and revised budgets, identify the following.

       (1)   The variable cost of material and labour per Fasta
       (2)   The fixed and unit variable cost within heat, light and power

(ii)   Prepare a flexible budget, including variances, for Rivermede Ltd after correcting for the miscoding of the invoice.

(b)   On receiving your flexible budget statement, Steven Jones states that the total adverse variance is much less than the £46,400 shown in the original statement. He also draws your attention to the actual sales volume being greater than in the revised budget. He believes these results show that a participative approach to budgeting is better for the company and wants to discuss this belief at the next board meeting. Before doing so, Steven Jones asks for your comments.

Task

Write a memo to Steven Jones. Your memo should do the following.

(i) **Briefly** explain why the flexible budgeting variances differ from those in the original statement given in the data to task (a).

(ii) Give TWO reasons why a favourable cost variance may have arisen other than through the introduction of participative budgeting.

(iii) Give TWO reasons why the actual sales volume compared with the revised budget's sales volume may not be a measure of improved motivation following the introduction of participative budgeting.

36 Viking Smelting Company (120 mins)

(a) The Viking Smelting Company established a division, called the reclamation division, in April 20X5, to extract silver from jewellers' waste materials. The waste materials are processed in a furnace, enabling silver to be recovered. The silver is then further processed into finished products by three other divisions within the company.

A performance report is prepared each month for the reclamation division which is then discussed by the management team. Sharon Houghton, the newly appointed financial controller of the reclamation division, has recently prepared her first report for the four weeks to 31 May 20X8. This is shown below.

Performance Report – Reclamation Division – 4 weeks to 31 May 20X8

	Actual	Budget	Variance	Comments
Production (tonnes)	200	250	50 (A)	
	£	£	£	
Wages and social security costs	46,133	45,586	547 (A)	Overspend
Fuel	15,500	18,750	3,250 (F)	
Consumables	2,100	2,500	400 (F)	
Power	1,590	1,750	160 (F)	
Divisional overheads	21,000	20,000	1,000 (A)	Overspend
Plant maintenance	6,900	5,950	950 (A)	Overspend
Central services	7,300	6,850	450 (A)	Overspend
Total	100,523	101,386	863 (F)	

(A) = adverse, (F) = favourable

In preparing the budgeted figures, the following assumptions were made for May.

- The reclamation division was to employ four teams of six production employees.

- Each employee was to work a basic 42 hour week and be paid £7.50 per hour for the four weeks of May.

- Social security and other employment costs were estimated at 40% of basic wages.

- A bonus, shared amongst the production employees, was payable if production exceeded 150 tonnes. This varied depending on the output achieved.

  - If output was between 150 and 199 tonnes, the bonus was £3 per tonne produced.
  - If output was between 200 and 249 tonnes, the bonus was £8 per tonne produced.
  - If output exceeded 249 tonnes the bonus was £13 per tonne produced.

- The cost of fuel was £75 per tonne.

- Consumables were £10 per tonne.

- Power comprised a fixed charge of £500 per four weeks plus £5 per tonne for every tonne produced.

- Overheads directly attributable to the division were £20,000.

- Plant maintenance was to be apportioned to divisions on the basis of the capital values of each division.

- The cost of Viking's central services was to be shared equally by all four divisions.

You are the deputy financial controller of the reclamation division. After attending her first monthly meeting with the board of the reclamation division, Sharon Houghton arranges a meeting with you. She is concerned about a number of issues, one of them being that the current report does not clearly identify those expenses and variances which are the direct responsibility of the reclamation division.

Task

Sharon Houghton asks you to prepare a flexible budget report for the reclamation division for May 20X8 in a form consistent with responsibility accounting.

(b) On receiving your revised report, Sharon tells you about the other questions raised at the management meeting when the original report was presented. These are summarised below.

- Question 1: Why are the budgeted figures based on two year old data taken from the proposal recommending the establishment of the reclamation division?

- Question 2: Should the budget data be based on what we are proposing to do or what we actually did do?

- Question 3: Is it true that the less we produce the more favourable our variances will be?

- Question 4: Why is there so much maintenance in a new division with modern equipment and why should we be charged with the actual costs of the maintenance department even when they overspend?

- Question 5: Could the comments explaining variances be improved?

- Question 6: Should all the variances be investigated?

- Question 7: Does showing the cost of central services on the divisional performance report help control these costs and motivate the divisional managers?

Task

Prepare a memo for the management of the reclamation division. Your memo should:

(i) answer their queries and justify your comments;

(ii) highlight the main objective of your revised performance report developed in task (a) and give two advantages of it over the original report.

37 Parkside Manufacturing Ltd (80 mins) 12/00

(a)   You have recently been appointed as the management accountant of Parkside Manufacturing Ltd. Parkside Manufacturing makes a single product, the Delta. The previous management accountant has already prepared an analysis of budgeted and actual results for the year to 30 November 20X0. These are reproduced below.

Parkside Manufacturing Ltd						
Operating statement for year ended 30 November 20X0						
	Budget		Actual		Variance	
Volume (number of Deltas)	100,000		125,000			
	£'000	£'000	£'000	£'000	£'000	
Turnover		2,000		2,250	250	(F)
Material	600		800		200	(A)
Light, heat and power	200		265		65	(A)
Production labour	120		156		36	(A)
Rent, rates and depreciation	140		175		35	(A)
Administrative expenses	110		110		–	
		1,170		1,506		
Profit		830		744	86	(A)
Key. (F) = favourable, (A) = adverse						

Judith Green, the production director, tells you that the following assumptions were made when the budget was originally prepared.

- Material is entirely a variable cost.

- Light, heat and power is a semi-variable cost. The fixed element included in the budgeted figure was £40,000.

- Production labour is a stepped cost. Each production employee can make up to 10,000 Deltas. Each production employee was budgeted to receive a basic wage of £12,000 per year with no overtime and no bonuses.

- There are no part-time employees.

- Rent, rates and depreciation, and administrative expenses are fixed costs.

Tasks

(i)   In preparation for the next board meeting of Parkside Manufacturing Ltd, calculate the following.

    (1)   Budgeted cost of material per Delta
    (2)   Budgeted variable cost per Delta of light, heat and power
    (3)   Number of production employees assumed in the budget

(ii)   Prepare a statement which compares the actual results of Parkside Manufacturing with the flexible budget, and identify any variances.

(b)   On receiving your flexible budget and variances, Judith Green gives you the following information.

- She does not understand why there is a need for the two types of budget, the one prepared by the previous management accountant and the flexible budget prepared by yourself.

- She does not know if it is necessary to investigate all variances.

- She is concerned that the original budgeted sales volume was so different from the actual sales volume and is considering the use of linear regression to improve sales forecasting of Deltas.

Tasks

Judith Green asks you to write a brief report in preparation for the board meeting. In your report, you should do the following.

(i)   Briefly explain the different purposes of the two types of budget, and explain which one should be used to compare with the actual results.

(ii)   Suggest THREE general factors that need to be taken into account in deciding whether or not to investigate variances.

(iii) Briefly explain THREE limitations to the use of linear regression in sales forecasting.

38 HFD plc (120 mins)   12/99

(a)   HFD plc opened a new division on 1 December 20X0. The division, HFD Processes Ltd, produces a special paint finish. Because of the technology, there can never be any work in progress. The original budget was developed on the assumption that there would be a loss in the initial year of operation and that there would be no closing stock of finished goods.

One year later, HFD Processes Ltd prepared its results for its first year of operations. The chief executive of HFD plc was pleased to see that, despite budgeting for an initial loss, the division had actually returned a profit of £74,400. As a result, the directors of HFD Processes were entitled to a substantial bonus. Details of the budget and actual results are reproduced below.

HFD Processes Operating results for year ended 30 November 20X1				
	Budget		Actual	
Volume (units)		20,000		22,000
	£	£	£	£
Turnover		960,000		1,012,000
Direct costs				
Materials	240,000		261,800	
Production labour	260,000		240,240	
Light, heat and power	68,000		65,560	
	568,000		567,600	
Fixed overheads	400,000		370,000	
Cost of sales		968,000		937,600
Operating profit/(loss)		(8,000)		74,400

You are employed as a management accountant in the head office of HFD plc and have been asked to comment on the performance of HFD Processes Ltd. Attached to the budgeted and actual results were the relevant working papers. A summary of the contents of the working papers is reproduced below.

- The budget assumed no closing finished stocks. Actual production was 25,000 units and actual sales 22,000 units.

- Because of the technology involved, production employees are paid per week, irrespective of production levels. The employees assumed in the budget are capable of producing up to 26,000 units.

- The cost of material varies directly with production.

- The cost of light, heat and power includes a fixed standing charge. In the budget this fixed charge was calculated to be £20,000 per year. However, competition resulted in the supplier reducing the actual charge to £12,000 for the year.

- During the year, HFD Processes Ltd produced 25,000 units. The 3,000 units of closing finished stock were valued on the basis of direct cost plus 'normal' fixed overheads.

  The number of units was used to apportion direct costs between the cost of sales and closing finished stock.

  The budgeted fixed overhead of £20 per unit was used to calculate the fixed overheads in closing finished stocks.

  The detailed composition of the cost of sales and closing stocks using these policies was as follows.

	Closing finished stocks	Cost of sales	Cost of production
Units	3,000	22,000	25,000
	£	£	£
Material	35,700	261,800	297,500
Production labour	32,760	240,240	273,000
Light, heat and power	8,940	65,560	74,500
Fixed overheads	60,000	370,000	430,000
	137,400	937,600	1,075,000

Tasks

(i) Calculate the following.

   (1) The budgeted unit selling price
   (2) The budgeted material cost per unit
   (3) The budgeted marginal cost of light, heat and power per unit
   (4) The actual marginal cost of light, heat and power per unit

(ii) Prepare a flexible budget statement for the operating results of HFD Processes Ltd using a **marginal costing** approach, identifying fixed costs for the year and showing any variances.

(b)   You present your flexible budget statement to the chief executive of HFD plc who is concerned that your findings appear different to those in the original operating results.

Task

You are asked to write a **brief** memo to the chief executive. In your memo, you should do the following.

(i)   Give TWO reasons why the flexible budget operating statement shows different results from the original operating results.

(ii)   Give ONE reason why the flexible budget operating statement might be a better measure of management performance than the original operating results.

39 Hall Ltd (110 mins)   12/01

(a)   Hall Ltd makes a product called the Omega. The budgeted and actual results for the year ended 30 November 20X1 are shown below.

Hall Ltd: Budgeted and actual operating statement Year ended 30 November 20X1		
	Budget	*Actual*
Sales volume (units)	36,000	35,000
	£	£
Turnover	1,440,000	1,365,000
Direct costs		
Material	432,000	500,000
Labour	216,000	232,000
Light, heat and power	92,000	96,000
Fixed overheads		
Depreciation	100,000	70,000
Other fixed overheads	400,000	420,000
Costs of production	1,240,000	1,318,000
less closing stock	–	164,750
Cost of sales	1,240,000	1,153,250
Operating profit	200,000	211,750

Ann Jones, the senior management accountant gives you the following information.

*   Material and labour are variable costs.

*   The budgeted total cost of light, heat and power includes a fixed element of £20,000.

*   The actual cost of light, heat and power includes a fixed element of £12,000.

*   There were no budgeted or actual opening stocks.

*   During the year, **actual** production was 40,000 Omegas, of which 5,000 were unsold at the year end.

- The closing stock of 5,000 Omegas were valued at their actual direct cost plus an appropriate proportion of fixed overheads.

- The company did not purchase or sell any fixed assets during the year.

- There was no work in progress at any time.

Tasks

(i)   Calculate the following.

(1)   Budgeted selling price per Omega
(2)   Budgeted material cost per Omega
(3)   Budgeted labour cost per Omega
(4)   Budgeted variable cost of light, heat and power per Omega
(5)   The percentage of cost of production carried forward in closing stock
(6)   Total actual variable cost of sales by expenditure type
(7)   Total actual fixed costs

(ii)   Prepare a flexible budget statement using variable (or marginal) costing, showing the budgeted and actual results and any variances.

(b)   The chief executive of Hall Ltd is Harry Easton. On receiving the original budgeted and actual operating statement, he had been very pleased with the performance of Hall Ltd. After reading your revised statement, however, he is concerned about the changes in both the budgeted profits and actual profits and is considering investigating whether or not the managers of Hall Ltd were responsible for the differences. Ann Jones suggests you write a memo to the chief executive.

Task

Write a short memo to Harry Easton, the chief executive. In your memo you should do the following.

(i)   Briefly explain the main reason for the following.

(1)   The difference between the original budget and the budget you prepared in task (a)

(2)   The difference between the original operating profit and the operating profit you prepared in task (a)

(ii)   Give TWO possible reasons why the actual operating profit shown in task (a) was greater than the budgeted operating profit despite a lower sales volume.

Spreadsheets are also covered in activity 27.

---

chapters 12 and 13

Measurement of performance

Activity checklist

This checklist shows which activities cover the performance criteria, range statements and knowledge and understanding points dealt with in Chapters 12 and 13 of the BPP *Managing Costs and Controlling Resources* Interactive Text.

Performance criteria		Activities
8.2A	Analyse routine cost reports, compare them with other sources of information and identify any implications	40, 42, 43, 45, 49, 51
8.2B	Prepare and monitor relevant performance indicators, interpret the results, identify potential improvements and estimate the value of potential improvements	40, 41, 44-47
8.2D	Prepare exception reports to identify matters which require further investigation	48, 50

Range statement

8.2	Performance indicators to measure: efficiency, effectiveness and productivity; financial, customer, internal business and learning and growth perspectives; unit costs; resource utilisation; profitability; quality of service	40, 41, 43-51
8.2	Recommendations: benchmarking	45, 51

Knowledge and understanding

Unit 8 Accounting techniques

6	Performance indicators: efficiency, effectiveness; productivity; balanced scorecard, benchmarking; unit costs; control ratios (efficiency, capacity and activity), scenario planning ('what-if' analysis)	40, 41, 43-51

40 Melsoven Ltd (65 mins)

Melosoven Ltd is a subsidiary company of Rengbaud plc and manufactures motor components. It is run as a separate entity from the parent company, however. Rengbaud plc monitors the performance of subsidiaries using a quarterly financial ratio analysis. Melosoven Ltd's factory is in Swansea.

You are employed as a financial analyst in Rengbaud plc's corporate finance department at the group's Leicestershire headquarters. Louise Simpson, the managing director of Melosoven Ltd, is at group head office for a meeting. She has called into your office with the last quarter's summary results which have just been faxed to her. Louise needs to have these figures analysed as quickly as possible and has obtained the agreement of Rob Hutchings, your immediate superior, for you to assist her.

Melosoven Ltd Financial results for quarter 4					
Operating statement			**Operating net assets at quarter end**		
	£'000	£'000		£'000	£'000
Sales		4,759	Fixed assets (NBV)		7,253
Materials	1,583				
Labour	1,196		Current assets		
Production overheads	1,201		Materials stocks	305	
		3,980	Work in progress	224	
Gross profit		779	Finished goods stocks	1,326	
Admin overheads		427	Debtors	2,040	
Operating profit		352	Bank and cash	83	
				3,978	
			Current liabilities		
Stock changes			Trade creditors	2,362	
Materials		+ 43	Other creditors	758	
Work in progress		0		3,120	
Finished goods		+ 231	Working capital		858
			Net assets		8,111

Tasks

(a) Given that there are 91 days in quarter 4, prepare a table containing the following performance indicators for Melosoven Ltd for quarter 4.

 (i) The quarterly return on capital employed
 (ii) The operating profit margin as a percentage
 (iii) The quarterly asset turnover
 (iv) The average age of period-end debtors in days
 (v) The average age of period-end trade creditors in days
 (vi) The average age of period-end materials stocks in days
 (vii) The average age of period-end finished goods stocks in days

(b) Louise needs a comparison between the quarter 4 results and those for the earlier quarters to take with her to a meeting at which Rengbaud plc's board will be reviewing the performance of Melosoven Ltd.

You are able to extract the following figures from Rengbaud plc's corporate information system.

Performance indicators for Melosoven Ltd for quarters 1 to 3			
	Q1	Q2	Q3
Return on capital employed	4.3%	1.2%	2.8%
Operating profit margin	9.0%	2.6%	5.3%
Quarterly asset turnover	0.54	0.55	0.52
Age of debtors in days	39	38	44
Age of trade creditors in days	192	167	158
Age of materials stocks in days	29	24	18
Age of finished goods stocks in days	51	41	28

(i) Given that Melosoven Ltd's business is *not* seasonal, update the above table to include Melosoven Ltd's quarter 4 figures.

(ii) Write a briefing note to Louise comparing Melosoven Ltd's quarter 4 figures with those for quarters 1 to 3.

41 Chain of hotels

You are employed as a management accountant in the head office of a chain of hotels.

Task

List measures of performance that should be used to monitor the performance of the managers in the hotel chain.

42 Regent Hotel (30 mins)

The Regent Hotel is experiencing some problems with its full-time employees. They have been complaining for some time that their weekly earnings are beginning to fall behind the amount which they could earn in other hotels in the area. In the past, pay rises have always been based approximately on the annual increase in the Retail Prices Index (RPI).

The new manager is keen to be fair in the rates that he pays and he has asked you as assistant to the management accountant to prepare some information to help him in negotiations with the employees. You have collected the following data.

Regent Hotel: average weekly earnings of full-time employees.

	£ per week
20X4	195
20X7	208

Source: Hotel records

Hotel and Catering Industry: index of average weekly earnings of full-time employees in UK

	Index number
20X4	173.4
20X7	191.2

Source: Trade Association Statistics

Tasks

(a) Calculate what the average weekly earnings of Regent Hotel's full-time employees would have been in 20X7 if, since 20X4, they had increased at the same rate as average earnings in the hotel and catering industry.

(b) Prepare a memorandum for the manager which contains the following.

(i) A statement of whether his employees are correct in claiming that their earnings have lagged behind the industry average

(ii) Two limitations of a comparison between the hotel's employees' earnings and the average for the hotel and catering industry

(iii) An explanation of the Retail Prices Index (RPI), describing what the RPI is designed to show and the likely reason why the manager was using it as a basis for calculating wage increases

43 Traders plc (50 mins)

You are the assistant management accountant to Traders plc, a small retailing chain, and you have just left a meeting with the company's managing director who is concerned about the threat posed by the superior profitability of a major competitor, Sellars plc. Sellars have just published their annual report which shows profits of £1,956,760 generated by shareholders' funds of £5,765,000. A board meeting has been called for two weeks' time to discuss the board's development of a strategy to meet this threat. The summarised profit and loss accounts and balance sheets for both companies are reproduced below.

Trading and profit and loss accounts for the year ended 30 June 20X8

	Traders plc £	*Sellars plc* £
Turnover	24,000,000	26,800,000
Cost of sales	18,000,000	19,564,000
Gross profit	6,000,000	7,236,000
Administration expenses	4,060,000	4,330,000
Operating profit	1,940,000	2,906,000
Interest		150,000
Profit before taxation	1,940,000	2,756,000
Taxation	640,200	799,240
Profit after taxation	1,299,800	1,956,760
Dividends	800,000	1,200,000
Retained profits	499,800	756,760

Balance sheets as at 30 June 20X8

	Traders plc £	Sellars plc £
Fixed assets (see note 1)	4,320,000	5,270,000
Net current assets	1,500,000	1,995,000
Total assets	5,820,000	7,265,000
Long-term loans		1,500,000
	5,820,000	5,765,000
Financed by:		
Shareholders' funds	5,820,000	5,765,000
	5,820,000	5,765,000
Number of employees	170	200

Note 1

	Traders plc			Sellars plc		
	Cost £	Accumulated depreciation £	Net book value £	Cost £	Accumulated depreciation £	Net book value £
Fixed assets						
Land and buildings	5,000,000	1,200,000	3,800,000	12,000,000	7,200,000	4,800,000
Fixtures and fittings	800,000	480,000	320,000	700,000	350,000	350,000
Motor vehicles	400,000	200,000	200,000	600,000	480,000	120,000
Total	6,200,000	1,880,000	4,320,000	13,300,000	8,030,000	5,270,000

	Traders plc			Sellars plc		
	Land and buildings £	Fixtures and fittings £	Motor vehicles £	Land and buildings £	Fixtures and fittings £	Motor vehicles £
Depreciation charge for the year	100,000	160,000	100,000	240,000	70,000	120,000

Tasks

(a)   The management accountant of Traders plc has already analysed your company's results, focusing on the following six key ratios.

Return on capital employed (before interest and taxation)	33.33%
Gross profit margin	25%
Net (or sales) margin (before interest and taxation)	8.08%
Asset turnover	4.12 times
Turnover per employee	£141,176
Average age of working capital	30 days

The average age of working capital is defined as $\dfrac{\text{Working capital}}{\text{Cost of sales}} \times 365$

As the assistant management accountant to Traders plc, you are asked to calculate the above ratios for Sellars plc. Present your results in the form of a table alongside the ratios for your own company.

(b)   The turnover for Traders plc for the year to 30 June 20X7 was £23,000,000. A trade association index of retail prices stood at 224.50 for June 20X7 and 237.90 for June 20X8.

In anticipation of the board meeting, prepare a briefing paper for circulation to the directors of Traders plc.

Your paper should do the following.

(i)   Explain **in outline** the meaning and limitations of each ratio, making use of the given data where possible.

(ii)   Comment on any strengths and weaknesses found within Traders plc.

(iii) Use the trade association's statistics to show the percentage growth in Traders' sales volume since last year.

(iv)   Suggest two reasons why your estimate of sales volume growth might not be accurate.

44 Middle plc (25 mins)

Middle plc owns two subsidiaries, East Ltd and West Ltd, producing soft drinks. Both companies rent their premises and both use plant of similar size and technology. Middle plc requires the plant in the subsidiaries to be written off over ten years using straight-line depreciation and assuming zero residual values.

East Ltd was established five years ago but West Ltd has only been established for two years. Goods returned by customers generally arise from quality failures and are destroyed. Financial and other data relating to the two companies are reproduced below.

Profit and loss accounts year to 30 November 20X8	West Ltd £'000	East Ltd £'000	Balance sheets extracts at 30 November 20X8	West Ltd £'000	East Ltd £'000
Turnover	18,000	17,600	Plant	16,000	10,000
Less Returns	90	176	Depreciation to date	3,200	5,000
Net turnover	17,910	17,424	Net book value	12,800	5,000
Material	2,000	2,640	Current assets	4,860	3,000
Labour	4,000	4,840	Current liabilities	(2,320)	(1,500)
Production overheads*	3,000	3,080	Net assets	15,340	6,500
Gross profit	8,910	6,864			
Marketing	2,342	1,454			
Research & development	1,650	1,010			
Training	950	450			
Administration	900	1,155			
Operating profit	3,068	2,795			

*Includes plant depreciation of £1,600,000 for West Ltd and £1,000,000 for East Ltd

Other data (000's litres)	West Ltd	East Ltd
Gross sales	20,000	22,000
Returns	100	220
Net sales	19,900	21,780
Orders received in year	20,173	22,854

You are employed by Middle plc as a member of a team monitoring the performance of subsidiaries within the group. Middle plc aims to provide its shareholders with the best possible return for their investment and to meet customers' expectations. It does this by comparing the performance of subsidiaries and using the more efficient ones for benchmarking.

Tasks

Your team leader, Angela Wade, has asked you to prepare a report evaluating the performance of West Ltd and East Ltd. Your report should do the following.

(a)   Calculate and explain the meaning of the following financial ratios for each company.

      (i)   The return on capital employed

      (ii)   The asset turnover

      (iii)   The sales (or operating profit) margin

(b)   Calculate the percentage of faulty sales as a measure of the level of customer service for each company.

(c)   Identify one other possible measure of the level of customer service which could be derived from the accounting data.

(d)   Identify TWO limitations to your analysis in task (a), using the data in the accounts.

45 Grand Hotel (50 mins)

(a)   The Grand Hotel is a privately-owned hotel and restaurant located in a major business and tourist centre. Because of this, demand for accommodation is spread evenly throughout the year. However, in order to increase overall demand, the Grand Hotel has recently joined World Rest, an association of similar hotels. World Rest publicises member hotels throughout the world and provides advice and control to ensure common standards amongst its members. In addition, it provides overall performance indicators by location and category of hotel, allowing members to compare their own performance.

You are employed by Green and Co, the Grand Hotel's auditors, and your firm has been asked to calculate the hotel's performance statistics required by World Rest. A colleague informs you that the Grand Hotel:

- operates for 365 days of the year;
- has 80 double or twin bedrooms;
- charges £80 per night for each bedroom;
- charges guests separately for any meals taken.

Your colleague also gives you a copy of World Rest's performance indicators' manual. The manual details the performance indicators required and gives guidance on their calculation. The relevant performance indicators and a summary of Grand Hotel's latest set of accounts are reproduced below.

Extract from World Rest's performance indicators' manual

Indicator	Definitions
Maximum occupancy	Number of days in year × number of bedrooms
Occupancy rate	Annual total of rooms let per night as percentage of maximum occupancy
Gross margin: accommodation	Contribution from accommodation ÷ accommodation turnover
Gross margin: restaurant	Contribution from restaurant ÷ restaurant turnover
Operating profit: hotel	Profit before interest but after all other expenses
Sales margin: hotel	Operating profit ÷ total turnover
Return on capital employed: hotel	Operating profit ÷ net assets
Asset turnover: hotel	Standard definition

Grand Hotel
Profit and loss account
12 months ended 30 November 20X8

	Accommodation £	Restaurant £	Total £
Turnover	1,635,200	630,720	2,265,920
Variable costs	1,308,160	473,040	1,781,200
Contribution	327,040	157,680	484,720
Fixed costs			
Depreciation – land and buildings			24,000
Depreciation – fixtures and fitting			29,000
Administration			160,224
Rates and insurance			158,200
Debenture interest			80,000
Profit for the year			33,296

Extract from balance sheet at 30 November 20X8

	Land and buildings £	Fixtures and fitting £	Total £
Fixed assets			
Net book value	1,200,000	145,000	1,345,000
Net current assets			
Debtors		594,325	
Cash		88,125	
Creditors		(611,250)	
			71,200
Net assets			1,416,200

Task

Your colleague asks you to calculate the performance indicators listed above for the Grand Hotel using the definitions laid down by World Rest.

(b)   A few days later you receive a letter from Claire Hill, the manager of the Grand Hotel. She enclosed a summary sent to her by the World Rest organisation showing the average performance indicators for hotels in similar categories and locations. This is reproduced below.

World Rest Hotel Association Performance Summary

Location Code B	*Category Code 4*
Occupancy rate	80%
Gross margin: accommodation	22%
Gross margin: restaurant	20%
Sales margin: hotel	10%
Return on capital employed: hotel	20%
Asset turnover: hotel	2 times

In her letter to you, Claire Hill expresses her concern about the performance of the Grand Hotel and provides you with the following information.

- The restaurant is currently working at maximum capacity. Any volume improvement must, therefore, come from the accommodation side of the hotel's activities.

- It is not possible to change the level of the fixed assets nor the net current assets without adversely affecting the business.

    Claire Hill proposes increasing the return on capital employed to 20% by:

- increasing the occupancy rate to 80% of capacity while maintaining current prices; and

- increasing restaurant prices by 5% while decreasing the restaurant's variable costs by 5% without any change in demand.

Task

Write a letter to Claire Hill. Your letter should do the following.

(i)   Calculate the operating profit required on the existing capital employed to give a 20% return.

(ii)   Show the revised profit of the Grand Hotel if she achieves *both* her proposed occupancy rate and her proposed changes to the restaurant's pricing and costing structure.

(iii)   List the following revised performance indicators assuming her proposals are achieved without changing the amount of the capital employed.

    (1)   Return on capital employed
    (2)   Asset turnover
    (3)   Sales margin

(iv)   Use the performance indicators calculated in (iii) to suggest the following.

    (1)   What proportion of the planned increase in profits is due to the increased occupancy rates and what proportion is due to the change in the restaurant's pricing and costing structure

    (2)   ONE possible area of investigation if profits are to be further increased

46 Student Housing Society (50 mins)

(a)   You work as an accounting technician with the Student Housing Society. The Student Housing Society is a registered charity, formed to provide low-cost accommodation for students. The accommodation consists of 100 student bedrooms. The invoiced rent per bedroom is £2,400 per year.

Following the resignation of the previous manager, Helen Brown has recently been appointed as the general manager to the housing society. The society has laid down the following financial objectives for managing the society.

- The affairs of the society must be carried out in an efficient and effective manner.

- The society must attempt to achieve a return on its net assets of between 6% and 8%.

- The annual operating surplus should be at least 15% but no more than 20% of rents receivable.

- The general manager should attempt to achieve a 95% occupancy rate.

- The target average age of rent arrears should be no more than one month.

- In order to avoid liquidity problems, the year-end cash and bank balance should be sufficient to meet the payment of two months' expenses.

In a few days time, the Student Housing Society is due to hold its annual general meeting and an extract from the accounts for the year to 31 May 20X8 is reproduced below.

Operating statement year ended 31 May 20X8		Balance sheet extract at 31 May 20X8			
		Fixed assets	Cost £	Accumltd amortis'n £	Net book value £
	£				
Rent receivable	192,000	Land	200,000	0	200,000
Expenses		Buildings	700,000	336,000	364,000
Cleaning	16,000		900,000	336,000	564,000
Lighting and heating	4,800				
Maintenance	11,200	Net current assets			
Rates payable	76,000	Debtors*		48,000	
Amortisation	14,000	Cash and bank		4,500	
Administration costs	58,000	Creditors		(16,500)	36,000
		Net assets			600,000
Operating surplus	12,000				

* Debtors arise entirely from arrears of rent.

Task

Helen Brown wishes to know whether or not the charity has achieved the financial objectives laid down and asks you to calculate the following performance indicators in preparation for the annual general meeting.

(i)   The return on net assets

(ii)   The operating surplus as a percentage of rents receivable

(iii)   The occupancy rate for the society

(iv)   The average age of rent arrears in months

(v)   The number of months that expenses could be paid from the cash and bank balance

(b)   On receiving your calculations, Helen Brown discovers that the housing society has failed to meet all its objectives. Helen had previously worked in a commercial organisation and was uncertain how an organisation could be both efficient and effective while restricting the return on net assets and operating surplus margins. She also needs to make proposals at the annual general meeting which will ensure that all of the objectives are met next year. Helen believes it is possible to achieve the 95% occupancy rate and reduce the average age of rent arrears to the one month laid down in the objectives.

Helen Brown wants to know the effect on the other performance indicators if these two objectives had been achieved this year. She gives you the following information.

- The only marginal or variable costs relate to cleaning, lighting and heating, and maintenance.
- All other expenses are fixed costs.
- The creditors entirely relate to rates payable and administration costs.
- The figure for creditors would not change with any change in occupancy rates.

Task

Write a memo to Helen Brown. Your memo should do the following.

(i)   Identify the revised operating surplus if a 95% occupancy rate had been achieved.

(ii)   Show the value of debtors and cash as a result of achieving the 95% occupancy rate and the one month average age of rent arrears.

(iii)   Assuming the occupancy rate is 95% and the average age of rent arrears is one month, use your answers to parts (i) and (ii) of this task to calculate the following.

    (1)   The revised return on net assets

    (2)   The revised operating surplus as a percentage of rents receivable

    (3)   The number of months that expenses could be paid from the revised cash and bank balance

(iv)   **Briefly** explain:

    (1)   what is meant by efficiency;

    (2)   what is meant by effectiveness;

    (3)   why the return on net assets might not be an appropriate measure of efficiency for the housing society.

47 Micro Circuits Ltd (85 mins)   12/98

(a)   You are employed by Micro Circuits Ltd as a financial analyst reporting to Angela Frear, the Director of Corporate Strategy. One of your responsibilities is to monitor the performance of subsidiaries within the group. Financial and other data relating to subsidiary A is reproduced below.

Subsidiary A

Profit and loss account year to 30 November 20X8	£'000	£'000	Extract from balance sheet at 30 November 20X8	£'000	£'000	£'000
			Fixed assets	Land and buildings	Plant and machinery	Total
Sales		4,000				
less returns		100				
Turnover[1]		3,900	Cost	2,000	2,500	4,500
Material	230		Additions	–	1,800	1,800
Labour	400			2,000	4,300	6,300
Production overheads[2]	300		Accumulated depreciation	160	1,700	1,860
Cost of production	930			1,840	2,600	4,440
Opening finished stock	50					
Closing finished stock	(140)		Raw material stock	15		
Cost of sales		840	Finished goods stock	140		
Gross profit		3,060		155		
Marketing	500		Debtors	325		
Customer support	400		Cash and bank	40		
Research and development	750		Creditors	(85)		
Training	140					
Administration	295	2,085				435
Operating profit		975	Net assets			4,875

Other information

Notes

1. **Analysis of turnover**

	£'000			£'000
Regular customers	3,120	New products		1,560
New customers	780	Existing products		2,340
	3,900			3,900

2. Production overheads include £37,200 of reworked faulty production.

3. Orders received in the year totalled £4,550,000.

Task

Angela Frear asks you to calculate the following performance indicators in preparation for a board meeting.

(i)   The return on capital employed
(ii)   The asset turnover
(iii) The sales (or operating profit) margin
(iv)   The average age of debtors in months
(v)   The average age of finished stock in months

(b)   One of the issues to be discussed at the board meeting is the usefulness of performance indicators. Angela Frear has recently attended a conference on creating and enhancing value.

Three criticisms were made of financial performance indicators.

- They could give misleading signals.
- They could be manipulated.
- They focus on the short term and do not take account of other key, non-financial performance indicators.

At the conference, Angela was introduced to the idea of the balanced scorecard. The balanced scorecard looks at performance measurement from four perspectives.

The financial perspective
This is concerned with satisfying shareholders. Examples include the return on capital employed and sales margin.

The customer perspective
This asks how customers view the business and is concerned with measures of customer satisfaction. Examples include speed of delivery and customer loyalty.

The internal perspective
This looks at the quality of the company's output in terms of technical excellence and customer needs. Examples would be striving towards total quality management and flexible production as well as unit cost.

The innovation and learning perspective
This is concerned with the continual improvement of existing products and the ability to develop new products as customers' needs change. An example would be the percentage of turnover attributable to new products.

Task

Angela Frear asks you to prepare briefing notes for the board meeting. Using the data from part (a) where necessary, your notes should do the following.

(i)   Suggest ONE reason why the return on capital employed calculated in (a) might be misleading.
(ii)   Identify ONE way of manipulating the sales (or operating profit) margin.
(iii) Calculate the average delay in fulfilling orders.
(iv)   Identify ONE other possible measure of customer satisfaction other than the delay in fulfilling orders.
(v)   Calculate TWO indicators which may help to measure performance from an internal perspective.
(vi)   Calculate ONE performance indicator which would help to measure the innovation and learning perspective.

48 ALV Ltd (95 mins)   6/99

(a)   You are employed by ALV Ltd as an accounting technician. Two companies owned by ALV Ltd are ALV (East) Ltd and ALV (West) Ltd. These two companies are located in the same town and make an identical electrical product which sells for £84.

Financial data relating to the two companies is reproduced below. In addition, performance indicators for ALV (East) Ltd are also shown. Both companies use the same straight-line depreciation policy and assume no residual value.

ALV (East) Ltd				
Extract from balance sheet at 31 May 20X3			**Income statement** **Year to 31 May 20X3**	
	Cost	Accumulated depreciation	Net book value	
Fixed assets	£'000	£'000	£'000	£'000
Buildings	1,000	700	300	Turnover 840
Plant and machinery	300	240	60	Material and bought-in
	1,300	940	360	services 340
Net current assets				Production labour 180
Stock		45		Other production
Debtors		30		expenses 52
Cash		5		Depreciation –
Creditors		(40)	40	buildings 20
			400	Depreciation –
				plant and machinery 30
				Administration and
				other expenses 50
				Operating profit 168

Other data

Number of employees	18	Units produced	10,000

Performance indicators for ALV (East) Ltd

Asset turnover	2.1 times	Production labour	
Net profit margin	20.00%	cost per unit	£18.00
Return on capital employed	42.00%	Output per employee	556
Wages per employee	£10,000	Added value per employee	£27,778
		Profit per employee	£9,333

ALV (West) Ltd					
Extract from balance sheet at 31 May 20X3				**Income statement** **Year to 31 May 20X3**	
	Cost	*Accumulated depreciation*	*Net book value*		
Fixed assets	£'000	£'000	£'000		£'000
Buildings	1,500	120	1,380	Turnover	2,520
Plant and					
machinery	900	180	720	Material and bought-in	
	2,400	300	2,100	services	1,020
Net current assets				Production labour	260
Stock		20		Other production	
Debtors		30		expenses	630
Cash		5		Depreciation –	
Creditors		(55)	nil	buildings	30
			2,100	Depreciation –	
				plant and machinery	90
				Administration and	
				other expenses	112
				Operating profit	378
Other data					
Number of employees			20	Units produced	30,000

ALV Ltd is considering closing one of the companies over the next two years. As a first step, the board of directors wish to hold a meeting to consider which is the more efficient and productive company.

Task

In preparation for the board meeting, calculate the following performance indicators for ALV (West) Ltd.

(i) Asset turnover
(ii) Net profit margin
(iii) Return on capital employed
(iv) Wages per employee
(v) Production labour costs per unit
(vi) Output per employee
(vii) Added value per employee
(viii) Profit per employee

(b) Shortly after preparing the performance indicators for ALV (West) Ltd, the chief executive of ALV Ltd, Jill Morgan, issued a statement to a local newspaper. In that statement, she said that the workforce at ALV (West) Ltd was far less productive than at the other company despite both companies making an identical product. She concluded that it was up to the workforce to improve productivity. In response, the employees stated that the normal way of measuring efficiency is profit, and therefore, ALV (West) was more efficient than ALV (East).

Jill Morgan asks you to prepare a report for the next board meeting to explain the issues involved so that all board members can be properly briefed.

Task

Write a report to Jill Morgan for distribution to the board of directors. Your report should do the following.

(i) Explain what is meant by the following.
   (1) Productivity
   (2) Efficiency

(ii) Identify the best TWO performance indicators used by ALV Ltd to measure efficiency and use those indicators to identify which of the two companies is the more efficient.

(iii) Identify the best TWO performance measures used by ALV Ltd to measure productivity and use those indicators to identify which of the two companies has the higher productivity.

(iv) Use the NET FIXED ASSETS to derive a different measure of productivity for both companies.

(v) Use the data in task (a) and your answer to task (b)(iv) to explain ONE reason why the productivity and efficiency measures might give different rankings.

49 Cam Car Company (60 mins)

(a) The Cam Car Company is a multinational manufacturer of motor vehicles. It operates two divisions, one producing cars and the other producing vans. You are employed as a management accountant in the van division. The labour content for each type of vehicle is very similar although the material content of a car is much greater than that of a van. Both divisions apply straight-line depreciation to fixed assets.

You have been asked to prepare information to be used in the company's annual wage negotiations. Each year, the van employee representatives make comparisons with the car division and one of your tasks is to calculate performance indicators for your division. Financial and other information relating to both divisions is reproduced below along with some of the relevant performance indicators for the car division.

Balance sheet extracts at 31 May 20X8

	Van division			Car division		
	Cost	Dep'n to date	Net	Cost	Dep'n to date	Net
	£m	£m	£m	£m	£m	£m
Buildings at cost	500	400	100	1,200	240	960
Plant and machinery at cost	400	320	80	800	240	560
	900	720	180	2,000	480	1,520
Stock		60			210	
Trade debtors		210			285	
Cash		(140)			150	
Trade creditors		(30)			(265)	
			100			380
Net assets			280			1,900

Profit and loss accounts for year to 31 May 20X8

	Van division		Car division	
	£m	£m	£m	£m
Turnover		420		1,140
Materials and bought-in components	95		790	
Production labour	110		138	
Other production expenses	26		32	
Depreciation – buildings	10		24	
Depreciation – plant and machinery	40		80	
Administrative expenses	27		28	
		308		1,092
Profit		112		48

Other information

	Van division	Car division
Vehicles produced	50,000	84,000
Number of production employees	10,000	12,000

Yearly performance indicators for the car division

Return on capital employed	2.53%	Profit margin	4.21%
Asset turnover	0.6 times	Profit per employee	£4,000
Wages per employee	£11,500	Output per employee	7 vehicles
Production labour cost per unit	£1,643	Added value per employee	£29,167

Task

You have been asked to calculate the yearly performance indicators for the van division and to present them in a table with the comparable figures for the car division.

(b) Shortly after preparing the performance indicators, you receive a telephone call from Peter Ross, a member of the management team. Peter explains that the employee representatives of the van division wish to negotiate an increase in wages. The representatives are arguing that employees in the van division are paid less than the equivalent staff in the car division despite the van division being more profitable. In addition, the representatives state that their productivity is higher than in the car division. Peter explains that he is not an accountant. He is not clear how productivity is measured nor what is meant by added value.

Task

You are asked to write a memo to Peter Ross. The memo should do the following.

(i) Briefly explain what is meant by the following terms.
    (1)   Productivity
    (2)   Added value

(ii) Identify those performance indicators that could be used by the employees of the van division to justify their claims in terms of the following.
    (1)   Profitability
    (2)   Productivity

(iii)   Give ONE example from the performance indicators that could be used to counter those claims and use the financial data given in task (a) to identify one possible limitation to the indicator.

(iv)   Use BOTH the return on capital employed AND the added value per employee to show why the indicators calculated in task (a) might be overstated.

50 Travel Bus Ltd (80 mins)   12/00

(a)   Travel Bus Ltd is owned by Travel Holdings plc. It operates in the town of Camford. Camford is an old town with few parking facilitates for motorists. Several years ago, the Town Council built a car park on the edge of the town and awarded Travel Bus the contract to carry motorists and their passengers between the car park and the centre of the town.

Originally, the Council charged motorists £4.00 per day for the use of the car park but, to encourage motorists not to take their cars into the town centre, parking has been free since 1 December 20W9.

The journey between the car park and the town centre is the only service operated by Travel Bus Ltd in Camford. A summary of the results for the first two years of operations, together with the net assets associated with the route and other operating data, is reproduced below.

Operating statement year ended 30 November			Extract from balance sheet at 30 November		
	20W9	20X0		20W9	20X0
	£	£		£	£
Turnover	432,000	633,600	Buses	240,000	240,000
Fuel	129,600	185,328	Accumulated depreciation	168,000	180,000
Wages	112,000	142,000	Net book value	72,000	60,000
Other variable costs	86,720	84,512	Net current assets	14,400	35,040
Gross profit	103,680	221,760		86,400	95,040
Bus road tax and insurance	22,000	24,000			
Depreciation of buses	12,000	12,000			
Maintenance of buses	32,400	28,512			
Fixed garaging costs	29,840	32,140			
Administration	42,000	49,076			
Net profit/(loss)	(34,560)	76,032			

Other operating data	20W9	20X0
Fare per passenger journey	£0.80	£1.00
Miles per year	324,000	356,400
Miles per journey	18.0	18.0
Days per year	360	360
Wages per driver	£14,000	£14,200

Throughout the two years, the drivers were paid a basic wage per week, no bonuses were paid and no overtime was incurred.

In two weeks there will be a meeting between officials of the Town Council and the chief executive of Travel Holdings to discuss the performance of Travel Bus for the year to 30 November 20X0. The previous year's performance indicators were as follows.

Gross profit margin	24%
Net profit margin	–8%
Return on capital employed	–40%
Asset turnover	5 times
Number of passengers in the year	540,000
Total cost per mile	£1.44
Number of journeys per day	50
Maintenance cost per mile	£0.10
Passengers per day	1,500
Passengers per journey	30
Number of drivers	8

Task

In preparation for the meeting, you have been asked to calculate the following performance indicators for the year to 30 November 20X0.

(i) Gross profit margin
(ii) Net profit margin
(iii) Return on capital employed
(iv) Asset turnover
(v) Number of passengers in the year
(vi) Total cost per mile
(vii) Number of journeys per day
(viii) Maintenance cost per mile
(ix) Passengers per day
(x) Passengers per journey
(xi) Number of drivers

(b) On receiving your performance indicators, the chief executive of Travel Holdings raises the following issues with you.

- The drivers are claiming that the improved profitability of Travel Bus reflects their increased productivity.

- The managers believe that the change in performance is due to improved motivation arising from the introduction of performance related pay for managers during the year to 30 November 20X1.

- The officials from the Town Council are concerned that Travel Bus is paying insufficient attention to satisfying passengers needs and safety.

The chief executive asks for your advice.

Task

Write a memo to the chief executive of Travel Holdings plc. Where relevant, you should make use of the data and answers to task (a) to do the following.

(i) **Briefly** discuss whether or not increased productivity always leads to increased profitability.

(ii) Develop ONE possible measure of driver productivity and suggest whether or not the drivers' claim is valid.

(iii)   Suggest ONE reason, other than improved motivation, why the profitability of Travel Bus might have improved.

(iv)   (1)   Suggest ONE **existing** performance indicator which might measure the satisfaction of passenger needs.

        (2)   Suggest ONE other possible performance indicator of passenger needs which cannot be measured from the existing performance data collected by Travel Bus.

(v)   (1)   Suggest ONE existing performance indicator which might measure the safety aspect of Travel Bus's operations.

        (2)   Suggest ONE other possible performance indicator which cannot be measured from the existing performance data collected by Travel Bus.

51 Bon Repose (80 mins)   12/01

(a)   The Bon Repose hotel group is a French company. It builds and operates economy class hotels close to major roads to provide overnight accommodation for motorists. Each bedroom is a standard size and the only food provided for guests is breakfast.

        Recently, Bon Repose formed a UK subsidiary and shortly afterwards you were appointed its management accountant. You report to Helene de la Tour, the chief executive of the UK subsidiary who provides you with the following information.

        •   All Bon Repose hotels have 80 bedrooms and operate for 365 days per year

        •   Sales volume is measured in room-nights. Customers are charged for the use of the room per night for either single or double occupancy. A customer staying three nights will therefore be charged for three room-nights.

        •   Creditors relate only to the variable costs incurred by the hotel.

        •   The company does not provide for depreciation.

        The first Bon Repose UK hotel was opened one year ago. Its financial and operating information is shown below.

Operating statement year ended 30 November 20X1	£	£	Net assets at 30 November 20X1	£	£
Turnover		560,640	Fixed assets		669,556
Variable costs					
Breakfast and laundry		175,200	Net current assets		
Contribution		385,440	Debtors	35,040	
Fixed costs			Cash	10,804	
Labour	133,865			45,844	
Light and heat	89,045		Creditors	(14,600)	
Rates, insurance, maintenance	120,482				31,244
		343,392	Net assets		700,800
Net profit		42,048			
Actual number of room-nights sold		17,520			

Task

Helene de la Tour asks you to prepare the following performance indicators for the hotel.

(i) Gross (or contribution) margin
(ii) Net profit (or sales) margin
(iii) Return on capital employed
(iv) Asset turnover
(v) Average age of debtors in months
(vi) Average age of creditors in months
(vii) The number of months that expenses could be paid from the cash balance
(viii) Maximum capacity of the hotel in room-nights
(ix) The percentage room-night occupancy rate of the hotel

(b) On receiving your performance indicators, Helene de la Tour tells you that similar hotels in France are more profitable. She believes one of the reasons for the poor profits at the UK hotel is because the manager has been giving discounts. She tells you of the following company policies.

• The price of each room is £40.00 per night but the manager can reduce this to £20 where necessary.

• The average age of debtors should be 0.5 months.

• The company should take twice as many months to pay its creditors as it currently does.

• The cash balance at the hotel should only be £3,000. Any surplus cash should be transferred to the head office bank account.

You agree to investigate the reasons for the poor profits.

Task

Write a memo to Helene de la Tour. In your memo, you should do the following.

(i) Calculate the following.

(1) What the turnover would have been had there been no discounts
(2) The total discount
(3) The number of discounted room-nights
(4) The percentage of room-nights discounted

(ii) Prepare a revised operating statement and statement of net assets assuming that the company's policies had been met but no discounts offered.

(iii) Calculate the following revised indicators.

(1) Gross (or contribution) margin
(2) Net profit (or sales) margin
(3) Return on capital employed

(iv) **Briefly** discuss whether or not the discounting of prices would have been the reason for the reduced profits.

chapters 14 and 15

Cost management

Activity checklist

This checklist shows which activities cover the performance criteria, range statements and knowledge and understanding points dealt with in Chapters 14 and 5 of the BPP *Managing Costs and Controlling Resources* Interactive Text.

Performance criteria		Activities
8.1E	Analyse the effect of organisational accounting policies on reported costs	52-54
8.2C	Consultant relevant specialists and assist in identifying ways to reduce costs and enhance value	55
8.2E	Make specific recommendations to management in a clear and appropriate form	56

Range statement

8.1	The build up of costs: activity-based costing	52-54
8.2	Performance indicators to measure: cost of quality	16, 55, 56
8.2	Recommendations: efficiencies; modifications to work processes	16

Knowledge and understanding

Unit 8 Accounting principles and theory

9	Cost management: activity based costing; principles of Total Quality Management (including cost of quality)	16, 52-56

52 Fill in the table

(a)   In the table below fill in the following values.

  (i)   Overhead per cost driver unit
  (ii)   Total overhead per product per activity
  (iii) Cost per item

(b)   What do you understand by the term 'cost driver unit'? Give an example for each activity listed in the table below.

Activity	Total ovh'd £	Total cost driver units Units	Ovh'd per cost driver unit £	Cost driver units per product X Units	Y Units	Z Units	Total overhead per product per activity X £	Y £	Z £
Machinery set-ups	32,000	320		140	80	100			
Materials handling	16,000	40		12	14	14			
Quality control	25,800	200		75	55	70			
Supervision	7,400	50		10	15	25			
Maintenance	6,585	15		4	6	5	_____	_____	_____
Number of units produced							1,250	500	550
Cost per item							£	£	£

53 Charleroi Aircon Ltd (60 mins)

You are employed as an accounts assistant in the management accounting department of Charleroi Aircon Ltd, the UK subsidiary of a major French group. Charleroi design and install industrial air-conditioning systems. The company is based in Birmingham.

Charleroi's usual pricing policy is to use direct costs (equipment and installation labour) plus a mark-up of 50% to establish the selling price for an air-conditioning installation.

Alice Devereaux, Charleroi's sales manager, is about to tender for a contract (quotation HMG/012) to install air-conditioning in some government offices in Exeter which are being refurbished.

Alice is also about to bid for a contract (quotation CFG/013) to install the air-conditioning in a furniture store which is being built in Gloucester. This job is very similar to an earlier one for the same customer.

Alice has asked Mark Langton, Charleroi's management accountant, to second you to the sales department to assist her in developing better pricing and cost models. Alice is particularly keen to experiment with activity based costing (ABC) as Mark is in the process of designing an ABC system for the company. She has asked you to investigate the profitability of quotations HMG/012 and CFG/013.

You have obtained the following information about the two jobs.

Estimates related to contracts HMG/012 and CFG/013

Contract number:	HMG/012	CFG/013
Equipment: cost	£175,000	£120,000
number of items purchased	650	410
Direct labour: hours	10,000	6,000
hourly rate	£13	£11
Design hours	1,280	620
Distance from Birmingham office (miles round-trip)	320	90
Engineer site visits required	30	10

You have managed to obtain the following overhead information from Mark's ABC working papers.

ABC details for overhead activities connected with air conditioning installation contracts

Activity	Budgeted cost pool £pa	Cost driver	Cost driver units pa
Design department	675,000	Design hours	25,000
Site engineers	370,000	Miles travelled	185,000
Purchasing department	105,000	Items purchased	15,000
Payroll department	75,000	Direct hours	300,000
Site management	750,000	Direct hours	300,000
Post-installation inspection	80,000	Items purchased	20,000

Tasks

(a) Calculate the price for each of jobs HMG/012 and CFG/013.

(b) Prepare a schedule setting out the activity-based overhead costs for each of jobs HMG/012 and CFG/013.

(c) Write a memo to Alice setting out the profitability of each contract. Include a breakdown of costs into their main elements, plus details of the projected profits as a percentage of selling price and as a percentage of total cost.

54 Benefits of ABC

You have recently been employed by the legal firm of Thomson, Simons and Barfleet as their management accountant. The senior partner, Lucy Thomson, has doubts about the usefulness of the figures produced by the previous management accountant. She has heard that activity based costing (ABC) may be an appropriate system for the firm to adopt.

Task

In response to a request from Ms Thomson, prepare a brief paper setting out the way in which ABC works and what benefits the firm may expect from introducing the system.

Include a simple illustration.

55 BeePee plc

A Total Quality Management (TQM) Programme has been introduced in BeePee plc, a large manufacturing organisation. Senior management have found the results of the programme so far very useful and so there are plans to extend it from manufacturing to the whole of the organisation. You have been asked to help devise a TQM programme for the management accounting section of the finance department.

Tasks

(a)   Briefly explain each of the four categories of quality cost.

(b)   Give ONE example of each category appropriate to a manufacturing environment.

(c)   Give ONE example of each category appropriate to a management accounting department.

56 Local Engineering Ltd (50 mins)

(a)   You are employed as the assistant management accountant with Local Engineering Ltd, a company which designs and makes a single product, the X4, used in the telecommunications industry. The company has a goods received store which employs staff who carry out random checks to ensure materials are of the correct specification. In addition to the random checks, a standard allowance is made for failures due to faulty materials at the completion stage and the normal practice is to charge the cost of any remedial work required to the cost of production for the month. Once delivered to the customer, any faults discovered in the X4 during its warranty period become an expense of the customer support department.

At the end of each month, management reports are prepared for the Board of Directors. These identify the cost of running the stores and the number of issues, the cost of production and the number of units manufactured, and the cost of customer support.

Jane Greenwood, Local Engineering's management accountant, has just returned from a board meeting to discuss a letter the company recently received from Universal Telecom, Local Engineering's largest customer. In the letter, Universal Telecom explained that it was determined to maintain its position as a world-class provider of telecommunication services and that there was serious concern about the quality of the units delivered by your company. At the meeting, Local Engineering Ltd's board responded by agreeing to establish a company-wide policy of implementing a Total Quality Management (TQM) programme, commencing with a revised model of the X4. Design work on the new model is scheduled to commence in six month's time.

One aspect of this will involve the management accounting department collecting the *cost of quality*. This is defined as the total of all costs incurred in preventing defects plus those costs involved in remedying defects once they have occurred within the accounting system – attributable to producing output that is not within its specification.

Task

As a first step towards the implementation of TQM, a meeting of the senior staff in the management accounting department has been called to discuss the role the department can play in making TQM a success. Jane Greenwood has asked you to prepare a *brief* background paper for the meeting.

Your paper should do the following.

(i)   Explain in outline what is meant by Total Quality Management.

(ii)   Briefly discuss why the current accounting system fails to highlight the *cost of quality*.

(iii)   Identify FOUR general categories (or classifications) of Local Engineering's activities where expenditure making up the explicit *cost of quality* will be found.

(iv)   Give ONE example of a cost found within each category.

(v)   Give ONE example of a *cost of quality* not normally identified by the accounting system.

(b)   Local Engineering Ltd has capacity to produce no more than 1,000 X4s per month and currently is able to sell all production immediately at a unit selling price of £1,250. A major component of the X4 is a complex circuit board. Spot checks are made on these boards by a team of specialist employees when they are received into stores. In May, 100 units were found to be faulty. Good components are then issued to production along with other material.

Upon completion, each X4 is tested. If there is a fault, this involves further remedial work prior to dispatch to customers. For the month of May, 45 units of the X4 had to be reworked because of subsequent faults discovered in the circuit board. This remedial work cost an additional £13,500 in labour charges.

Should a fault occur after delivery to the customer, Local Engineering is able to call upon a team of self-employed engineers to rectify the fault as part of its customer support function. The cost of the remedial work by the self-employed engineers carried out in May – and the number of times they were used – is shown as contractors under customer support.

Extract from the accounting records of Local Engineering Ltd for the month of May

	Units	£		Units	£
Purchases:			Production:		
Printed circuits	1,000	120,000	Printed circuits	900	108,000
Less returns	(100)	(12,000)	Other material		121,500
Net costs	900	108,000	Labour		193,500
Other material		121,500	Direct prod'n o/hd		450,000
Total purchases issued to production		229,500	Cost of production		873,000
Other direct stores costs:					
Goods received, labour costs and rent		54,000	Customer support:		
Inspection costs		10,000	Direct costs		36,000
Costs of returns	100	4,500	Contractors	54	24,300
Costs of stores		68,500			60,300

Task

As part of the continuing development of Total Quality Management, you are asked by Jane Greenwood to calculate the following:

(i)   The explicit **cost of quality** for Local Engineering Ltd for the month of May

(ii)   A further **cost of quality** not reported in the above accounting records.

Cost management is also covered in activity 16.

Full Assessments

UNIT 8 FULL ASSESSMENT 1 (JUNE 2002)

NVQ/SVQ IN ACCOUNTING, LEVEL 4

UNIT 8

CONTRIBUTING to the MANAGEMENT of PERFORMANCE and the ENHANCEMENT of VALUE (PEV)

This examination paper is in TWO sections.

You have to show competence in BOTH sections.

You should therefore attempt and aim to complete EVERY task in BOTH sections.

You should spend about 90 minutes on Section 1 and 90 minutes on Section 2.

Include all essential workings within your answers, where appropriate.

SECTION 1

You should spend about 90 minutes on this section.

DATA

You are employed as a financial analyst at Drampton plc, a computer retailer. One of your duties is to prepare a standard costing reconciliation statement for the finance director.

The company sells two types of computer, desktop computers for individual use and mainframe computers for large organisations. Desktop computers are sold by advertising in newspapers. Customers telephone Drampton to place an order and the telephone call is answered by trained operators. Drampton pays the cost of the telephone call. The total standard cost of one phone call is shown below.

Standard cost of one call			
Expense	Quantity	Cost	Cost per call
			£
Telephone cost	1 unit	£0.07 per unit	0.07
Operators' wages	6 minutes	£3.50 per hour	0.35
Fixed overheads [1]	6 minutes	£6.50 per hour	0.65
Standard cost of one telephone call			1.07

[1] Fixed overheads are based on budgeted operator hours.

Drampton's finance director gives you the following information for the three months ended 31 May 20X2.

• Budgeted number of calls		900,000 calls
• Actual number of calls		1,000,000 calls
• Actual expenses	Quantity	Cost
		£
Telephone cost	1,200,000 units	79,200
Operators' wages	114,000 hours	478,800
Fixed overheads		540,400
Actual cost of actual operations		1,098,400

Task 1.1

(a)   Calculate the following information.

   (i) .   Actual cost of a telephone unit
   (ii)   Actual hourly wage rate of operators
   (iii)   Standard number of operator hours for 1,000,000 calls
   (iv)   Budgeted cost of fixed overheads for the three months ended 31 May 20X2
   (v)   Budgeted number of operator hours for the three months ended 31 May 20X2
   (vi)   Standard cost of actual operations

(b) Using the data given and your answers to part (a), calculate the following variances.

(i)   Price variance for telephone calls
(ii) Usage variance for telephone calls
(iii) Labour rate variance for the telephone operators
(iv) Labour efficiency variance for the telephone operators
(v)   Fixed overhead expenditure variance
(vi) Fixed overheard volume variance
(vii) Fixed overhead capacity variance
(viii) Fixed overhead efficiency variance

(c) Prepare a statement for the three months ended 31 May 20X2 reconciling the standard cost of actual operations to the actual cost of actual operations.

DATA

Drampton plc has recently taken over Little Ltd, a small company making mainframe and desktop computers. Little appears to make all of its profits from mainframe computers. Drampton's finance director tells you that Little's fixed overheads are currently charged to production using standard labour hours and gives you their standard cost of making mainframe and desktop computers. These are shown below.

Little Ltd: Standard cost per computer

Model	Mainframe	Desktop
Annual budgeted volume	5	5,000
Unit standard cost	£	£
Material and labour	50,000	500
Fixed overhead	4,000	40
Standard cost per computer	54,000	540

The finance director asks for your help and suggests you reclassify the fixed overheads between the two models using activity based costing. You are given the following information.

- **Budgeted total annual fixed overheads**

	£
Set-up costs	10,000
Rent and power (production area)	120,000
Rent (stores area)	50,000
Salaries of store issue staff	40,000
Total	220,000

- Every time Little makes a mainframe computer, it has to stop making desktop computers and rearrange the factory layout. The cost of this is shown as set-up costs. If the factory did not make any mainframe computers these costs would eliminated.

- **Cost drivers**

	Mainframe	Desktop	Total
Number of set-ups	5	0	5
Number of weeks of production	10	40	50
Floor area of stores (square metres)	400	400	800
Number of issues of stock	2,000	8,000	10,000

Task 1.2

Prepare a note for Drampton's finance director. In the note, you should use the cost drivers to do the following.

(a)   Reallocate Little's budgeted total fixed annual overheads between mainframe and desktop production.

(b)   Show the revised **unit** fixed overheads for each of the two types of computer.

SECTION 2

You should spend about 90 minutes on this section.

DATA

Drampton plc is considering purchasing Hand Power Systems Ltd. Hand Power Systems Ltd makes a hand-held computer and has provided Drampton with its latest operating statement and balance sheet. These are shown below together with details of the orders received during the year and information about the sales returns.

Hand Power Systems Ltd: Operating statement for the year ended 31 May 20X2

	Volume	£'000	£'000
Gross sales	21,000		6,300
Less sales returns	1,000		300
Turnover	20,000		6,000
Material		3,360	
Labour		960	
Production fixed overheads		480	
Cost of production	24,000	4,800	
Add opening finished stock	1,000	300	
Less closing finished stock	(5,000)	(1,350)	
Cost of sales	20,000		3,750
Gross profit			2,250
Research and development		768	
Training		576	
Customer support		240	
Marketing		200	
Administration		226	2,010
Net operating profit			240

Extract from balance sheet at 31 May 20X2

	£'000	£'000
Fixed assets		
Machinery and equipment		
Cost		5,000
Accumulated depreciation		4,000
Net book value		1,000
Net current assets		
Stock of finished goods	1,350	
Debtors	1,500	
Cash	(426)	
Creditors	(424)	2,000
Net assets		3,000

Additional information

- Orders for 26,000 hand-held computers were received during the year ended 31 May 20X2.
- Sales returns represent hand-held computers found to be faulty by customers. Customers had these replaced by fault-free computers.

Task 2.1

Prepare the following performance indicators for Drampton's finance director.

(a)	Gross profit margin
(b)	Net profit (or sales) margin
(c)	Return on capital employed
(d)	Asset turnover
(e)	Average age of debtors in months
(f)	Research and development as a percentage of the cost of production
(g)	Training as a percentage of the cost of production
(h)	Customer support as a percentage of turnover
(i)	Returns as a percentage of turnover
(j)	Average delay in months between placing an order and receiving a fault-free, hand-held computer

DATA

The finance director believes that a balanced scorecard will help in the analysis on Hand Power Systems' performance and gives you the following information.

The balanced scorecard views performance measurement from four perspectives.

- The financial perspective: this is concerned with satisfying shareholders and measures used include the return on capital employed.

- The customer perspective: this attempts to measure how customers view the organisation and with measuring customer satisfaction. Examples include the speed of delivery and customer loyalty.

- The internal perspective: this measures the quality of the organisation's output in terms of technical excellence and consumer needs. Examples include unit cost and total quality measurement.

- The innovation and learning perspective: this emphasises the need for continual improvement of existing products and developing new products to meet customers' changing needs. In a 'for profit' organisation, this might be measured by the percentage of turnover attributable to new products.

Task 2.2

Name **ONE** balanced scorecard perspective being measured for each of the performance indicators in task 2.1.

DATA

The finance director gives you the following additional information relating to Hand Power Systems for the year to 31 May 20X3.

Accounting policies

- **Stocks**: the closing stock of finished goods is valued on a **last-in, first-out** basis and material prices have been falling throughout the year ended 31 May 20X2.

  There are no raw material or work in progress stocks at any time.

- **Depreciation**: this is calculated on a straight line basis assuming no residual value.

  The depreciation charge for the year was £1,000,000.

  Similar fixed assets in other companies have an average life of 10 years.

Other information

- Indices for this year and next year:

	Selling prices	Material costs	Sales volumes
Index year ended 31 May 20X2	120	175	100
Forecast index year ended 31 May 20X3	100	140	130

- Total quality management will be introduced. As a result, there will no longer be any sales returns.

- The hand-held computers will be made to order so there will be no closing stocks.

- As a result of this year's research and development, new machinery and equipment will be introduced from 1 June 20X2. This will result in a 25% saving in the labour cost per hand-held computer.

- The new machinery and equipment will also result in savings of £160,000 in the production fixed overheads.

TASK 2.3

Write a memo to the finance director. In your memo you should do the following.

(a)   Briefly state and explain the effect of the following accounting policies on Hand Power Systems' profit for the year ended 31 May 20X2.

   (i)   Stock valuation
   (ii)   Depreciation

(b)   Calculate the following FORECAST data for the year ending 31 May 20X3.

   (i)   Selling price per hand-held computer
   (ii)   Sales volume
   (iii)   Sales turnover
   (iv)   Material per hand-held computer
   (v)   Labour cost per hand-held computer
   (vi)   Production volume
   (vii)   Cost of production
   (viii)   Cost of sales
   (ix)   Gross profit

UNIT 8 FULL ASSESSMENT 2 (DECEMBER 2002)

NVQ/SVQ IN ACCOUNTING, LEVEL 4

UNIT 8

CONTRIBUTING to the MANAGEMENT of PERFORMANCE and the ENHANCEMENT of VALUE (PEV)

This examination paper is in TWO sections.

You have to show competence in BOTH sections.

You should therefore attempt and aim to complete EVERY task in BOTH sections.

You should spend about 90 minutes on Section 1 and 90 minutes on Section 2.

Include all essential workings within your answers, where appropriate.

SECTION 1

You should spend about 90 minutes on this section.

DATA

You are a newly appointed trainee accounting technician with Primary Chemicals plc. One of your responsibilities is to prepare and monitor standard costing variances for the distillation department. The distillation department prepares barrels of a refined chemical using a continuous process.

Fixed overheads are charged to production on the basis of machine hours. This is because the machine hours required determines the speed of production.

The budgeted and actual results of the distillation department for the week ended 30 November 20X2 are shown below.

Distillation department: operating results – week ended 30 November 20X2				
	Budget			*Actual*
Production	2,500 barrels			2,400 barrels
		Standard cost		*Actual cost*
		£		£
Material	12,500 litres	106,250	11,520 litres	99,072
Labour	10,000 labour hours	60,000	10,080 labour hours	61,488
Fixed overheads	20,000 machine hours	200,000	18,960 machine hours	185,808
Total cost		366,250		346,368

Task 1.1

(a)   Calculate the following information.

   (i)   Standard price of material per litre
   (ii)   Actual price of material per litre
   (iii)   Standard litres of material per barrel
   (iv)   Standard labour rate per hour
   (v)   Standard labour hours per barrel
   (vi)   Standard machine hours per barrel
   (vii)   Budgeted fixed overheads per budgeted machine hour
   (viii) Standard absorption cost per barrel

(b)   Using the data provided in the operating results and your answers to part (a), calculate the following variances.

   (i)   Material price variance
   (ii)   Material usage variance
   (iii)   Labour rate variance
   (iv)   Labour efficiency variance
   (v)   Fixed overhead expenditure variance

(vi)   Fixed overhead volume variance

(vii)   Fixed overhead capacity variance

(viii) Fixed overhead efficiency variance

(c)   Prepare a statement reconciling the standard absorption cost of actual operations to the actual absorption cost of actual operations.

DATA

Anthony Bush is the financial controller of Primary Chemicals. Shortly after you prepare the reconciliation statement, he tells you how he calculates the standard material cost per litre.

- He forecasts a trend price per litre for each of the four quarters of the year. He then divides the total by four. This forecast average trend price then becomes the standard cost per litre for the year.

- He ignores seasonal variations in the price of materials.

Anthony tells you that he ignores the seasonal variations as, on average, they equal zero and that, by taking the average trend figure, the standard cost per litre is still accurate. He also tells you that production volume varies according to demand throughout the year.

The data used by Anthony for the year to 31 December 20X2 is shown below.

	Quarter 1 1/1 – 31/3	Quarter 2 1/4 – 30/6	Quarter 3 1/7 – 30/9	Quarter 4 1/10 – 31/12
Forecast quarterly trend	£7.00	£8.00	£9.00	£10.00
Seasonal variations	–10%	–20%	+10%	+20%

Task 1.2

Write a memo to Anthony Bush. In your memo you should do the following.

(a)   Briefly explain the following.

(i)   Whether or not his way of calculating the forecast average trend price produced a valid forecast of the average trend price for the year

(ii)   Whether or not it was valid to ignore seasonal variations when calculating variances

(b)   Use the data provided to calculate a revised standard cost of material per litre for the week ended 30 November 20X2.

(c)   Subdivide the material price variance into that part due to the revised standard cost per litre being different from the original standard cost and that part due to other reasons.

SECTION 2

You should spend about 90 minutes on this section.

DATA

You are the management accountant of Care4, a registered charity. You report to Carol Jones, the chief executive. Care4 owns Highstone School, a residential school for children with special needs. One of your duties is to prepare performance indicators for Highstone School. The accounts for the year to 31 August 20X2 are shown below.

Operating statement – year to 31 August 20X2		
	£	£
Fee income		1,760,000
Teacher salaries	600,000	
Nursing and support staff salaries	480,000	
Administrative expenses	120,000	
Power	128,000	
Housekeeping	160,000	
Depreciation *old*	236,800	
Total expenses		1,724,800
Operating surplus		35,200

Balance sheet extract at 31 August 20X2			
Fixed assets	*Land*	*Buildings and equipment*	*Total*
	£	£	£
Cost	4,502,800	11,840,000	16,342,800
Depreciation to date		9,708,800	9,708,800
Net book value	4,502,800	2,131,200	6,634,000
Net current assets			
Debtors	440,000		
Cash	62,000		
Creditors	(96,000)		406,000
Net assets			7,040,000

Local authorities refer children with special needs to the school and pay the school fees. There is a standard contract that states the number of children per teacher and the number of nursing and support staff required.

You are provided with the following additional information.

- The school fee per child for the year ended 31 August 20X2 was £22,000.

- The contract states the following.

- There must be one teacher for every four children. (The average salary per teacher is £30,000.)

- There must be one member of the nursing and support staff for every two children. (The average salary per member of the nursing and support staff is £12,000.)

- The school can accommodate a maximum of 100 children.

- The buildings and equipment are depreciated by equal amounts each year and are assumed to have no residual value.

- Creditors entirely relate to power and housekeeping.

Task 2.1

Prepare the following school performance indicators for Carol Jones.

(a)   Operating surplus as a percentage of fee income
(b)   Return on net assets
(c)   Average age of debtors in months
(d)   Average age of creditors in months
(e)   Number of children in the school
(f)   Occupancy rate of the school
(g)   Number of teachers in the school
(h)   Number of nursing and support staff in the school
(i)   Total of cash-based expenses
(j)   Number of months that cash-based expenses could be paid from the cash balance

DATA

On receiving your performance indicators, Carol Jones tells you that she is worried about the financial viability of the school. Some creditors are objecting to the late payment of their invoices and the cash balance is insufficient to pay expenses when due. She also tells you that the school wants to purchase new equipment costing £400,000 in September 20X3.

Carol Jones feels that the productivity and efficiency of the school must be improved and sets the following targets for the year to 31 August 20X3.

- Operating surplus as a percentage of fee income should double.

- Return on net assets should double.

- The school should generate sufficient cash to be able to do the following.

  - Pay for the new equipment
  - Have a cash balance equivalent to one month's cash-based expenses

She proposes the following action plan for the year to 31 August 20X3.

> **Action plan – year to 31 August 20X3**
>
> - The number of children will increase by 10%.
> - The school fee per child will not change.
> - The number of teachers and the number of nursing and support staff will increase according to the contract.
> - There will be no change in the average salaries of either teachers or nursing and support staff.
> - No other expenses will change.
> - Debtors will only be allowed 1½ months to pay.
> - The average age of creditors will be two months.
> - There will be no additional funding by Care4 nor will the school make any payments to Care4.

Task 2.2

Prepare the following forecast information for the year to 31 August 20X3 using the assumptions of the action plan and before the purchase of the new equipment.

(a) Operating statement
(b) Year-end debtors
(c) Year-end creditors
(d) Year-end net book value of fixed assets
(e) Year-end cash balance
(f) Year-end net assets

Task 2.3

Write a memo to Carol Jones. In your memo you should do the following.

(a) Calculate the following forecast information for the year ended 31 August 20X3.

   (i)   Operating surplus as a percentage of fee income

   (ii)   Return on net assets

   (iii) Cash available after buying the new equipment

   (iv)   Number of months that cash-based expenses could be paid from the cash balance after allowing for buying the new equipment

(b) State if the action plan achieves all of the proposed targets.

(c) Explain the difference between productivity and efficiency.

(d) Give ONE example of increased productivity as a result of implementing the action plan.

UNIT 9 FULL ASSESSMENT 1 (JUNE 2002)

NVQ/SVQ in ACCOUNTING, LEVEL 4

UNIT 9

CONTRIBUTING to the PLANNING and CONTROL of RESOURCES (PCR)

This examination paper is in TWO sections.

You have to show competence in BOTH sections.

You should therefore attempt and aim to complete EVERY task in BOTH sections.

You are advised to spend about 80 minutes on Section 1 and 100 minutes on Section 2.

Include all essential workings within your answers, where appropriate.

SECTION 1

You should spend about 80 minutes on this section.

DATA

You are employed as an accounting technician by Guildshot Ltd, a company that makes statues. Statues are made in batches. A special powdered rock is added to water and poured into moulds. These moulds are then placed in ovens. Afterwards, the statues are removed from their moulds and inspected before being sold. At this inspection stage, some of the statues are found to be faulty and have to be destroyed. The faulty statues have no residual value.

Guildshot makes two types of statues, the Antelope and the Bear. Both use the same type of material and labour but in different amounts.

One of your duties is to prepare the production, material purchases and labour budgets for each four-week period. You are given the following information for period 8, the four weeks ending 26 July 20X2.

Forecast sales	Antelope	Bear
• Sales volume, period 8, four weeks ending 26 July 20X2	141,120 units	95,000 units

Product information		
• Opening finished stocks	30,576 units	25,175 units
• Kilograms of powdered rock per statue	0.75 kg	0.50 kg
• Production labour hours per statue	0.10 hours	0.05 hours
• Faulty production	2%	5%

Material information	
• Material: opening stock of powdered rock	30,000 kg
• Material: closing stock of powdered rock	40,000 kg
• Price per kilogram of powdered rock	£8.00

Labour information	
• Number of production employees	140 employees
• Days per week	5 days
• Weeks per period	4 weeks
• Hours per production employee per week	38 hours
• Guaranteed weekly wage *	£228.00

The guaranteed weekly wage is paid even if hours produced are less than hours worked.

Closing finished stocks

The closing finished stocks are based on the forecast sales volume for period 9, the four weeks ending 23 August 20X2.

- Demand for the Antelope in period 9 is forecast to be 50% more than in period 8. The closing finished stock of Antelope statues for period 8 must be equal to four days' sales in period 9.

- Demand for the Bear statue in period 9 is forecast to be 30% more than in period 8. The closing finished stock of Bear statues for period 8 must be equal to five days' sales in period 9.

Other information

- The faulty production is only discovered after the statues have been made.
- For technical reasons, the company can only operate the ovens for five days per week.

Task 1.1

Prepare the following information for period 8, the four weeks ending 26 July 20X2.

(a) Production budget in units for Antelopes and Bears
(b) Material purchases budget in kilograms
(c) Cost of the materials purchases budget
(d) Labour budget in hours
(e) Cost of the labour budget

DATA

Hilary Green is the production director for Guildshot. She tells you that there are likely to be material and labour shortages in period 9. For commercial reasons, the company must fully meet the demand for Bear statues. As a result it will not be able to meet all the demand for Antelope statues.

Hilary suggests it might be possible to meet the demand by producing extra Antelope statues in period 8. She gives you the following information.

- Because of the technology involved, Guildshot cannot increase the number of production employees and the existing employees cannot work any overtime. The maximum hours are limited to the 38 hours per week for each production employee.

- It would be possible to buy up to a maximum 3,000 extra kilograms of powdered rock in period 8.

Task 1.2

(a) Calculate the maximum number of extra fault-free Antelope statues that could be made in period 8.

(b) Prepare a revised purchases budget in kilograms to include the production of the extra fault-free statues.

SECTION 2

You should spend about 100 minutes on this section.

DATA

Just over a year ago, Guildshot formed a subsidiary, Alderford Ltd, to make a new type of chemical. The chemical is sold in drums to the building industry where it is used to dry out new buildings.

You have been asked to help James Alexander, Alderford's managing director, prepare a report on the first twelve months of Alderford's operations.

James gives you a copy of the company's operating statement for the first twelve months of operations. This is shown below.

Alderford Ltd: operating statement – 12 months ended 31 May 20X2		
	Budget	*Actual*
Number of drums produced and sold	80,000	125,000
	£'000	£'000
Turnover	2,400	4,000
Variable costs		
Material A	240	425
Material B	480	680
Material C	320	500
Semi-variable costs		
Power	270	440
Water	122	200
Stepped costs		
Supervisors	160	258
Fixed costs		
Rent and rates	250	250
Lighting and heating	120	118
Administration expenses	200	240
Operating profit	238	889

James also gives you the following information.

- The budgeted fixed cost element of power was £110,000.
- The budgeted fixed cost element of water was £90,000.
- Each supervisor can supervise the production of up to 10,000 drums of the chemical.
- All other expenses are either totally fixed or vary directly with production and sales.
- There are no opening or closing stocks of any sort.

Task 2.1

(a)   Calculate the budgeted variable cost per drum of the following inputs.

      (i)   Material A
      (ii)   Material B
      (iii)   Material C
      (iv)   Power
      (v)   Water

(b)   Prepare a statement showing Alderford's actual results, the flexible budget and any variances.

DATA

James Alexander notices that there is a significant difference between the budgeted and actual number of drums sold during Alderford's first twelve months of trading.

He tells you that he has three strategies to increase the number of drums sold.

*   More sales to existing customers
*   Sales to new customers in the building industry
*   The development of new markets

James wants to increase the accuracy of forecasting for the year to 31 May 20X3 and asks for your advice.

Task 2.2

Write a memo to James Alexander. In your memo, you should explain the following.

(a)   FOUR forecasting techniques that Alderford could currently use

(b)   One forecasting technique that Alderford is currently unable to use

(c)   The most appropriate forecasting technique available for each of the three strategies to increase the number of drums sold

UNIT 9 FULL ASSESSMENT 2 (DECEMBER 2002)

NVQ/SVQ in ACCOUNTING, LEVEL 4

UNIT 9

CONTRIBUTING to the PLANNING and CONTROL of RESOURCES (PCR)

This examination paper is in TWO sections.

You have to show competence in BOTH sections.

You should therefore attempt and aim to complete EVERY task in BOTH sections.

You are advised to spend about 90 minutes on Section 1 and 90 minutes on Section 2.

Include all essential workings within your answers, where appropriate.

SECTION 1

You should spend about 90 minutes on this section.

DATA

You are employed by JDJ plc as a management accountant where you help to prepare budgets for all of the company's divisions. One division makes a single product, the Zeta, and its sales forecast for all of the five accounting periods to Friday 1 August 20X3 is shown below.

Sales forecast for Zetas to 1 August 20X3					
Accounting period ending	14 February	28 March	9 May	20 June	1 August
	Period 1	Period 2	Period 3	Period 4	Period 5
Sales volume (Zetas)	14,400	15,000	15,600	16,800	16,800

The production director gives you the following information.

Production

- The division works a five-day week for both production and sales.
- There are six weeks in each accounting period.
- The opening finished stock for period 1 will be 5,760 Zetas.
- The current policy of the division is that finished stocks in each period must equal 12 working days' sales volume of the next period.

Material

- Raw material has to be purchased in the period it is used and so there are no stocks.
- There is a 4% wastage of material due to evaporation before being issued to production.
- The division can purchase up to 130,000 litres of material in any six-week accounting period under an existing contract at a price of £7.00 per litre. Any extra purchases of material have to be bought on the open market at a cost of £12.00 per litre.
- Each Zeta requires eight litres of material.

Labour

- Employees work a guaranteed, 40-hour, five-day week.
- The guaranteed weekly wage is £240.00.
- There are 130 production employees in the division.
- It takes two labour hours to produce one Zeta.
- Any overtime required is payable at £7.00 per labour hour.

Task 1.1

Prepare the following budgets for EACH of the four periods 1 to 4 in accordance with the division's policy on finished stocks.

(a)   Production budget in Zetas
(b)   Purchases budget in litres
(c)   Cost of purchases budget
(d)   Labour hours required for budgeted production
(e)   Cost of labour budget

DATA

After presenting your budgets to the production director, she tells you that budgeted profits are less then planned because of two factors.

- The large amount of overtime
- Purchasing materials on the open market

She tells you that the policy on finished stocks is to be amended. There must always be sufficient stock to meet customer needs. Closing stocks cannot, therefore, be less than 12 working days, but can be more than 12 working days if this results in cost savings. This would involve producing more Zetas than required in some periods in order to make savings in later periods.

The production director asks you to revise your budgets to take account of the revised stock policy.

Task 1.2

(a)   Prepare the following REVISED budgets for each of the periods 1 to 4 to maximise any possible cost savings.

(i)   Purchases budget in litres
(ii)   Cost of purchases budget
(iii)   Production budget in Zetas
(iv)   Labour hours required for the revised budgeted production
(v)   Cost of labour budget

(b)   Write a memo to the production director. In the memo, you should do the following.

(i)   Calculate the total cost savings possible.
(ii)   Identify TWO possible costs that might be necessary to achieve savings.

SECTION 2

You should spend about 90 minutes on this section.

DATA

JDJ plc has another division that also makes a single product, the Omicron. Just over a year ago the senior managers of the Omicron division prepared a budget for the year ended 30 November 20X2. The managing director of the division, Robert Maxton, rejected their budget. In its place, he imposed a budget of his own that assumed a 10% increase in sales volume. The original budget prepared by the senior managers, the revised budget prepared by Robert Maxton and the actual results for the year are shown below.

Budgeted and actual operating results year ended 30 November 20X2			
	Original budget	Revised budget	Actual results
	Vol '000	Vol '000	Vol '000
Sales volume (Omicrons)	400	440	450
Production volume (Omicrons)	400	440	600
	£'000	£'000	£'000
Turnover	6,400	7,040	6,840
Expenditure type			
Material	1,600	1,760	2,520
Labour	2,000	2,200	3,180
Electricity	880	960	1,200
Depreciation	500	500	300
Maintenance	300	300	200
Other fixed costs	700	700	800
Cost of production	5,980	6,420	8,200
Less closing finished stock	nil	nil	2,050
Cost of sales	5,980	6,420	6,150
Operating profit	420	620	690

You are provided with the following information.

Budget data

- The difference between the original and revised budgets arose entirely from the change in volume. Both budgets used the same selling price and the same prices for all of the expenses,

- Material and labour are variable (or marginal) costs and electricity is a semi-variable cost. All other costs are fixed costs.

Actual data

- There was no opening finished stock and no opening or closing work in progress.

- The closing finished stock of 150,000 Omicrons included an appropriate proportion of overheads. The value of this closing stock was based on the absorption cost of production.

- From 1 November 20X1, the electricity supplier no longer imposed a fixed charge for electricity.

Task 2.1

(a)   Calculate the following budgeted data.

    (i)   Selling price per Omicron
    (ii)   Variable cost of material per Omicron
    (iii) Variable cost of labour per Omicron
    (iv) Variable cost of electricity per Omicron
    (v)   Fixed cost of electricity

(b)   Calculate the following actual data.

    (i)   Variable cost of material per Omicron
    (ii)   Variable cost of labour per Omicron
    (iii) Variable cost of electricity per Omicron

(c)   Prepare a variable (or marginal) costing statement showing *actual expenses by expenditure type* for the actual 450,000 Omicron sales volume.

(d)   Using the task data and your answer to part (c), prepare a variable (or marginal) costing flexible budget statement for the sales volume of 450,000 Omicrons. Your statement should show the budgeted and actual results and any variances.

DATA

Robert Maxton believes that the improved actual operating profit of £690,000 over the original budgeted profit of £420,000 is evidence that his imposed budget motivated managers.

Task 2.2

Write a memo to Robert Maxton. In your memo you should do the following.

(a)   Identify TWO situations where an imposed budget might be preferable to one prepared with participation of senior managers.

(b)   Identify THREE reasons, other than increased sales, why the original operating profit of £690,000 was greater than the revised budget's operating profit of £620,000.

(c)   Briefly explain why the actual operating profit used in the flexible budget statement prepared in task 2.1(d) is different from the £690,000 actual operating profit originally shown.

AAT Specimen Exams

AAT SPECIMEN EXAM PAPER- 2003 STANDARDS

NVQ/SVQ in ACCOUNTING, LEVEL 4

UNIT8

CONTRIBUTING to the MANAGEMENT of PERFORMANCE
and the ENHANCEMENT of VALUE (PEV)

This examination paper is in TWO sections.

You have to show competence in BOTH sections.

You should therefore attempt and aim to complete EVERY task in BOTH sections.

You should spend about 100 minutes on Section 1 and 80 minutes on Section 2

Include all essential workings within your answers, where appropriate.

SECTION 1

You should spend about 100 minutes on this section

DATA

You are employed as the assistant management accountant at Disc Makers Ltd where you report to Jennifer Oldham, the managing director. The company makes compact discs for customers in other companies at its factory.

The factory has two departments that share the factory's fixed costs. The pressing department uses expensive machinery to write digital data from a master disc onto blank discs. The second department, the finishing department, then prints information on the front of the pressed discs, packages them and sends the completed discs to the customers.

Disc Makers uses standard costing in both departments. The standard costs for the pressing department are based on *machine hours* and planned production is 800 compact discs per machine hour. Each standard machine hour requires eight standard labour hours.

The standard costs for the pressing department, together with other data for the week ended 14 November 2003, are shown below.

Standard cost per *machine* hour - Pressing Department	
Blank compact discs: 800 × £0.20 each	£160.00
Labour: 8 *labour* hours × £7.00	£56.00
Fixed overheads	£200.00
Standard cost of pressing 800 compact discs per machine hour	£416.00

Pressing Department information:

- Actual cost of blank compact discs issued to production   £20,790
- Actual price paid for each blank compact disc   £0.21
- Actual number of *fault-free* pressed compact discs produced   96,000 CDs
- Budgeted labour hours   880 hours
- Actual labour hours worked   980 hours
- Actual cost of labour   £7,252

Factory information:

- Budgeted *total* factory fixed costs   £33,000
- Budgeted *total* factory labour hours   1,320 hours
- Actual *total* factory fixed costs   £34,500
- Both budgeted **and** actual fixed overheads are apportioned between the pressing and finishing departments on the basis of **budgeted labour hours**.

PROFESSIONAL EDUCATION

Task 1.1

a) Calculate the following information for the Pressing Department for the week ended 14 November 2003:

    i)   actual number of blank compact discs issued to production;

    ii)   budgeted *machine* hours of the department;

    iii)   standard number of compact discs produced per *labour* hour;

    iv)   standard labour hours produced;

    v)   budgeted fixed overheads of the pressing department;

    vi)   actual fixed overheads of the pressing department;

    vii)   standard fixed overhead rate per *labour* hour;

    viii)   actual cost of actual production, including fixed overheads;

    ix)   standard cost of actual production, including fixed overheads.

b) Calculate the following variances for the Pressing Department:

    i)   material price variance;

    ii)   material usage variance;

    iii)   labour rate variance;

    iv)   labour efficiency variance;

    v)   fixed overhead expenditure variance;

    vi)   fixed overhead volume variance;

    vii)   fixed overhead capacity variance;

    viii)   fixed overhead efficiency variance.

c) Prepare a statement reconciling the standard absorption cost of actual production to the actual absorption cost of actual production.

3

DATA

After reading your reconciliation statement, Jennifer Oldham tells you:

- she is not certain if all variances should be investigated. She explains that for every 100 **fault-free** compact discs produced in the week ended 14 November 2003, 2 had to be scrapped because they were faulty. As the unit cost of a blank CD is so small, she feels it is not worth investigating the other reasons for the material usage variance;

- the standard costs are also used for quoting prices to potential customers. When the standard costs were developed, Disc Makers assumed that customers would want their discs to be both pressed and finished. The demand for disc pressing is so high that it exceeds the capacity of the CD pressing department but most customers then take the pressed compact discs elsewhere for finishing;

- the pressing department requires a dust-free, air-conditioned environment using an expensive machine but the finishing department does not use any expensive resources.

Jennifer Oldham gives you an analysis of the budgeted factory fixed overheads showing their usage by department. This is reproduced below.

	Pressing	Finishing	Total
Rents, rates and insurance	£8,600	£1,300	£9,900
Air conditioning, heat, light and power	£9,600	£900	£10,500
Depreciation and maintenance	£12,600		£12,600
	£30,800	£2,200	£33,000

Task 1.2

Write a memo to Jennifer Oldham. In your memo you should:

a) identify FOUR issues to consider before deciding to investigate a variance;

b) subdivide the material usage variance into that part due to discs being scrapped because they were faulty and that part due to other reasons;

c) *briefly* explain, with reasons, why the use of budgeted labour hours to apportion fixed overheads between departments might cause the excess demand for the pressing department and the reduced demand for the finishing department.

4

SECTION 2

You should spend about 80 minutes on this section.

DATA

Dolio Ltd makes a single product, the Uno. The Uno is sold directly to domestic customers and Dolio is able to sell as many Unos as it can produce. Each Uno requires one X24, a specialist part which is in short supply.

The internal accounts of Dolio for the year to 30 November 2003, together with other data, are shown below.

Operating statement for the year ended 30 November 2003			
	Units	£	£
Turnover			6,480,000
Purchases X24	12,000	1,200,000	
Less returns	1,200	120,000	
Net purchases	10,800	1,080,000	
Add opening stocks	1,200	120,000	
Less closing stocks	(1,200)	(120,000)	
X24 issued to production	10,800	1,080,000	
Other material and bought-in services		108,000	
Production wages		1,296,000	
Variable cost of production and sales			2,484,000
Contribution			3,996,000
Production overhead		3,024,000	
Inspection cost of X24 goods received		69,600	
Cost of X24 returns		48,000	
Cost of remedial work		120,000	
Customer support for faulty products		194,400	
Administrative and distribution expenses		216,000	
Total fixed overheads			3,672,000
Net operating profit			324,000

Balance sheet at 30 November 2003		
	£	£
Net fixed assets		1,600,000
Stock	120,000	
Cash	80,000	
Creditors	(180,000)	
Net current assets		20,000
Net assets		1,620,000
Financed by		£
Shareholders' funds		800,000
Loans		820,000
		1,620,000

5

OTHER DATA

- Number of production employees   140
- Maximum production capacity per year   12,000
- Dolio operates a Just-in-Time stock policy for the oher material and bought-in services but not for the X24.
- Closing stock only consists of units of X24.
- Creditors only arise from purchases of X24.
- Dolio does not offer credit facilities to customers or hold any stock of Unos.

You are employed by Dolio as its management accountant. One of your duties is to prepare management accounting information for Lewis Green, the Managing Director of Dolio.

Task 2.1

Lewis Green asks you to prepare the following performance indicators for Dolio:

a)   sales (or net profit) margin;

b)   return on capital employed;

c)   asset turnover;

d)   average age of stock in months;

e)   average age of creditors in months;

f)   added value per production employee;

g)   wages per production employee;

h)   capacity ratio (defined as actual production as a percentage of maximum production);

i)   contribution per Uno.

DATA

At a board meeting to consider the performance indicators, the Directors express concern about the *high cost of quality*. This is defined as the total of all costs incurred in preventing faults plus those costs involved in correcting faults once they have occurred. It is a single figure measuring all the explicit costs of quality - that is, those costs collected within the accounting system.

The Directors have also asked the supplier of the X24 to implement a Total Quality Management (TQM) programme to avoid faulty units of X24 being purchased and to also operate a Just-in-Time (JIT) policy to eliminate the need for Dolio to carry stocks.

Lewis Green tell you that:

- all costs making up the cost of quality are caused by the faulty units of X24;
- the supplier would agree to the TQM and JIT proposals but:
    - the cost per X24 would increase by £10;
    - supplies of the X24 would be limited to the 12,000 currently provided but each X24 would be guaranteed fault-free;
    - supplies of the X24 would have to be paid for in the month received and no credit would be allowed;
- Dolio's cost of quality would be saved and stocks eliminated if the supplier implemented the TQM and JIT proposals;
- Dolio would want to keep its cash balance at £80,000;
- any surplus cash arising from the proposals would be used to reduce the £820,000 of loans.

Lewis Green is interested in knowing what the results of Dolio would have been if the TQM and JIT proposals had been applied to the results for the year ended 30 November 2003.

Task 2.2

Lewis Green asks you to calculate the following:

a) cost of quality for Dolio Ltd;

b) revised operating profit if the supplier's conditions were accepted;

c) increase in cash balance before reducing the amount of the loans;

d) revised capital employed if there were no stocks or creditors and if any surplus cash had been used to reduce the amount of the loans;

e) revised return on capital employed.

AAT SPECIMEN EXAM PAPER - 2003 STANDARDS

NVQ/SVQ in ACCOUNTING, LEVEL 4

UNIT 9

CONTRIBUTING to the PLANNING and CONTROL of
RESOURCES (PCR)

This examination paper is in TWO sections.

You have to show competence in BOTH sections.

You should therefore attempt and aim to complete EVERY task in BOTH sections.

You should spend about 100 minutes on Section 1 and 80 minutes on Section 2.

Include all essential workings within your answers, where appropriate.

2

SECTION 1

You should spend about 100 minutes on this section.

DATA

Berry Ltd makes a product called the Delta. The only use for Deltas is as part of a machine made by World Products plc and World Products requires Berry to keep a minimum closing stock of Deltas.

You are the newly appointed management accountant employed by Berry Ltd and report to Nicola Brown, the managing director. She gives you the following information.

Accounting periods

- Both Berry Ltd and World Products plc divide the year into four-week periods. Each week consists of five days and each day comprises eight hours.

Forecast demand for Deltas - first five periods of 2004

• Four-weeks ending	30 January	27 February	26 March	23 April	21 May
	Period 1	Period 2	Period 3	Period 4	Period 5
Number of Deltas required	5,700	5,700	6,840	6,460	6,080

Finished Stocks and Work-in-progress

- World Products requires that closing stocks of Deltas at the end of *each* period must equal 3 days demand of the next period.
- The opening stock of Deltas for period 1, the four weeks ending 30 January 2004, will be 1,330 Deltas.
- There is no work-in-progress at any time.

Material

- Each Delta requires 6 litres of material.
- The material is currently supplied under a long-term contract at a cost of £8.00 per litre and is made exclusively for Berry Ltd.
- The supplier of the material can only make a maximum of 34,000 litres in any four-week period and Berry normally purchases the material in the same four-week period it is used.
- Should Berry require more than 34,000 litres in a four-week period, the supplier would be willing to supply additional material in the preceding period, providing it had spare capacity.
- There is a readily available alternative source for the material but the cost is £12.00 per litre.
- Before buying from the alternative source, any shortage of material in a period should be overcome, where possible, by first purchasing extra material from the supplier in the **immediately preceding** period.

Labour

- There are 78 production employees who are paid a guaranteed basic wage of £160 per 40-hour week.
- Each Delta should take 2 labour-hours to make but, due to temporary technical difficulties, the workforce is only able to operate at 95 per cent efficiency in periods 1 to 4.
- Any overtime incurred is payable at a rate of £6.00 per hour.

3

131

Task 1.1

Nicola Brown asks you to prepare the following budgets for EACH of the periods 1 to 4:

a) the production budget in Deltas, using the 3-day stock levels required by World Products;

b) the material purchases budget in litres;

c) the cost of the material purchases;

d) the labour budget in hours, including any overtime hours;

e) the cost of the labour budget, including the cost of any overtime.

DATA

On receiving your budgets, Nicola Brown, the managing director, tells you that:

• she is concerned about the cost of the planned overtime and the extra cost of purchasing materials from the alternative source;

• the minimum demand in any four-week period is forecast to be 5,700 Deltas;

She also believes that some immediate and longer-term cost savings are possible if Delta stocks at the end of each period were sometimes more than the 3-days required by World Products.

Task 1.2

Write a memo to Nicola Brown. In your memo, you should:

a) use the budget information prepared in task 1.1 to identify ONE immediate possible cost saving proposal other than reducing the 3-day stock requirement imposed by World Products;

b) calculate the value of the cost savings in the proposal identified in part a);

c) use the forecast of demand for Deltas to show whether or not:

  i) the need to obtain material supplies from the alternative supplier is a short-term problem; and

  ii) the need for overtime payments is also a short-term problem;

d) suggest TWO cost savings which may be possible in the longer term.

4

SECTION 2

You should spend about 80 minutes on this section.

DATA

Just over twelve months ago, Berry Ltd started selling a new product, the Zeta, that no one else can make or sell. A budget was prepared at the time but this was then amended to take account of revised forecasts. The original and amended budgets, and the actual results for the year to 30 November 2003, are shown below in an operating statement prepared by the previous management accountant

Zeta: Budgeted and actual operating results for the year to 30 November 2003						
	Original budget		**Amended budget**		**Actual results**	
	Units	*£000*	*Units*	*£000*	*Units*	*£000*
Turnover	20,000	700	22,000	770	23,000	782
Material		160		176		225
Labour		300		330		350
Production overhead		74		74		75
Cost of production	20,000	534	22,000	580	25,000	650
less closing stock	nil	nil	nil	nil	2,000	52
Cost of sales	20,000	534	22,000	580	23,000	598
Gross profit		166		190		184
General expenses		110		114		125
Operating profit		56		76		59

Nicola Brown, the managing director of Berry Ltd, tells you that:

- the only change in costs and revenues between the two budgets arose from the forecast change in volume;
- material and labour are variable (or marginal) costs, production overhead is a fixed cost and general expenses is a semi-fixed cost;
- both budgets assumed there would be no opening and no closing stocks.

She also gives you the following information about the **actual results**:

- the actual results have been prepared using absorption costing;
- the closing stock valuation includes a proportion of production overhead;
- general expenses include £71,000 which do not vary with changes in either sales or production volumes;
- the balance of general expenses are selling expenses and vary with Zetas sold;
- the actual unit cost of material and labour has remained the same throughout the year.

Nicola Brown is concerned that the actual profit for the year is less than the revised budgeted profit. She asks you to prepare an analysis showing why the two profit figures are different.

5

Task 2.1

Prepare an analysis for Nicola Brown. In your analysis you should:

a) calculate the following BUDGETED data:
    i) selling price per Zeta;
    ii) material cost per Zeta;
    iii) labour cost per Zeta;
    iv) variable (or marginal) cost of general expenses per Zeta;
    v) fixed cost of general expenses;

b) identify the ACTUAL production fixed costs incurred during the year;

c) redraft the ACTUAL results for the year on a marginal costing basis;

d) prepare a variable (or marginal) costing flexible budget statement for the year to 30 November 2003 showing:
    i) the actual results on a marginal costing basis;
    ii) the appropriate flexible budget; and
    iii) any variances.

Data

After receiving your statement comparing the actual marginal costing results with the flexible budget, Nicola Brown tells you that:
- she does not understand why the budget in your statement is different from the agreed revised budget nor why some costs have changed but others have remained the same;
- she does not understand why the actual results in your statement are different from the actual results in the operating statement prepared by the previous management accountant;
- she is concerned that the actual sales volume was significantly different from the budgeted sales volume.

Task 2.2

Write a memo to Nicola Brown. In your memo you should *briefly*:

a) give ONE reason why the budget in your statement answering task 2.1 d) is different from the revised budget;

b) explain why the actual results in your statement are different from the actual results given in the task data;

c) explain THREE forecasting techniques Berry Ltd can currently use to estimate the demand for Zetas;

d) explain ONE forecasting technique that Berry Ltd is currently unable to use to estimate the demand for Zetas.

6

Answers to Practice Activities

Chapters 1 and 2 Introduction/Behaviour and recording and reporting of costs

1 Productivity, efficiency, effectiveness

Term	Productivity
Definition	The relationship between output and input
Measures	Output per £ of fixed assets
	Output per employee
Term	Efficiency
Definition	The relationship between the value generated by output and input
Measures	Profit margin
Term	Effectiveness
Definition	The relationship between output and an organisation's objectives
Measures	Sales volume compared with budgeted market share (units)
	Number of hospital patients treated within six months of going on a waiting list

2 Absorption costing and marginal costing

Tutorial note. Several alternative methods of presenting the profit statement in task (a)(iii) would be acceptable. But remember that an absorption costing statement should include the overheads absorbed in production costs and the adjustment for under/over absorption of overhead.

The difference between the profits in (a)(iii) and (b) of £7,500 is caused by the difference in closing stock values, which amounts to the fixed production overhead absorbed on the 3,000 units at £2.50 per unit. Had there been any opening stocks, the difference in their valuation would also have affected the comparative figures.

	Production costs £	Sales etc costs £
Total costs of 60,000 units (fixed plus variable)	510,000	150,000
Total costs of 36,000 units (fixed plus variable)	366,000	126,000
Difference = variable costs of 24,000 units	144,000	24,000
Variable costs per unit	£6	£1

	Production costs £	Sales etc costs £
Total costs of 60,000 units	510,000	150,000
Variable costs of 60,000 units	360,000	60,000
Fixed costs	150,000	90,000

The **rate of absorption** of fixed production overheads will therefore be:

$$\frac{£150,000}{60,000} = £2.50 \text{ per unit}$$

Total absorption costing production cost = £(6 + 2.50) = £8.50

(a)   (i)   The fixed production overhead absorbed by the products would be 16,500 units produced × £2.50 = £41,250.

(ii)   Budgeted annual fixed production overhead = £150,000

	£
Actual quarterly fixed production o/hd = budgeted quarterly production o/hd	37,500
Production o/hd absorbed into production (see (i) above)	41,250
Over absorption of fixed production o/hd	3,750

(iii)   **Profit for the quarter, using absorption costing**

	£	£	£
Sales (13,500 × £12)			162,000
Costs of production (no opening stocks)			
Value of stocks produced (16,500 × £8.50)		140,250	
Less value of closing stocks			
(3,000 units × full production cost of £8.50)		(25,500)	
		114,750	
Sales etc costs			
Variable (13,500 × £1)	13,500		
Fixed (¼ of £90,000)	22,500		
		36,000	
Total cost of sales		150,750	
Less over-absorbed production overhead		3,750	
			147,000
Profit			15,000

(b)   **Profit statement using marginal costing**

	£	£
Sales		162,000
Variable costs of production (16,500 × £6)	99,000	
Less value of closing stocks (3,000 × £6)	18,000	
Variable production cost of sales	81,000	
Variable sales etc costs	13,500	
Total variable cost of sales (13,500 × £7)		94,500
Contribution (13,500 × £5)		67,500
Fixed costs: production	37,500	
sales etc	22,500	
		60,000
Profit		7,500

3 Absorption costing and marginal costing again

(a)

	£
Actual overheads incurred	496,500
Over-absorbed overheads	64,375
Overheads absorbed	560,875

Overhead absorption rate = £560,875/22,435 = £25 per hour

(b)   Change in stock = (8,500 – 6,750) litres = decrease of 1,750 litres

There was a reduction in stock during the period and so more overhead was charged against profit via opening stock than carried forward via closing stock. Marginal costing therefore shows the higher profit.

∴ Absorption costing profit = marginal costing profit – (overhead absorbed in change in stock)
= £(27,400 – (1,750 × £2)) = £23,900

(c)   Overhead absorption rate = budgeted overheads/budgeted activity level

∴ Budgeted number of machine hours = budgeted overheads ÷ overhead absorption rate
= £475,200/£32 = 14,850

Chapter 3 Collecting data

4 Data collection

> **Tutorial note**. It is important that you not only understand the differences between the various sampling methods but also that you can relate the ideas to the particular scenario.

(a)   (i)   **Simple random sampling**

A simple random sample is one in which **every member of the population has an equal chance of being included**. A sampling frame of the entire adult population of the Northern sales territory would have to be drawn up if this method were to be used. Such a sampling frame would probably be constructed by combining the electoral registers for the area in question. Each person on the electoral register would then need to be allocated a number and a sample of 10,000 (500,000 × 2%) would be selected using random number tables or a random number generator on a computer.

(ii)   **Cluster sampling**

Cluster sampling involves selecting **one definable subsection of the population** as the sample, that subsection taken to be **representative of the population in question**. In the Northern sales territory, where a sample of 10,000 is required, the regions might be split into groups (or clusters) of size 10,000 each. Northia would, for instance, contain 9 clusters while Wester would contain only one. In total there would be 50 clusters from which one would be selected randomly by numbering them and using random number tables as in (i). Every member of the selected cluster would then be surveyed. A more representative cluster sample could be obtained at greater cost by dividing the population into 500 geographic groups of 1,000 people each and then randomly selecting ten groups to be surveyed.

(iii)   **Stratified sampling**

It is possible that people's responses to the survey will depend on the region in which they live and so, in order to obtain a representative sample, it is important to ensure that all regions contribute to the sample in proportion to their population sizes. This is achieved **by dividing the total population into strata** (the regions in this case), **sampling separately in the** six **strata** (regions) and then pooling the samples. Regional samples must be proportional to regional sizes so, for instance, Northia's population of 90,000 would require a sample of 2% of 90,000 which is 1,800 people. The members of this sample would be selected randomly from the population of Northia by numbering and using random numbers as outlined in (i). The other sample sizes required would be as follows.

Wester	2% of 10,000	=	200
Southam	2% of 140,000	=	2,800
Eastis	2% of 40,000	=	800
Midshire	2% of 120,000	=	2,400
Centrasia	2% of 100,000	=	2,000

The total of the six smaller samples is 10,000.

(iv)   **Systematic sampling**

This method selects the sample by **choosing every nth person from a list of the population**, having first made a **random start** at some point between 0 and fifty on the list (we require a sample of 2% of the population so every fiftieth (500,000 ÷ 2% of 500,000) name will be chosen). Assuming that the territory does not have a single list of the adult population but does have electoral registers spanning the entire area, these could constitute a single list provided agreement could be reached on the order they were to be taken. A computer could randomly select one number between 0 and 50 and the person on the list in that position could be the random start. Thereafter every fiftieth person would be selected, with counting running on from one electoral list to the next until the total sample of 10,000 was selected.

(b)   The method likely to give the **most representative** sample is **stratified sampling** since this method deliberately selects from the different groups in the population in a representative fashion. The groups used in this case would be geographic, however, and it may be that people's characteristics regarding sales intentions do not vary according to the region in which they live. It may be that the sample would be more representative were it stratified by age or by gender. It would be very difficult, perhaps impossible, to stratify in such a way, however. With the caveat therefore that the **basis of stratification needs to be relevant to the subject of the survey**, stratification can be expected to give the most representative sample. Its disadvantages are that both the initial division of the sampling frame into strata and the process of numbering all population members, generating the required random numbers and identifying the corresponding people are **difficult** and **time-consuming** and therefore very **costly.**

The **disadvantage of simple random sampling** is that it is **theoretically possible**, although unlikely, to **select highly unrepresentative samples**. For example, every single sample member could live in Northia. Additional problems are that a **sampling frame** for the entire sales territory could be **difficult to construct** and, as for stratified sampling, the method of numbering and selecting by random numbers is **cumbersome** and **costly.**

In general, **systematic sampling** is just as likely to give unrepresentative samples as simple random sampling, but it has the added problems of **bias** if the sampling frame contains any cyclical patterns which correspond to the cycle of selection, such as every fiftieth person being elderly. The method we have suggested above would at least remove the danger of geographic imbalance, however. The combination of electoral registers into a single sampling frame would also be difficult.

Cluster sampling, although a relatively simple and cheap process by comparison with the other methods, is very open to **bias**. Indeed it would be surprising if one single geographic group could possibly be representative of the entire population. Even the selection of ten groups could easily prove to be very unrepresentative. There would also be some difficulty in dividing the population into clusters of exactly 10,000 each.

5 Surveys

(a)   The major **advantage** of using **personal interviews** is that they are associated with **high response rates**. Other advantages are as follows.

(i)   The interviewer can clarify what the questions mean.

(ii)   The interviewer completes the questionnaire so it doesn't need to look especially attractive, responses can start being coded straight away and the questionnaire will be completed accurately and professionally.

(iii)   Answers may be entered immediately into a hand-held computer.

(iv)   Depending on the answers given to various questions, the interviewer need not bother the respondent with certain groups of questions.

There are however a number of **disadvantages** in using personal interviews. The main ones are that the method is **costly and slow** and is therefore associated with **relatively small sample sizes**. Other disadvantages are as follows.

(i)   People may be tempted to 'show off' or to try to give the responses that they think the interviewer favours.

(ii)   The interviewer may introduce bias by unintentionally letting his opinions show. This can be dealt with by training interviewers but this will only exacerbate the cost and time problem.

(iii)   In a personal interview, people may be reluctant to answer questions of an intimate nature.

(iv)   Generally speaking, it is not possible to schedule personal interviews at a time to suit the respondent. The respondent may be out or busy when the interviewer calls.

(v)   It is often impractical to use personal interviews if the survey covers a wide geographic area.

(vi)   The respondent may need time to reflect on certain questions or to look for information. The time available to the respondent and the interviewer is often too brief to allow this.

(b)   Postal surveys have more or less opposite advantages and disadvantages to personal interviews, and so will be dealt with next.

The major **advantages** of the use of **postal questionnaires** are that they are very **easy, quick** and **cheap** and hence **relatively large samples** can be used. Other advantages are as follows.

(i)   There is no possibility of interviewer bias and people are less inclined to give what they perceive to be the desired responses.

(ii)   People are less reluctant to answer questions of an intimate nature.

(iii)   The respondent can complete the questionnaire at a convenient time and can take as long to reflect on questions or to find information as he needs, subject to sending the questionnaire back in time.

(iv)   There are fewer problems in locating respondents than there are when using personal interviews.

(v)   The survey can spread over an area of any size provided that it is covered by the postal service.

The **disadvantages** of using postal surveys tend to mirror the advantages of personal interviews. The main disadvantage is that **low response rates** are very common and it is not possible to know whether the views of non-respondents are similar to those of respondents. There are consequently great difficulties in judging the reliability of these surveys. Other disadvantages are as follows.

(i)   A great deal of thought and effort goes into making the questionnaire look attractive and approachable.

(ii)   Ideally the questionnaire should be short and simple but it will often have to involve complex formulations like 'if "yes", answer questions 8 and 9, otherwise go straight to question 10'. Interviewers are capable of dealing with these types of question more easily than are postal questionnaires.

(iii)   Questions should be short and simple but, since there is no possibility of clarifying them, they often have to be long and complicated in order to be as clear as possible.

(iv)   Postal questionnaires are often filled in very badly and many respondents give up and fail to complete them.

(v)   Respondents who do not walk past post boxes in their day-to-day routine need to make an effort to go out of their way to return the form.

(c)   The **advantages** of **telephone surveys** fall somewhere between those of personal interviews and postal surveys. For example, telephone surveys will generally achieve **higher response rates than postal surveys** but **lower response rates than personal interviews**. They are **not as cheap or as quick as postal surveys** but they are quite a bit **cheaper and easier than personal interviews**. Their advantages are as follows.

(i)   They have reasonable response rates.

(ii)   The interviewer can clarify questions and can omit any irrelevant questions.

(iii) The appearance of the questionnaire does not matter. Responses can be coded immediately. This type of survey is the best method for immediate data entry into a computer.

(iv)   There is less interviewer bias than there is with personal interviews.

(v)   They are reasonably quick and cheap to carry out provided the questionnaire is kept short. They are therefore associated with larger samples than personal interviews but smaller samples than postal surveys.

(vi)   The survey can encompass any area provided that it is covered by the telephone network.

The main **disadvantage** is that there are still quite a lot of people who do not have telephones and this can lead to **unrepresentative samples** being selected. Other disadvantages are as follows.

(i)   As with personal interviews, there can be a tendency to 'show off', intimate questions can cause problems, the respondent cannot generally select a convenient time for the interview and the respondent does not have time to reflect or to gather information.

(ii)   If the respondent is not at home, this is less of a problem than it is with personal interviews since it is simple enough to phone again.

(iii) It is not possible to show any forms of identification to the respondent. This is thought to contribute to the response level for this type of survey being lower than that of personal interviews.

Chapter 4 Analysing data

6 Using index numbers

(a)   Updated standard cost = £3.50 × 145/115 = £4.41

(b)   Planned cost   = 100,000/10 = £10,000
       Actual cost   = 100,000/11.2 = £8,929
       Difference   = £1,071

Chapter 5 Forecasting

7 Blue Diamond Recovery

Blue Diamond Recovery – Forecast membership and call outs

	(a)	(b)		(c)
		Call outs	*Seasonal*	*Call outs*
Month	*Members*	*(unadjusted)*	*variation*	*(adjusted)*
December (actual)	240,000	8,000	+ 20%	9,600
January	260,000	8,800		8,800
February	280,000	9,600	−10%	8,640
March	300,000	10,400	+ 20%	12,480
April	340,000	11,200	−10%	10,080
May	380,000	12,000	−10%	10,800
June	420,000	13,600	−10%	12,240
July	460,000	15,200		15,200
August	500,000	16,800	+20%	20,160
September	540,000	18,400		18,400
October	580,000	20,000	−10%	18,000
November	620,000	21,600	−10%	19,440
December	660,000	23,200	+20%	27,840
January	700,000	24,800		24,800

8 Forecasting

Tutorial note. In computing the seasonally adjusted sales, we must remember that data = trend + seasonal adjustment, so trend = data − seasonal adjustment. Thus a positive seasonal adjustment must be subtracted, and a negative one added.

(a)

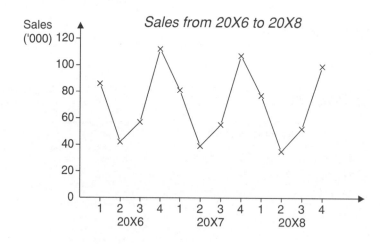

There are very marked **seasonal fluctuations**, with the fourth quarter of each year showing the highest sales and the second quarter the lowest sales. There does appear to be a **steadily falling trend**, with each peak and each trough slightly lower than the previous one.

(b)

Year	Quarter	Data £'000	4-quarter total £'000	Moving average of 4-quarter total £'000	Trend £'000
20X6	1	86			
	2	42			
			297	74.25	73.625
	3	57	292	73.00	72.625
	4	112	289	72.25	72.000
20X7	1	81	287	71.75	71.125
	2	39	282	70.50	70.000
	3	55	278	69.50	69.000
	4	107	274	68.50	68.125
20X8	1	77	271	67.75	66.750
	2	35	263	65.75	
	3	52			
	4	99			

(c) **20X8**

Quarter	Data £'000	Adjustment £'000	Adjusted data £'000
1	77	−9	68
2	35	+32	67
3	52	+16	68
4	99	−39	60

(d) We can forecast sales by **extrapolating the trend and then making seasonal adjustments**.

Over the period from 20X6, quarter 3 to 20X8, quarter 2 (a duration of seven quarters, not eight) the trend fell by 73.625 − 66.75 = 6.875, giving an average fall per quarter of 6.875/7 = 0.982.

Forecasts can then be prepared as follows, extrapolating the trend at this rate from the value for 20X8, quarter 2. Forecasts have been **rounded to avoid giving a false impression of great precision**.

20X9

Quarter	Trend £'000	Adjustment £'000	Forecast £'000
1	*63.804	+9	73
2	62.822	−32	31
3	61.840	−16	46
4	60.858	+39	100

* 66.750 − 3 × 0.982

These forecasts should **not be assumed to be reliable**. Although the decline in the trend has been steady, and the pattern of seasonal variations consistent, from 20X6 to 20X8, it is always dangerous to extrapolate into the future. The trend or seasonal patterns may break down, or random variations may have a substantial effect.

9 Time series analysis

Tutorial note. In this question you need to calculate a moving total of four quarters' sales. The moving average calculated from this moving total does not 'line up' with actual time periods, however, and so you need to take a second set of moving averages (which will be the mid-points of two of the first moving averages).

(a)

Year	Revenue	Sales	Moving total of 4-quarters' sales	Moving average of 4-quarters' sales	Mid-point of two moving averages Trend	Variation
20X2	1	200				
	2	110				
	3	320	870	217.5	219	+101
	4	240	884	221.0	222	+18
20X3	1	214	892	223.0	225	-11
	2	118	906	226.5	229	-111
	3	334	926	231.5	232	+102
	4	260	932	233.0	234	+26
20X4	1	220	938	234.5	235	-15
	2	124	944	236.0	238	-114
	3	340	962	240.5		
	4	278				

(b)

		Quarter				
Year		1	2	3	4	Total
20X2				+101	+18	
20X3		-11	-111	+102	+26	
20X4		-15	-114			
		-26	-225	+203	+44	-4
Unadjusted average		-13.0	-112.5	+101.5	+22.0	-2
Adjustment		+0.5	+0.5	+0.5	+0.5	+2
Adjusted average		-12.5	-112.0	+102.0	+22.5	0

ANSWERS TO PRACTICE ACTIVITIES

10 Eskafeld Industrial Museum

Tutorial note. In task (a) the seasonal variations sum to zero and so no averaging or adjustments are required. In task (d), discuss the product life cycle in general *and* in relation to the museum.

(a)

Year	Quarter	Number of visitors (actual)	Moving annual total	Moving average	Midpoint of two moving averages (trend)	Seasonal variations
20X7	1	5,800				
	2	9,000				
			35,200	8,800		
	3	6,000			8,900	− 2,900
			36,000	9,000		
	4	14,400			9,100	+ 5,300
			36,800	9,200		
20X8	1	6,600			9,300	− 2,700
			37,600	9,400		
	2	9,800			9,500	+ 300
			38,400	9,600		
	3	6,800				
	4	15,200				

(b)

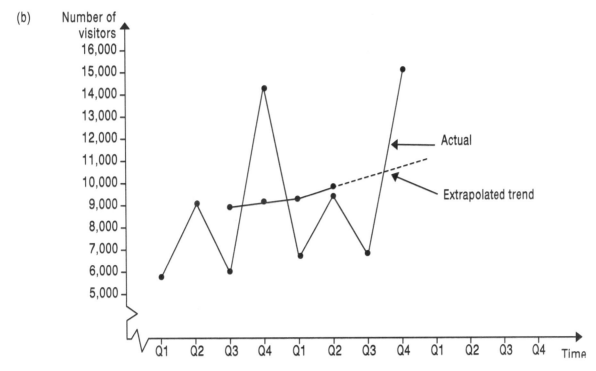

(c)   The **trend figures calculated above indicate an increase of 200 visitors per quarter. (Alternatively you could read the figures from the graph.)**

Year	Quarter	Trend		Seasonal variation	Forecast
20X9	1	9,500 + (3 × 200)*	= 10,100	– 2,700	7,400
	2	10,100 + 200	= 10,300	+300	10,600
	3	10,300 + 200	= 10,500	– 2,900	7,600
	4	10,500 + 200	= 10,700	+5,300	16,000

*For the three quarters between 20X8 Quarter 2 and 20X9 Quarter 1

(d)   **Notes on forecasting for John Derbyshire**

(i)   There are a number of steps that we can take to **improve the forecasting** of visitor numbers.

We should attempt to **analyse the visitor numbers in more detail**, perhaps by day of the week, week or month of the year. Time series analysis could then be applied to this more detailed data and a more accurate trend determined. The use of time series analysis assumes that the pattern of trend and seasonal variations will continue into the future, however, and this may not necessarily be true.

We could also consider **surveying past, present and future visitors** to the museum to obtain information about their possible plans to visit the museum in the future. Visitors may not always tell the truth when questioned, however.

Secondary sources of data could also be examined. Tourist industry data, data obtained by other museums and so on could be analysed with a view to determining future visitor numbers. But it should be borne in mind that such data will have been collected for another purpose and we will not be aware of its limitations.

(ii)   If we wish to **obtain the views of past, present and future visitors** to the museum (as suggested above), we could use either **telephone sampling or postal questionnaires. Telephone sampling might be preferable** for a number of reasons.

(1)   The response is rapid.

(2)   It is relatively cheap.

(3)   A wide geographical area can be covered from a central location without the need for an interviewer to travel between respondents.

(4)   The interview does not take up so much of the respondent's time.

(5)   Large numbers of postal questionnaires may not be returned or may be returned only partly completed.

(6)   Misunderstanding is more likely with postal questionnaires because there is nobody to explain questions that the respondent does not understand.

(7)   Interviewers can ask for clarification of answers given.

(8)   Additional questions can be asked if necessary.

(iii) Information about the stage the museum has reached in its product life cycle may provide an important indicator of likely future visitor numbers.

The **product life cycle** is an attempt to recognise distinct stages in a product's (in this case a museum's) sales history.

The **introduction phase** of a product requires heavy investment; this would have been the situation when the museum opened ten years ago, the major investment being in working exhibits. Significant marketing expenditure would have been necessary to bring the museum to the public's attention.

During the **growth phase**, a product gains a bigger market as demand build up. The museum's growth phase would have seen a significant increase in visitor numbers as a result of the marketing activity and early investment.

The growth in demand for a product will slow down and enter a period of relative maturity during the **maturity stage**. The number of visitors to the museum would have reached a peak and then levelled off. Modifications and/or improvements to exhibits may be required as a means of sustaining visitor numbers.

At some stage, the market will have bought enough of a product and it will reach **'saturation point'**. Demand will start to fall. During this stage visitor numbers would have started to fall off as interest in the museum waned; this is probably the phase faced by the museum in recent years.

In order **to ensure continuous demand** for a product, **regular investment** is necessary so that each investment has its own product life cycle, overlapping with that of the previous investment, thereby resulting in sustained growth. As a result of the recent improvements which you made, the museum has completed the introduction phase of a life cycle and is at the beginning of a period of growth after a number of years of decline.

11 Star Fuels

> **Tutorial note**. Calculate residuals (the difference between actual values and forecast values) in task (b) to determine the best method of estimating turnover.

(a) **Calculation of trend sales values from the regression line**

Quarter

17		£(2,000,000 + (40,000 × 17))	=	£2,680,000
18		£(2,000,000 + (40,000 × 18))	=	£2,720,000
	or	£(2,680,000 + 40,000)	=	£2,720,000
19		£(2,720,000 + 40,000)	=	£2,760,000
20		£(2,760,000 + 40,000)	=	£2,800,000

ANSWERS TO PRACTICE ACTIVITIES

Calculation of seasonally-adjusted sales

Quarter	Trend value £	Seasonal variation	Absolute variation £	(i) Forecast £	Percentage variation %	(ii) Forecast £
17	2,680,000	A	+350,000	3,030,000	+15	3,082,000*
18	2,720,000	B	+250,000	2,970,000	+10	2,992,000
19	2,760,000	C	−400,000	2,360,000	−15	2,346,000**
20	2,800,000	D	−200,000	2,600,000	−10	2,520,000

* £2,680,000 × 115%
** £2,760,000 × 85%

(b) (i)

Quarter	Actual £	Absolute forecast £	Residual error £	Percentage forecast £	Residual error £
17					
18	3,079,500	3,030,000	+49,500	3,082,000	−2,500
19	3,002,400	2,970,000	+32,400	2,992,000	+10,400
20	2,346,500	2,360,000	−13,500	2,346,000	+500
20	2,490,200	2,600,000	−109,800	2,520,000	−29,800

In each of the four quarters, the residual error associated with percentage seasonal variations is lower than that associated with absolute seasonal variations. On the basis of the sample of four quarters, the **percentage seasonal variations method appears to be the more accurate forecasting method.**

(ii)

Quarter	Season	Trend £	Seasonal variation %	Forecast £
21	A	2,840,000*	+15	3,266,000
22	B	2,880,000	+10	3,168,000
23	C	2,920,000	−15	2,482,000
24	D	2,960,000	−10	2,664,000

*Trend for Q20 + £40,000

(c)

Memorandum

To: Managing Director
From: Assistant Management Accountant
Date: 17 June 20X8
Subject: **Forecasting, seasonal variations and seasonally-adjusted data**

I have recently tested a statistical software package which can be used for estimating demand for fuel oil. I set out below some information which you may find useful.

(i)   **Seasonal variations** are regular, predictable and consistent changes in recorded values due to different circumstances which affect results at different times of the year, on different days of the week, at different times of day or whatever. For oil distribution, it is likely that demand will be higher in winter than in summer and this is reflected in the seasonal variations for our organisation produced by the software package. The sales revenue in Quarter A, which includes the winter months, is 15% above the average quarterly sales revenue whereas the sales revenue in Quarter C, which includes the summer months, is 85% of the average quarterly sales revenue.

Seasonally-adjusted data is actual data from which seasonal variations (derived from historic data) have been removed, to leave a figure which might be taken to indicate the trend (if we assume that any random variations are negligible). For example, the estimated seasonal variations within the actual sales revenue for Quarter 17 = 15/115 × £3,079,500 = £401,674, say £402,000. Deducting this from the actual sales revenue leaves an underlying figure of £(3,079,500 − 402,000) = £2,677,500.

(ii)   The **percentage seasonal variations method of seasonal adjustment might be more accurate than the absolute seasonal variations method because the trend in sales turnover is increasing over time**. When a trend is increasing, it is likely that absolute seasonal variations are also increasing. The absolute seasonal variations method simply adds absolute and unchanging seasonal variations to the trend figures whereas the percentage seasonal variations method, by multiplying the increasing trend values by a constant factor, produces seasonal variations which increase in time with the trend in sales.

(iii) There are a number of ways in which an **understanding of seasonal variations and seasonally-adjusted data** can help us to be more efficient. For example, it **helps in stock control**. If we are able to forecast demand we will not have to hold excessive stock. This helps cash flow in two ways.

(1)   It reduces cash tied up in stocks.
(2)   It minimises the interest charges on amounts owing to Star Fuels.

Accurate forecasts of demand will also enable us to forecast future profit levels more accurately.

(iv)   There are, however, a number of **limitations** to this forecasting technique

(1)   The use of the least squares regression equation assumes that there is a linear relationship between sales turnover and time.

(2)   The use of the equation also assumes that sales turnover is dependent only upon time. In reality it might depend on several other variables such as the actions of competitors or the state of the economy.

(3)   It assumes that what has happened in the past will provide a reliable guide for what will happen in the future. If, for example, a new competitor has entered the market, this will not be the case.

(4) The data used was measured in monetary terms but part of any increase in sales turnover may be due to rising prices rather than increased demand. It might therefore be better to measure sales in litres rather than value.

(5) The choice of a quarterly seasonal variation may be inappropriate. Forecasting on a weekly basis may be more suitable.

Chapter 6 and 7 Variances

12 Standard costing

Tutorial note. This is a very straightforward introduction to standard costing. The three types of variance required in task (b) are calculated as follows.

- The total labour variance is calculated as the difference between what the actual output should cost in terms of labour and what it did cost.

- The labour rate variance is calculated as the difference between what the actual labour hours should cost and what they did cost.

- The labour efficiency variance is calculated as the difference between the number of hours the actual output should have taken and the number of hours actually taken, valued at the standard rate per hour.

(a) **Standard production cost per unit**

		Major £	Major £		Minor £	Minor £
Direct materials	(2.2kgs × £15.00)		33.00	(1.4kgs × £15.00)		21.00
Direct labour						
Machining dept	(4.8 hrs × £6.00)	28.80		(2.9hrs × £6.00)	17.40	
Assembly dept	(3.6hrs × £5.00)	18.00		(3.1hrs × £5.00)	15.50	
			46.80			32.90
Standard direct cost			79.80			53.90
Overheads						
Machining dept	(3.5hrs × £16.00)	56.00		(0.9hrs × £16.00)	14.40	
Assembly dept	(3.6hrs × £9.50)	34.20		(3.1 hrs × £9.50)	29.45	
			90.20			43.85
Standard product cost per unit			170.00			97.75

(b) **Major**

Total – machining department

	£
650 units should cost (× £28.80)	18,720
but did cost	18,239
	481 (F)

Total – assembly department

	£
650 units should cost (× £18.00)	11,700
but did cost	11,700
	–

Rate – machining department

	£
2,990 hrs should have cost (× £6)	17,940
but did cost	18,239
	299 (A)

Rate – assembly department

	£
2,310 hrs should have cost (× £5)	11,550
but did cost	11,700
	150 (A)

Efficiency – machining department

650 units should have taken (× 4.8 hrs)	3,120 hrs
but did take	2,990 hrs
Efficiency variance in hrs	130 hrs (F)
× standard rate per hour	× £6
Efficiency variance in £	£780 (F)

Efficiency – assembly department

650 units should have taken (× 3.6 hrs)	2,340 hrs
but did take	2,310 hrs
Efficiency variance in hrs	30 hrs (F)
× standard rate per hour	× £5
Efficiency variance in £	£150 (F)

Minor

Total – machining department

	£
842 units should cost (× £17.40)	14,650.80
but did cost	15,132.00
	481.20 (A)

Total – assembly department

	£
842 units should cost (× £15.50)	13,051
but did cost	12,975
	76 (F)

Rate – machining department

		£
2,480 hrs should have cost (× £6)		14,880
but did cost		15,132
		252 (A)

Rate – assembly department

		£
2,595 hrs should have cost (× £5)		12,975
but did cost		12,975
		–

Efficiency – machining department

842 units should have taken (× 2.9 hrs)	2,441.8 hrs
but did take	2,480.0 hrs
Efficiency variance in hours	38.2 hrs (A)
× standard rate per hour	× £6
Efficiency variance in £	£229.20 (A)

Efficiency – assembly department

842 units should have taken (× 3.1 hrs)	2,610.2 hrs
but did take	2,595.0 hrs
Efficiency variance in hours	15.2 hrs (F)
× standard rate per hour	× £5
Efficiency variance in £	£76 (F)

(c) **Direct labour rate variances indicate whether rates of pay above standard rates have been paid**. An adverse variance would indicate that rates were higher, perhaps because of a wage increase or perhaps because labour with a higher rate of pay than the type of labour anticipated in the standard were used. A favourable variance might indicate that less skilled, and therefore lower paid, labour were used than anticipated in the standard.

Direct labour efficiency variances indicate whether labour took more time or less time than anticipated by the standard to produce the output. An adverse variance might indicate that less skilled labour were used, who consequently took more time than allowed by the standard or that the labour had to use poor quality materials and could not work so quickly. A favourable variance would indicate that labour took less time than standard, possibly because a more skilled labour force was used.

In the example above, the analysis of variances by both product and department will enable management to **pinpoint more accurately the areas of operations which need investigation** because they are not operating to standard and to **capitalise on the benefits offered by those areas which are operating above standard**.

13 Gransden Ltd

Tutorial note. In task (a)(i) you were not provided with the actual cost per metre of wood. By adding the variance to the standard cost you can determine the actual cost, however, and by dividing this actual cost by the actual usage of wood you can determine the actual cost per metre.

(a)   (i)

	£
Standard cost of 5,000 cabinets	2,500,000
Variance	200,000 (A)
Actual cost	2,700,000

Actual usage = 22,500 metres

∴ Actual cost per metre = £2,700,000 ÷ 22,500 = £120

	£
22,500 metres of wood should have cost (× £100)	2,250,000
but did cost (× £120)	2,700,000
Material price variance	450,000 (A)

5,000 cabinets should have used (× 5m)	25,000 m
but did use	22,500 m
Material usage variance in metres	2,500 m (F)
× standard cost per metre	× £100
Material usage variance	£250,000 (F)

(ii)   Current index   168
      Index when standards agreed   160

∴ Increase = 8 index points = 8/160 × 100% = 5%

∴ Price inflation = increase in RPI = 5%

(b)

	Usage Metres	Price £
Standard cost of 5,000 cabinets	25,000	100
Actual cost of 5,000 cabinets	22,500	120
Difference	2,500	20

Part of the difference of £20 in price per metre is due to inflation. This element = £100 × 5% = £5. The remaining increase of £15 is due to other factors.

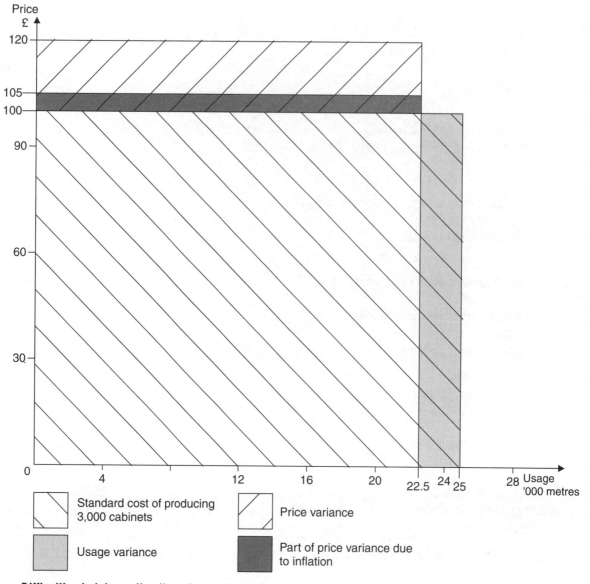

Legend:
- Standard cost of producing 3,000 cabinets
- Price variance
- Usage variance
- Part of price variance due to inflation

(c)   **Difficulties in interpreting the price variance**

(i)   The original standard may have been inappropriate given the conditions in May.

(ii) There may be an interrelationship between the adverse price variance and the favourable usage variance. If a superior but more expensive material is used (resulting in an adverse price variance), wastage should be less (and a favourable usage variance should occur).

(iii) The Retail Prices Index (RPI) is a measure of the cost of living of the average household in the UK. It may not reflect changes in prices in manufacturing generally or of wood in particular.

14 Priory Ltd

> **Tutorial note**. The additive model for time series analysis is Y = T + S. In task (a)(i) we want to calculate T and so we deduct S from Y. The signs of the seasonal variations as provided in the question therefore change. For example, if Y = 10 and T = − 1, then T = Y − S = 10 − −1 = 10 + 1.
>
> In task (a)(ii), we want to calculate a forecast Y as T + S, so the signs of the seasonal variations provided in the question do not change.

(a) (i)

	Quarter 1	Quarter 2	Quarter 3	Quarter 4
Actual price	£90	£105	£80	£75
Seasonal variation	−+£10	−+£20	−−£10	−−£20
	£80	£85	£90	£95

The **seasonally-adjusted price shows an increase of £5 per quarter**. The **trend** is therefore an **increase of £5 per quarter**.

(ii)

	Quarter 1	Quarter 2	Quarter 3	Quarter 4
Trend	£100	£105	£110	£115
Seasonal variation	+£10	+£20	−£10	−£20
Forecast price	£110	£125	£100	£95

(b) (i)

(1)

	£
18,200 litres should have cost (× £110)	2,002,000
but did cost	2,003,100
Material **price variance**	1,100 (A)

(2)

950 units should have used (× 21 litres)	19,950 l
but did use	18,200 l
	1,750 l (F)
× standard cost per litre	× £110
Material **usage variance**	£192,500 (F)

(3)

	£
7,100 hours should have cost (× £7)	49,700
but did cost	41,200
Labour **rate variance**	8,500 (F)

(4)

950 units should have taken (× 7 hrs)	6,650 hrs
but did take	7,100 hrs
	450 hrs (A)
× standard rate per hour	× £7
Labour **efficiency variance**	£3,150 (A)

(ii)   **Statement reconciling standard cost of actual production with actual cost of actual production**
(Week 7, control period 2)

	(F) £	(A) £	£
Standard cost of production (950 × £2,653)			2,520,350
Cost variances			
Material price		1,100	
Material usage	192,500		
Labour rate	8,500		
Labour efficiency		3,150	
Fixed overhead expenditure		81,900	
Fixed overhead efficiency		18,900	
Fixed overhead capacity		39,900	
	201,000	144,950	56,050 (F)
Actual cost of production			2,464,300

(c)   **Memorandum**

To: Production Director
From: Assistant Management Accountant
Date: XX July 20X8
Subject: **Meaning of variances**

(i)   **What variances are attempting to measure**

Most organisations have targets which they aim to reach in the course of one or more accounting periods. These targets are generally identified when an organisation plans for the future. Budgeting and standard costing are two methods whereby an organisation plans for the future.

Once an accounting period has been completed, it is useful to compare the actual results for the period with the budgeted results or standard costs for the same period. Any differences which arise are known as *variances*.

Variances are therefore attempting to measure any deviation between actual results and the original plan of action of the organisation.

(ii)   **Ways in which production variances can arise**

There are three main ways in which production variances can arise.

(1)   The actual cost per unit is different from the planned cost per unit
(2)   The actual input usage is different from the planned input usage
(3)   The actual production volume is different from the planned production volume

(iii)   **Reasons for errors in reporting variances**

There are a number of ways in which errors may arise when reporting variances.

(1)   If the original standards used are unrealistic or out-of-date.

(2)   If the actual results are recorded incorrectly.

(3)   If expenses are posted incorrectly, then the costs will not be matched with the budgeted costs.

(4)   If costs which have been incurred, but not invoiced are not accrued, then the costs will be understated, giving rise to an incorrect favourable variance.

(5)   If costs incurred by one department are due to the actions of another department, then the costs should be charged to the department responsible for them. If these costs are not identified correctly, then an incorrect adverse variance is likely to arise in the department which is not responsible for the costs.

(iv)   **Material price variance query**

Material A was forecast at a price of £125 per litre during control period 2. The standard price for material A is £110 per litre. During control period 2, the actual price paid per litre of A was £110.06 (£2,003,100 ÷ 18,200). The purchasing manager appears to have been efficient when buying litres of A, since he paid £110.06 per litre, when the standard cost was £110 per litre. The standard cost per litre of A may not be appropriate, however, since a forecast price of £125 per litre of A indicates that the purchasing manager may well have been very efficient when buying litres of A in control period 2. The standard price should possibly be higher.

15 Debussy Ltd

Tutorial note. Did you read the instructions carefully? Let's hope so. In task (b) you were told to calculate *total* variances (not variances for individual elements of fixed overhead). In task (c) you had to provide *one* possible reason for each of the variances that occurred.

(a)   (i)   Budgeted labour cost for quarter 4　　　　　　=　£48,000
               Budgeted rate per hour　　　　　　　　　　=　£8
               ∴ **Budgeted labour hours** for quarter 4　　=　£48,000 ÷ £8 = 6,000 hours

       (ii)   Actual labour cost for quarter 4　　　　　　=　£42,240
               Actual rate per hour　　　　　　　　　　　=　£8
               ∴ **Actual labour hours** for quarter 4　　　=　£42,240 ÷ £8 = 5,280 hours

       (iii) Budgeted output for quarter 4　　　　　　　=　3,000 tonnes
               Budgeted labour hours　　　　　　　　　　=　6,000 hours
               ∴ **Budgeted hours per tonne of fertiliser**　=　6,000 ÷ 3,000 = 2

       (iv)   Actual output for quarter 4　　　　　　　　=　2,400 tonnes
               Actual labour hours　　　　　　　　　　　=　5,280 hours
               ∴ **Actual hours per tonne of fertiliser**　　=　5,280 ÷ 2,400 = 2.2

(b)   We need to **begin by calculating the fixed overhead absorption rate per labour hour and per tonne.**

       Budgeted fixed overheads　　　　　　　　　　　=　£81,000
       Budgeted labour hours　　　　　　　　　　　　=　6,000
       ∴ Overhead absorption rate per hour　　　　　=　£13.50
       Budgeted hours per tonne of fertiliser　　　　=　2
       ∴ Overhead absorption rate per tonne　　　　=　2 × £13.50 = £27

(i)

	£
Budgeted fixed overheads	81,000
Actual fixed overheads	90,000
Fixed overhead expenditure variance	9,000 (A)

(ii)

Budgeted production	3,000 tonnes
Actual production	2,400 tonnes
	600 tonnes (A)
× standard absorption rate per tonne	× £27
Fixed overhead volume variance	16,200 (A)

(iii)

Budgeted hours of work	6,000 hrs
Actual hours of work	5,280 hrs
Capacity variance in hours	720 hrs (A)
× standard absorption rate per hour	× £13.50
Fixed overhead capacity variance	£9,720 (A)

(iv)

2,400 tonnes should have taken (× 2 hrs)	4,800 hrs
but did take	5,280 hrs
Efficiency variance in hours	480 hrs (A)
× standard rate per hour	× £13.50
Fixed overhead efficiency variance	£6,480 (A)

(c)

Memorandum

To: Claude Debussy
From: Accountant
Date: 13 December 20X8
Subject: **Fixed overhead variances**

(i) **Fixed overheads and changes in activity level**

Fixed overheads do not vary with changes in the level of production but remain fixed within a relevant range of production levels. For example, our plant and machinery can produce up to 15,000 tonnes of fertiliser per annum and so the insurance on this machinery should remain fixed provided output is 15,000 tonnes or less. If we were to produce 18,000 tonnes, however, we would need to invest in additional plant and machinery and hence the cost of insurance would increase.

Rather than vary in line with changes in output, fixed overheads vary with time. Rent and rates increase with time, the cost of leasing machinery increases the longer the machinery is leased and so on.

As actual output is within the relevant range of output, it is therefore most unlikely that fixed overheads have increased because actual output was greater than budgeted output. The difference between actual and budgeted fixed overheads is therefore due to either increases in the cost of fixed overheads since the budget was set or to poor planning and budgeting.

(ii) **Possible reasons for variances** (You were only required to provide one per variance.)

(1) The fixed overhead **expenditure variance** occurred because the overhead costs were actually higher than anticipated. This may be due to a rate of inflation that was higher than anticipated, the use of non-standard suppliers of insurance and power, sudden increase in costs or inappropriate standards.

(2)   The fixed overhead **capacity variance** occurred because actual hours of work were less than budgeted hours of work. This may be due to a reduction in demand for fertiliser compared with budget (and so the production workers were not required to work so many hours), a strike by workers or poor planning.

(3)   The fixed overhead **efficiency variance** occurred because the production workers worked less efficiently than anticipated. This may be due to poor motivation, weak supervision, machine breakdowns, production bottlenecks, poor quality materials that were difficult to work with or an inappropriate standard.

(d)   (i)

	Quarter 1	Quarter 2	Quarter 3	Quarter 4
Current budget	£30,000	£30,000	£30,000	£30,000
Seasonal variation (%)	+ 5%	− 10%	− 20%	+ 25%
Seasonal variation (£)	+ £1,500	− £3,000	− £6,000	+ £7,500
Revised budget	£31,500	£27,000	£24,000	£37,500

(ii)   **Use of revised budget for calculating variances**

The power which provides the heating for our ovens does not vary with changes in production output but it does depend on the outside temperature. If we take account of the seasonal variation in temperature and its effect on power consumption when budgeting, we will produce more accurate budgeted costs against which actual costs can be compared for control purposes. For example, the current figures shows an adverse power expenditure variance of £6,000 in quarter 4 but, by using the revised budget figure of £37,500, the variance is converted to a favourable variance of £1,500. Overall fixed overheads for the quarter would increase to £88,500, resulting in an overall adverse variance of £1,500, making it clear that the level of expenditure on fixed overheads was actually very close to the level budgeted.

The use of the revised figures for power costs would, however, increase the fixed overhead absorption rate in quarters when the seasonal variation is positive and decrease it in quarters when the seasonal variation is negative. This would in turn increase and decrease fixed overhead volume variances. The same volume variance in tonnes could therefore have a different monetary value in different quarters which would be extremely confusing and misleading for managers. Given that the seasonal variations balance each other out over the four quarters it would seem **more appropriate to use an annual fixed overhead absorption rate for calculating the volume variance**.

16 Hampstead plc

Tutorial note. Task (b) contained the tricky part of this question. You had to calculate the variances due to the machine breakdown and the price index change and then work out the variance due to normal operations. For example, if the total variance is £6,000 (F) and the variance due to the material shortage is £10,000 (A), the variance due to normal operations is *not* £4,000 (F) but £16,000 (F).

(a) (i) (1) **Standard marginal cost of a unit of Alpha**

	£
Material (36,000m ÷ 12,000) 3m × (£432,000 ÷ 36,000) £12 per m	36.00
Labour (72,000 hrs ÷ 12,000) 6 hours × (£450,000 ÷ 72,000) £6.25 per hr	37.50
	73.50

(2) **Standard cost of producing 10,000 units of Alpha**

	£
Material (£36 × 10,000)	360,000
Labour (£37.50 × 10,000)	375,000
Fixed overheads	396,000
	1,131,000

(ii) (1)

	£
32,000 m should have cost (× £12)	384,000
but did cost	377,600
Material price variance	6,400 (F)

(2)

10,000 units should have used (× 3 m)	30,000 m
but did use	32,000 m
Material usage variance in metres	2,000 m (A)
× standard cost per metre	× £12
Material usage variance in £	£24,000 (A)

(3)

	£
70,000 hrs should have cost (× £6.25)	437,500
but did cost	422,800
Labour rate variance	14,700 (F)

(4)

10,000 units should have taken (× 6 hrs)	60,000 hrs
but did take	70,000 hrs
Efficiency variance in hours	10,000 hrs (A)
× standard rate per hour	× £6.25
Labour efficiency variance in £	£62,500 (A)

(5)

	£
Budgeted fixed overhead expenditure	396,000
Actual fixed overhead expenditure (£(330,000 + 75,000))	405,000
Fixed overhead expenditure variance	9,000 (A)

(iii)

Report

To: Managing Director
From: Assistant Management Accountant
Date: 18 June 20X8
Subject: The **use of standard marginal costing** at Finchley Ltd

As discussed at our earlier meetings, because all companies within the Hampstead Group use standard marginal costing, Finchley Ltd will need to adopt the system from 1 August 20X8. This report is intended to **demonstrate and describe the use of standard marginal costing** in your company.

(1)   Set out below is a **statement reconciling the standard cost of production** for the three months ended 31 May 20X8 with the **actual cost of production** for that period.

		£		£
Standard cost of output((see (a)(i)(2))				1,131,000
Variances	*(A)*	*(F)*		
	£	£		
Material price		6,400		
Material usage	24,000			
Labour rate		14,700		
Labour efficiency	62,500			
Fixed overhead expenditure	9,000			
	95,500	21,100		74,400 (A)
Actual cost of output				1,205,400

(2)   The total labour variance in the statement above (£47,800 (A)) differs from that in your absorption costing management report for the three months ended 31 May 20X8 because the **original report compares the actual cost of producing 10,000 units and the budgeted cost of producing 12,000 units**. It therefore fails to compare like with like. The **report above**, however, **compares actual costs of producing 10,000 units and what costs should have been given the actual output of 10,000 units.** The total material variances in the two reports differ for this reason. There is very little point comparing a budgeted cost with an actual cost if the production level upon which the budgeted cost was based is not achieved.

The fixed overhead expenditure variance in the statement above also differs from the fixed overhead variance reported in the absorption costing statement. This is because the **absorption costing statement compares overhead absorbed whereas the marginal costing statement compares overhead expenditure.**

(3)   There are other **reasons why the marginal costing statement provides improved management information.**

(i)   It separates total variances into their components and so you will be able to determine whether, for example, the total material variance is the responsibility of the purchasing manager (price variance) or the production manager (usage variance).

(ii)   It avoids the use of under-or over-absorbed overhead, which is simply a bookkeeping exercise and does not reflect higher or lower cash spending.

(iii)   It allows management by exception.

(iv)   The original statement conveys the wrong message (that the overall variance was favourable).

I hope this information has proved useful. If I can be of further assistance or you have any questions, please do not hesitate to contact me.

(b)

		(A)	(F)	£
Standard cost of output				1,131,000
Variances		(A)	(F)	
		£	£	
Labour rate due to machine breakdown (W1)			2,520	
Labour rate due to normal working (W1)			12,180	
Labour efficiency due to machine breakdown (W2)		75,000		
Labour efficiency due to normal working (W2)			12,500	
Material price due to change in price index (W3)			38,400	
Material price due to other reasons (W3)		32,000		
Material usage		24,000		
Fixed overhead expenditure		9,000		
		140,000	65,600	74,400 (A)
Actual cost of output				1,205,400

Workings

1

	£
Total labour rate variance	14,700 (F)
Labour rate variance due to machine breakdown	
(12,000 × £14,700/70,000)	2,520 (F)
Labour rate variance due to normal working (balance)	12,180 (F)

2

	£
Total labour efficiency variance	62,500 (A)
Labour efficiency variance due to machine breakdown	
(12,000 hrs × £6.25)	75,000 (A)
Labour efficiency variance due to normal production	12,500 (F)

3

	£	£
Total material price variance		6,400 (F)
Variance due to price index change		
32,000 m should have cost (× £12 × 420.03/466.70)	345,600	
but should originally have cost (× £12)	384,000	
		38,400 (F)
Variance due to other reasons		32,000 (A)

(c)   (i)   The four general headings making up the cost of quality are as follows.

(1)   **Prevention** costs
(2)   **Appraisal** costs
(3)   **Internal failure** costs
(4)   **External failure** costs

(ii)   Examples of types of cost likely to be found in each category are as follows.

    (1)   **Prevention costs**. Maintenance of quality control and inspection equipment, training in quality control

    (2)   **Appraisal costs**. Inspection of goods inwards, inspection costs of in-house processing

    (3)   **Internal failure costs**. Losses from failure of purchased items, losses due to lower selling prices for sub-quality goods

    (4)   **External failure costs**. Costs of customer complaints section, cost of repairing products returned from customers

(iii)   **Implications for the existing costing system**

    (1)   If there are fixed price contracts with guaranteed levels of quality there are likely to be few, if any, material price variances or material usage variances due to poor quality.

    (2)   The cost of labour will effectively become a fixed cost, the actual unit cost of labour simply depending on the volume produced. Labour efficiency variances could therefore be calculated but they will not reflect costs saved or excess wages paid. Labour rate variances are likely to be minimal if there is a guaranteed weekly wage.

    (3)   Predetermined standards conflict with the TQM philosophy of continual improvement.

    (4)   Continual improvements should alter prices, quantities of inputs and so on, whereas standard costing systems are best used in stable, standardised, repetitive environments.

    (5)   Standard costing systems often incorporate a planned level of scrap in material standards. This is at odds with the TQM aim of 'zero defects'.

    Results of these implications

    (1)   There is less need for a standard costing system: variances are likely to be small or non-existent and, if incurred, non-controllable; the use of standards is inappropriate in a TQM environment.

    (2)   With the flexible work practices, capture of actual labour costs by individual jobs would be very difficult. Only material costs could be collected in the normal way. It is therefore unlikely that the full marginal cost of individual jobs could be collected.

(iv)   **A cost saving not recorded in the existing costing system**

With the introduction of a system of just-in-time, the cost of having money tied up in high levels of stocks will be saved. This cost would not normally be captured by Barnet Ltd's existing costing system.

17 Original Holidays Ltd

Tutorial note. You may have had trouble with task (a) but exchange rates should be one of the most familiar of all indices to you. Exchange rates are merely a special form of price index – the cost of one currency in terms of another (rather than the price of a product in terms of its price at a particular point in time).

(a)

	Quarter 1	Quarter 2	Quarter 3	Quarter 4
UK cost	£102.400	£137.760	£134.480	£68.921
Exchange rate (francs (F) to £)	2,000 F	2,000 F	2,800 F	3,000 F

(i)

	Quarter 1	Quarter 2	Quarter 3	Quarter 4
Cost in F (UK cost × exchange rate)	204,800 F	275,520 F	376,544 F	206,763 F
Seasonal variation*	– 20%	+ 5%	+ 40%	– 25%

* **Seasonal variations are expressed as a % of the trend**. If the trend is 100% and the seasonal variation is – 20%, the forecast (a) is 80%. To determine the trend you therefore need to multiply the forecast by 100/80 = 125% (not 120%).
Quarter 2 – multiply forecast by 100/105%
Quarter 3 – multiply forecast by 100/140%
Quarter 4 – multiply forecast by 100/75%

(ii)

	Quarter 1	Quarter 2	Quarter 3	Quarter 4
Trend in F	256,000F	262,400 F	268,960 F	275,684 F
Increase in F		6,400 F	6,560 F	6,724 F
(iii) Increase as %		**2.5%	2.5%	2.5%

Annual rate of increase $= (1 + 0.025)^4 - 1 = 10.38\%$

**6,400/256,000 × 100%

(iv)

Trend cost in F for quarter 4	275,684 F
Add quarterly increase of $2^1/_2$ %	6,892 F
	282,576 F
Seasonal adjustment (– 20%)	(56,515) F
Forecast in F (i)	226,061 F

Exchange rate (ii)	3,000 F
Forecast in £ ((i) ÷ (ii))	£75.35

(b) (i) **Standard absorption cost per holiday**

	£
Accommodation (£840,000 ÷ 6,000)	140
Air transport (£720,000 ÷ 6,000)	120
	260

(ii) Standard absorption cost of 7,800 holidays = £260 × 7,800 = £2,028,000

(iii) (1)

	£
Accommodation for 7,800 holidays should have cost (× £140)	1,092,000
but did cost	1,048,944
Material price variance (accommodation)	43,056 (F)

(2)

	£
Budgeted fixed overhead expenditure variance	720,000
Actual fixed overhead expenditure variance	792,000
Fixed overhead expenditure variance (air transport)	72,000 (A)

(3)

Budgeted number of return flights	80 flights
Actual number of return flights	78 flights
Fixed overhead capacity variance in flights	2 flights (A)
× standard overhead absorption rate per flight (£120 × 75)	£9,000
Fixed overhead capacity variance in £	£18,000 (A)

(4)

7,800 holidays should have used (÷ 75)	104 flights
but did use	78 flights
Fixed overhead efficiency variance in flights	26 flights (F)
× standard overhead absorption rate per flight	× £9,000
Fixed overhead efficiency variance in £	£234,000 (F)

(iv) **Original Holidays Cost Reconciliation Statement – 3rd quarter 20X7**

			£
Standard absorption cost for 7,800 holidays (7,800 × £260)			2,028,000

Variances	A	F	
	£	£	
Material price		43,056	
Fixed overhead expenditure	72,000		
Fixed overhead capacity	18,000		
Fixed overhead efficiency		234,000	
	90,000	277,056	187,056 (F)
Actual absorption cost			1,840,944

(v) The single most important reason **for the difference between budgeted and actual cost** is the **more intensive use of the aircraft**. 104 flights should have been used to transport 7,800 passengers but only 78 were required. This is represented by the favourable fixed overhead efficiency variance of £234,000.

(c)

Memorandum

To:	Jane Armstrong
From:	Accounting Technician
Date:	11 November 20X7
Subject:	**Fixed overhead variances**

Following our earlier telephone conversation, I set out below the information about fixed overhead variances that you requested.

(i) **Fixed overhead expenditure variance**

Provided that an organisation's activity level remains within what is known as the relevant range, fixed overheads remain the same regardless of the level of activity. The only reason they will therefore change is if the price paid for the overhead changes. This is represented by a fixed overhead expenditure variance. We reported an adverse fixed overhead expenditure variance of £72,000 in the third quarter of 20X7, caused by one or more of the costs associated with providing air transport increasing above the level budgeted. Maintenance, for example might have been more expensive than anticipated or the cabin crews might have had a salary increase which was not accounted for in the budget.

_25=_S

(ii)   **Fixed overhead capacity variance**

The capacity variance is a measure of resource usage. If it is favourable, a resource was used more than budgeted and so we would expect output to be greater than budgeted. If, on the other hand, a resource was used less than budgeted, there would be an adverse variance because we would expect output to be lower than budgeted.

The £18,000 adverse fixed overhead capacity variance reported in quarter 3 reflects the fact that there were actually two fewer flights than budgeted and hence, given budgeted passengers per flight, one would expect the total number of passengers carried to be lower than budgeted. There are a number of possible reasons why there were two fewer flights than budgeted: for example the aircraft may have been taken out of service to await spare parts that were not readily available; there may have been air traffic controller strikes which prevented the plane from taking off; or bad weather may have halted flights.

(iii)   **Fixed overhead efficiency variance**

The efficiency variance is a measure of resource productivity. If it is favourable, a resource was more productive than planned whereas if it is adverse, a resource was less productive than planned. In our case, the variance shows how intensively the aircraft was being used while it was operating.

The £234,000 favourable fixed overhead efficiency variance reported in quarter 3 reflects the fact that, for each of the 78 return flights which actually took place, 100 passengers (7,800 passengers ÷ 78 flights) were carried compared with the budgeted 75 passengers per return flight. In other words, the aircraft was used far more intensively than anticipated. More passengers may have been carried per return flight than planned because of the rising popularity of the island of Zed.

18 Pronto Ltd

Tutorial note. Remember in task (b)(ii)(3) that fixed overheads absorbed is based on the standard hours for actual production.

(a)   **Memo**

To: Richard Jones, Managing Director
From: Accounting Technician
Date: 11 December 20X8
Subject: **Variations in kit prices**

(i)   (1)   **UK cost per kit at the time the contract was agreed**

$54,243 ÷ $9.80 = £5,535

(2)   **UK cost of kits delivered**

	September	October	November
Kits delivered	2,000	2,100	2,050
Contract cost in $ (× $54,243)	$108,486,000	$113,910,300	$111,198,150
Exchange rate	$9.00	$10.00	$10.25
Contract cost in £($ cost/exchange rate)	£12,054,000	£11,391,030	£10,848,600

(3)   **Price variance due to exchange rate differences**

	September £	October £	November £
Contract cost of kits delivered			
should have been (from (2) ÷ $9.8)	11,070,000	11,623,500	11,346,750
but cost of kits delivered was (from (2))	12,054,000	11,391,030	10,848,600
Variance	984,000 (A)	232,470 (F)	498,150 (F)

(4)   Total variance = price variance + usage variance

∴ If price variance is as in (3) above, usage variance is total variance minus price variance in (3).

Usage variance

	September £	October £	November £
Kits delivered should			
have cost (see (3))	11,070,000	11,623,500	11,346,750
but did cost (given)	12,059,535	11,385,495	10,848,600
	989,535 (A)	238,005 (F)	498,150 (F)
less: price variance (see (3))	984,000 (A)	232,470 (F)	498,150 (F)
	5,535 (A)	5,535 (F)	Nil

(ii)   The price variances due to exchange rate differences should be excluded from any standard costing report prepared for the production manager of Pronto Ltd because they are not controllable by him and so he can do nothing to influence their occurrence. They do need to be recognised and monitored, however.

(b)   (i)   (1)   Budgeted overheads per machine (or track) hour = £840,000 ÷ 140 = £6,000 per hour

(2)   Budgeted number of cars produced per machine (or track) hour = 560/140 = 4 per hour

(3)   Standard hours of actual production = 500 cars ÷ 4 per hour = 125 hours

(ii)   (1)   **Fixed overhead expenditure variance**

	£
Budgeted expenditure	840,000
Actual expenditure	842,000
	2,000 (A)

(2)   Fixed overhead absorption rate per unit = £6,000/4 = £1,500

Fixed overhead volume variance

	£
Budgeted production at standard rate (560 × £1,500)	840,000
Actual production at standard rate (500 × £1,500)	750,000
	90,000 (A)

(3)   **Fixed overhead efficiency variance**

500 cars should have taken (from (b)(i)(3))	125 hrs
but did take	126 hrs
Variance in hours	1 hr (A)
× standard absorption rate per hour	× £6,000
	£6,000 (A)

(4)   **Fixed overhead capacity variance**

Budgeted hours of work	140 hrs
Actual hours of work	126 hrs
	14 hrs (A)
× standard absorption rate per hour	× £6,000
	£84,000 (A)

(iii)   **Reconciliation of fixed overheads incurred to fixed overheads absorbed**

	£	£	£
Fixed overheads incurred			842,000
Variances			
Expenditure		2,000 (A)	
Volume efficiency	6,000 (A)		
Volume capacity	84,000 (A)		
Volume		90,000 (A)	
			92,000 (A)
Fixed overheads absorbed (125 hrs × £6,000)			750,000

19 Malton Ltd

Tutorial note. Task (a) was very straightforward but task (b) was more difficult.

Task (b) required you to recalculate the same variances for a subsection of the original data. This is just like being asked to calculate the variances for different types of material and different classes of labour.

According to the assessor the weakest answers were to task (b)(iv). Too many candidates gave no consideration to the data in, or the requirements of, the question. For example, some candidates blamed the workforce for the adverse material usage variance on the special order even though it was specifically stated in the question that the additional material was below specification.

(a)   (i)   (1)

	£'000
78,000 litres of material should have cost (× £20)	1,560
but did cost	1,599
Material **price variance**	39 (A)

(2)	9,500 units of Beta should have used (× 8L)	76,000 L
	but did use	78,000 L
		2,000 L (A)
	× standard cost per litre	× £20
	Material **usage variance**	£40,000 (A)

(3)		£
	39,000 hours of labour should have cost (× £6)	234,000
	but did cost	249,600
	Labour **rate variance**	15,600 (A)

(4)	9,500 units of Beta should have taken (× 4)	38,000 hrs
	but did take	39,000 hrs
	Labour efficiency variance in hours	1,000 (A)
	× standard rate per hour	× £6
	Labour **efficiency variance**	£6,000 (A)

(ii) **Statement reconciling actual marginal cost of production to standard marginal cost of production**

	(F)	(A)	£
Standard marginal cost of production (9,500 × £184)			1,748,000
Cost variances	£	£	
Material price		39,000	
Material usage		40,000	
Labour rate		15,600	
Labour efficiency		6,000	
	−	100,600	100,600 (A)
Actual marginal cost of production May 20X7			1,848,600

(b) (i) Since 20% of the special purchase was scrapped *prior* to being issued to production, then the **amount of material purchased in order to make 1,500** units is as follows.

1,500 × 8L × 1/0.8 = 15,000L

(∴ 20% of 15,000L was scrapped = 3,000L scrapped and not issued to production)

	£
15,000L of material should have cost (× £20)	300,000
But did cost (× £22)	330,000
Material price variance due to extra order	30,000 (A)

Since 20% of the special purchase was scrapped prior to being issued to production, then of the 15,000L purchased for the extra order, 20% × 15,000L = 3,000L were scrapped. Therefore 15,000L − 3,000L = 12,000L were issued to production.

1,500 units of Beta should have used (× 8L)	12,000 L
but did use	15,000 L
	3,000 L (A)
× standard cost per litre	× £20
Material usage variance due to extra order	£60,000 (A)

	£
1,500 units of Beta should have cost (1,500 × 4 × £6)	36,000
but did cost (1,500 × 4 × £6 × 150%)	54,000
Labour rate variance due to extra order	18,000 (A)

(ii) (1) Standard price for materials was set with an index measuring 240.0.

Revised standard price for materials in May is £20 × $\frac{247.2}{240.0}$ = £20.60

(2) Materials price variance caused by general change in prices is therefore calculated as follows.

Total material used for 9,500 units	78,000 L
less: material used for special order	15,000 L
	63,000 L
× price increase	× £0.60
	£37,800 (A)

(iii) **Revised costing statement reconciling actual marginal cost of production with standard marginal cost of production**

			£
Standard marginal cost of production (9,500 × £184)			1,748,000

	Variances controllable by R Hill	Variances Not controllable by R Hill	
Cost variances			
Material price – due to inflation		37,800 (A)	
Material price – due to extra order		30,000 (A)	
Material price (W)	28,800 (F)		
Material usage	20,000 (F)	60,000 (A)	
Labour rate	2,400 (F)	18,000 (A)	
Labour efficiency	6,000 (A)		
	45,200 (F)	145,800 (A)	100,600 (A)
Actual marginal cost of production			1,848,600

Working

	£	£
Total variance		39,000 (A)
Variance due to inflation	37,800 (A)	
Variance due to extra order	30,000 (A)	
		67,800 (A)
Remaining variance		28,800 (F)

(iv) **Note to Richard Hill**

Following my review of the standard cost report for the Eastern Division, I should like to make the following comments.

The actual marginal cost of production was found to be £100,600 more than the standard marginal cost of production for May 20X7.

Inflation

There was an overall adverse materials price variance of £39,000. This was partly due to the fact that the original standard cost of material did not take into account inflation in May 20X7 (which caused a £37,800 (A) variance). This variance was out of your control, and I would like to suggest that the company revise standard material prices as soon as the indices for each month are known.

Extra order

The extra order which was accepted at late notice by the sales director was responsible for a number of adverse variances.

Firstly, materials for the extra order were purchased at a higher than normal price, giving rise to a material price variance (net of inflation) of £30,000.

Secondly, the extra material purchased was not up to normal specification and 20% of it had to be scrapped before being issued to production. This in turn gave rise to an adverse variance of £60,000.

Lastly the workforce could only produce the special order by working overtime. This overtime was in turn responsible for an adverse variance of £18,000.

All of the variances associated with the extra order were not within your control.

I would suggest that the company agrees to meet special orders at short notice only if the extra costs incurred (higher material prices, overtime costs) are recovered by charging a higher sales price.

20 Travel Holdings plc

Tutorial note. Don't get confused between labour hours and operating hours. Several people are employed to operate each ferry, so the number of labour hours is much higher than the number of ferry operating hours.

When you are calculating the overhead variances in part (a)(ii), you need to realise that overheads are absorbed on the basis of standard operating hours for the actual number of crossings. The assessor asks you to calculate this in (a)(i)(6), so you will already have the information available when it comes to the variance calculations.

(a) (i) (1)   Standard price of fuel = £497,664/1,244,160 litres = £0.40 per litre.

(2)   Standard litres of fuel per crossing = 1,244,160/6,480 = 192 litres
Standard litres of fuel for 5,760 crossings = 192 × 5,760 = 1,105,920 litres

(3)   Standard labour rate per hr = £466,560/93,312 hrs = £5 per hr

(4)   Standard labour hours per crossing = 93,312/6,480 = 14.4 hours
Std labour hrs for 5,760 crossings = 14.4 × 5,760 = 82,944 hrs

(5)   Standard fixed overhead cost per budgeted operating hour = £466,560/7,776 = £60 per hour

(6)   Standard operating hours per crossing = 7,776/6,480 = 1.2 hours

        Std operating hrs for 5,760 crossings = 1.2 × 5,760 = 6,912 hrs

(7)   Standard fixed overhead cost absorbed by 5,760 crossings = 6,912 hours (vi) × £60 per hour (from (5)) = £414,720

(ii)   (1)

	£
1,232,800 litres should cost (× £0.40 (a)(i)(1))	493,120
but did cost	567,088
Material price variance for fuel	73,968 (A)

(2)

5,760 crossings should have used ((a)(i)(2))	1,105,920 litres
but did use	1,232,800 litres
Usage variance in litres	126,880 litres (A)
× standard price per litre ((a)(i)(1))	× £0.40
Material usage variance for fuel	£50,752 (A)

(3)

	£
89,856 hours should have cost (× £5 (a)(i)(3))	449,280
but did cost	471,744
Labour rate variance	22,464 (A)

(4)

5,760 crossings should take ((a)(i)(4))	82,944 hours
but did take	89,856 hours
Efficiency variance in hours	6,912 hours (A)
× standard rate per hour ((a)(i)(3))	× £5
Labour efficiency variance	£34,560 (A)

(5)

	£
Budgeted fixed overhead expenditure	466,560
Actual fixed overhead expenditure	472,440
Fixed overhead expenditure variance	5,880 (A)

(6)

	£
Actual number of crossings (5,760) at standard rate ((a)(i)(7))	414,720
Budgeted number of crossings at standard rate	466,560
Fixed overhead volume variance	51,840 (A)

(7)

Budgeted operating hours	7,776
Actual operating hours	7,488
Capacity variance in hours	288 (A)
× std fixed o/hd cost per operating hour ((a)(i)(5))	× £60
Fixed overhead capacity variance	£17,280 (A)

(8) 5,760 crossings should take ((a)(i)(6))   6,912 operating hours
     but did take   7,488 operating hours
     Efficiency variance in operating hours   576 operating hours (A)
     × std fixed o/hd cost per op hr ((a)(i)(5))   × £60
     Fixed overhead efficiency variance   £34,560 (A)

(iii)

> **Tutorial note**. Remember that you must not include the overhead volume variance as well as the overhead capacity and overhead efficiency variances in your reconciliation. Since the volume variance is the total of the capacity variance and the efficiency variance, this would be double counting.

Statement reconciling the actual cost of operations to the standard cost of operations for year ended 30 November 20X0

Number of ferry crossings   5,760

	£	£
Actual cost of operations		1,511,272
Cost variances	Adverse	
Material price for fuel	73,968	
Material usage for fuel	50,752	
Labour rate	22,464	
Labour efficiency	34,560	
Fixed overhead expenditure	5,880	
Fixed overhead capacity	17,280	
Fixed overhead efficiency	34,560	
		239,464 (A)
Standard cost of operations		1,271,808*

* **Check.** 5,760/6,480 × £1,430,784 = £1,271,808

(b)

> **Tutorial note**. Remember to relate your answer to the task scenario. For example, the 'material' reflected in the material usage variance is fuel. It is not therefore really appropriate to suggest the use of inferior 'material' or pilferage as the cause of the adverse material usage variance.

Memo

To: Chief executive
From: Management accountant
Date: 6 January 20X1
Subject: **Variances for the year ended 30 November 20X0**

This memo addresses some of your concerns about the large number of adverse variances arising during the year.

(i)   **Subdivision of the material price variance for fuel**

Standard price of fuel per litre ((a)(i)(1)) = £0.40
Actual market price of fuel per litre = £0.40 × 1.2 = £0.48

	£	£
1,232,800 litres at standard price would have cost (× £0.40 (a)(i))		493,120
1,232,800 litres at actual market price would have cost (× £0.48)		591,744
Price variance due to difference between standard		
price and market price (part (1))		98,624 (A)
1,232,800 litres at actual market price should have cost (× £0.48)	591,744	
but did cost	567,088	
Price variance due to other reasons (part (2))		24,656 (F)
Total material price variance		73,968 (A)

(ii) The **fixed overhead efficiency variance** is **not controllable**. This variance is caused by the difference between the standard and actual operating hours for the 5,760 crossings. Since this difference arose entirely because of **weather conditions**, the corresponding variance is not controllable.

> **Tutorial note**. You could have given the labour efficiency variance as a non-controllable variance, but the discussion would be slightly more complicated.
>
> Overhead efficiency variance in operating hours ((a)(ii)(8)) = 576
>
> Ratio of standard labour hours to standard operating hours = 93,312/7,776
>
> ∴ Labour efficiency variance in terms of labour hours should be 93,312/7,776 × 576 = 6,912 labour hours
>
> This is the same as the calculated labour efficiency variance in terms of labour hours ((a)(ii)(4) above), and so the labour efficiency variance was also entirely due to adverse weather conditions.

(iii) The part of the **material price variance due to reasons** other than the difference between the standard price and the market price for fuel is **controllable**. This amount was calculated in (i) as £24,656 favourable. The adverse variance of £98,624 calculated in (i) is non-controllable, but the remainder of the price variance has arisen due to controllable factors, since the price paid was different to the prevailing market price.

The **labour rate variance** is also **controllable**. It is not affected by the uncontrollable factors of the change in the market price for fuel and the adverse weather conditions.

> **Tutorial note**. You could have also mentioned the fixed overhead capacity and expenditure variances.

21 Bare Foot Hotel complex

Tutorial note. You will need to think carefully when you calculate the variances because they are being applied in a slightly different situation in this task. For example, when you calculate the 'material usage' variance, you will be deciding 'how many meals 648 guests should have *used*'. The method and the reasoning remain the same, but you need to rethink your unit of measure.

(a) (i) (1) Actual number of meals served = 4 meals × 7 days × 648 guests = 18,144 meals

(2) Standard number of meals for actual number of guests = 3 meals × 7 days × 648 guests = 13,608 meals

(3) Actual hourly rate of pay = $5,280 ÷ 1,200 hours = $ 4.40 per hour

(4) Standard hours allowed for actual number of guests = (648 guests × 3 meals × 7 days) ÷ 12 meals per hour

= 1,134 hours

(5) Standard fixed overhead per guest = budgeted overheads ÷ budgeted number of guests

= $38,340 ÷ 540 = $71 per guest

(6) **Total standard cost for actual number of guests**

	$
Meal costs (13,608 meals × $3 per meal)	40,824
Catering staff costs (1,134 hours × $4 per hour)	4,536
Fixed overhead costs (648 × $71 per guest)	46,008
Total standard cost	91,368

(ii) (1)

	$
18,144 meals should cost (× $3)	54,432
but did cost	49,896
Material price variance for meals served	4,536 (F)

(2)

648 guests should have used ((a)(i)(2))	13,608 meals
but did use ((a)(i)(1))	18,144 meals
Usage variance in meals	4,536 meals (A)
× standard cost per meal	× $3
Material usage variance for meals served	$13,608 (A)

(3)

	$
1,200 hrs worked should have cost (× $4/hr)	4,800
but did cost	5,280
Labour rate variance for catering staff	480 (A)

177

(4) Meals for 648 guests should have taken ((a)(i)(4))   1,134 hours
       but did take   1,200 hours
     Labour efficiency variance in hours   66 hours (A)
     × standard rate per hour   × $4
     Labour efficiency variance for catering staff $264 (A)

(5) $
     Budgeted fixed overhead expenditure   38,340
     Actual fixed overhead expenditure   37,800
     Fixed overhead expenditure variance   540 (F)

(6) Actual number of guests   648
     Budgeted number of guests   540
     Volume variance – number of guests   108 (F)
     × standard fixed overhead per guest ((a)(i)(5))   × $71
     Fixed overhead volume variance $7,668 (F)

(iii) **Bare Foot Hotel complex**

Standard cost reconciliation for seven days ended 27 November 20X1

Budgeted number of guests   540
Actual number of guests   648

	$		$	
Standard cost for 648 guests (a(i)(6))			91,368	
Cost variances				
Material price variance ((a)(ii)(1))	4,536	(F)		
Material usage variance ((a)(ii)(2))	13,608	(A)		
			9,072	(A)
Catering labour rate variance ((a)(ii)(3))	480	(A)		
Catering labour efficiency variance ((a)(ii)(4))	264	(A)		
			744	(A)
Fixed overhead expenditure variance ((a)(ii)(5))	540	(F)		
Fixed overhead volume variance ((a)(ii)(6))	7,668	(F)		
			8,208	(F)
Actual cost for 648 guests			92,976	

Note. (A) denotes adverse variance, (F) denotes favourable variance.

(b)

Tutorial note. The assessor remarked that, as usual, the discursive elements in this assessment were less well answered than the computational ones.

Memorandum

To: Alice Groves, general manager
From: Assistant management accountant
Date: 8 December 20X1
Subject: **Performance report** for seven days ended 27 November 20X1

This memorandum deals with a number of issues arising from the standard cost reconciliation statement prepared for the seven days ended 27 November 20X1.

(i)   **Subdivision of the catering labour efficiency variance**

The adverse catering labour efficiency variance of $264 can be divided into that part due to guests taking more meals than planned and that part due to other efficiency reasons.

Standard hours allowed for 648 guests taking 3 meals ((a)(i)(4))	1,134 hours
Standard hours allowed for 648 guests taking 4 meals	
= (648 guests × 4 meals × 7 days) ÷ 12 meals per hour	1,512 hours
Excess hours due to guests taking more meals than planned	378 hours (A)
× standard rate per hour	× $4
Efficiency variance due to guests taking more meals than planned	$1,512 (A)

Standard hours allowed for 648 guests taking 4 meals (from above)	1,512 hours
Actual hours worked	1,200 hours
Efficiency variance due to other reasons (in hours)	312 hours (F)
× standard rate per hour	× $4
Catering labour efficiency variance due to other reasons	$1,248 (F)

(ii)   **The meaning of the fixed overhead capacity and efficiency variances**

The fixed overhead absorption rate for our hotel is based on the budgeted overhead expenditure for the period, divided by the budgeted number of guests.

$$\text{Fixed overhead absorption rate} = \frac{\text{budgeted fixed overhead}}{\text{budgeted number of guests}}$$

If the actual overhead, or the actual number of guests, or both, are different from budget then over or under absorption of overhead may occur, so that there may be a fixed overhead variance.

A **volume variance** arises when the activity level is different from that budgeted, in our case if the actual number of guests is different from the budgeted number. In some organisations it may be possible to sub-divide the volume variance into two parts: the capacity variance and the efficiency variance.

The **capacity variance** arises when the utilisation of the available capacity is higher or lower than budgeted. It is usually calculated as the difference between budgeted and actual hours worked, multiplied by the fixed overhead absorption rate. Under or over utilisation of capacity can potentially lead to under– or over-absorbed overhead.

The **efficiency variance** arises when employees are working at a more or less efficient rate than standard to produce a given output. Producing output at a faster or slower rate could also potentially lead to under– or over-absorbed overhead.

179

(iii)   **Calculating the fixed overhead capacity and efficiency variances for the Bare Foot Hotel complex**

The above descriptions of the fixed overhead capacity and efficiency variances highlight the need to be able to measure hours of work so that the volume variance can be subdivided.

It is not feasible to do this for the Bare Foot Hotel complex. We do have a measure of hours worked within the catering activity, but a large proportion of overheads are incurred on entertainment, for which we have no record of hours worked.

The absence of an activity measure based on hours worked therefore makes it difficult and meaningless to subdivide the fixed overhead volume variance into its capacity and efficiency elements.

Chapters 8 and 9 Budgets

22 Budget preparation

Tutorial note. You may think it's not worth the bother of writing out workings such as those in tasks (b) and (c). But, as we have said so often, if you make a mistake while putting numbers into your calculator, the assessor will not be able to see that, although you made an arithmetic mistake, you did know what to do.

(a)   **Production budget**

| | Cases | | | |
	June	July	August	September
Sales quantity	6,000	7,500	8,500	7,000
Closing stocks	750	850	700	650
	6,750	8,350	9,200	7,650
Less opening stocks	(750)	(750)	(850)	(700)
Budgeted production	6,000	7,600	8,350	6,950

(b)   **Ingredients purchase budget**

| | June | July | August |
	kg	kg	kg
Budgeted material usage (W)	15,000	19,000	20,875
Closing stocks	9,500	10,438	8,688
Less opening stocks	(5,800)	(9,500)	(10,438)
Budgeted ingredients purchases	18,700	19,938	19,125

Working

June   = 6,000 × 2.5 kg = 15,000 kg
July   = 7,600 × 2.5 kg = 19,000 kg
August = 8,350 × 2.5 kg = 20,875 kg

(c) **Budgeted gross profit for the quarter June – August**

	June £	July £	August £	Total £
Sales (W1)	150,000	187,500	212,500	550,000
Cost of sales (W2)	90,000	112,500	127,500	330,000
Budgeted gross profit	60,000	75,000	85,000	220,000

Workings

1	June	6,000 × £25 = £150,000
	July	7,500 × £25 = £187,500
	August	8,500 × £25 = £212,500
2	June	6,000 × £15 = £90,000
	July	7,500 × £15 = £112,500
	August	8,500 × £15 = £127,500

(d) A **flexible budget** is a budget which **recognises different cost behaviour patterns**, and therefore **changes as the volume of activity changes**. The **advantages** of adopting a system of flexible budgeting are therefore as follows.

(i) At the planning stage an organisation may wish to know what the consequences would be if the actual outcome differs from the prediction. For example, an organisation may prepare budgets at the planning stage to sell 100,000 units of product L, and it may also prepare flexible budgets based upon sales of say, 75,000 and 125,000 units of product L. Contingency plans could then be drawn up if considered necessary.

(ii) Managers are likely to have a more positive attitude to flexible budgets since they will feel that they are more realistic as they are adjusted for different volumes of activity.

(iii) At the end of a period, the actual results obtained by the organisation may be compared with the flexible budget. This comparison acts as a control procedure.

(iv) Since flexible budgets recognise whether costs are fixed, variable or semi-variable, such information can be used in the decision making process.

23 Product Q

Tutorial note. In task (a) you need to ensure that you take account of the losses and idle time correctly. In part (i) for example, the loss is 1/99 of the finished units required not 1/100. Likewise in part (ii) the idle time represents 7.5% of total hours, not 7.5% of worked hours.

The assessor reported that many candidates had great difficulty deriving a gross figure from a net figure in task (a) but that many were able to use their general business and commercial awareness to explain the implications of a shortage of material in task (b).

(a) (i) **Production budget for product Q**

		Units	Units
Budgeted sales			18,135
Closing stocks (1,200 × 115%)		1,380	
Opening stocks		1,200	
Increase in stocks			180
Finished units required			18,315
Loss through quality control check (1/99 × 18,315)			185
Budgeted production			18,500

(ii) **Direct labour budget for product Q**

	Hours
Worked hours (18,500 × 5 hours)	92,500
Idle time (7.5/92.5 × 92,500)	7,500
Budgeted paid hours	100,000
Budgeted labour cost (100,000 hrs × £6)	£600,000

(iii) **Material usage budget for material M**

	Kgs
Material for production (18,500 × 9kg)	166,500
Wastage (166,500 × 10/90)	18,500
Budgeted material usage	185,000

(iv) **Material purchases budget for material M**

	Kgs	Kgs
Required for production		185,000
Closing stocks (8,000 × 112%)	8,960	
Opening stocks	8,000	
Increase in stocks		960
Loss		1,000
Budgeted material purchases		186,960

(b) To achieve the budgeted production level of 18,500 units of product Q, 186,960 kgs of material M need to be purchased. If sufficient supplies are not available, however, budgeted production levels cannot be met, Alfred Ltd's plans cannot be achieved and material M is a limiting factor. **If the limiting factor cannot be alleviated material M will become the principal budget factor and the budget will need to be revised, the materials purchases budget being prepared first and all other budgets based around it**.

There are, however, a number of **ways in which this problem could be overcome**.

(i) Stock levels in the store could be kept as low as possible so that deterioration of material M is not possible. This would reduce the purchases requirement by 1,000 kg. Associated with such a policy, however, is the risk of stockouts (having insufficient stock when it is required for production) leading to disruptions to production and loss of sales and customer goodwill.

(ii) The planned closing stock levels of material M and product Q could be lowered. Again this could lead to stockouts (as in (a) above).

(iii) The rate of rejects due to the quality control check could be lowered, either by lowering the quality requirements or by improving the quality of the finished product. Alfred Ltd may be loath to reduce the quality requirements of product Q, however, as this could lead to a drop in sales. By implementing a programme of Total Quality Management, however, the company could attempt to raise the quality of the finished product, thereby reducing the number of units rejected.

(iv)   The implementation of the TQM programme should also reduce that part of the 10% wastage rate due to spillage.

(v)   The company could attempt to find alternative suppliers of material M but potential suppliers would need to be carefully vetted to ensure that they could guarantee the appropriate level of quality and reliability of supply.

(vi)   The budgeted level of sales could be reduced. Valuable customers may, however, move to competition on a permanent basis, affecting profits both next year and in subsequent years.

24 Arden Engineering Ltd

Tutorial note. In task (a), don't forget to calculate the fixed production overhead on the basis of gross production during the year rather than good production.

In task (b) you need to compare the marginal cost of production in Period 3 with the supplier's price for proposal 1. Since the labour cost is a fixed cost, the marginal labour cost is the £1.50 overtime payment.

The assessor reported that candidates had few problems with task (a) but were ill-prepared for task (b).

(a)   **Arden Engineering Ltd**

Production cost budget for periods 1 to 3 20X6

	Period 1 Units	Period 2 Units	Period 3 Units	Total Units
Gross production per period (W1)	240,000	280,000	320,000	840,000
Good production per period	228,000	266,000	304,000	798,000
	£	£	£	£
Wages	270,000	270,000	270,000	810,000
Overtime (W2)	–	–	45,000	45,000
Total labour cost	270,000	270,000	315,000	855,000
Material (W3)	840,000	980,000	1,120,000	2,940,000
Direct costs	1,110,000	1,250,000	1,435,000	3,795,000
Fixed production overheads (W4)	480,000	560,000	640,000	1,680,000
Production cost	1,590,000	1,810,000	2,075,000	5,475,000
Production cost per unit (based on good production)	£6.97	£6.80	£6.83	

Workings

1

	Period 1 Units	Period 2 Units	Period 3 Units	Period 4 Units
Sales	190,000	228,000	266,000	304,000
Good production	228,000	266,000	304,000	
Gross production				
(good production × 100/95)	240,000	280,000	320,000	

2   (320,000 – 290,000) units × £1.50 = £45,000

3   Material for period 1 = 240,000 × £3.50 = £840,000

4   Over the year, units sold equals good units produced = 3,296,500 units

  ∴ Gross production = 3,296,500 × 100/95 = 3,470,000

  ∴ Fixed production overhead per unit = £6,940,000 ÷ 3,470,000 = £2

  ∴ Fixed production overhead per period = gross production × £2

(b)   **Evaluation of proposal 1: outsourcing**

This is **not a viable proposal** because the marginal cost per unit is less than the price charged by the outside suppliers, even in the period when overtime is worked, as the working below shows.

Unit marginal cost in period 3 (with no wastage) =

	£
Material	3.50
Labour	1.50
	5.00

Note that the £270,000 labour cost is a fixed cost and hence will be paid regardless of the number of units produced. We included the £1.50 per unit overtime cost in our calculation above since this is what it costs in terms of labour to produce a unit over and above 290,000 units.

We need to adjust this unit cost to take account of wastage, however, since at the moment it represents the cost of producing a unit in a situation where all production is good.

  ∴ Unit marginal cost in Period 3 = £5 × 100/95 = £5.26

Evaluation of proposal 2: bringing forward production

30,000 of the units which it is planned to produce in Period 3 need to be produced in Periods 1 and 2. **Financing costs will be minimised if as many units as possible are produced in Period 2** since those produced in Period 1 will incur financing costs over two periods. We can produce another 10,000 units in Period 2 before the limit of 290,000 is reached.

Financing costs

	£
10,000 units in Period 2 × £0.50	5,000
20,000 units in Period 1 × (2 × £0.50)	20,000
	25,000

Savings

	£
Savings of overtime cost	45,000
Extra financing costs	25,000
Overall saving from proposal	20,000

Revised production schedule

	Period 1 Units	Period 2 Units	Period 3 Units
Planned production	240,000	280,000	320,000
Change to planned production	+20,000	+10,000	−30,000
Revised production schedule	260,000	290,000	290,000

25 Amber Ltd

> **Tutorial note**. You may have got confused with the rejection rate. Remember that if units are rejected, more units must initially be made than sold, and so sales is less than gross production.

(a)

		Week 1 Units	Week 2 Units	Week 3 Units	Week 4 Units
	Forecast sales	23,520	27,440	28,420	32,340
	Good production needed (W1)	27,440	28,420	32,340	
(i)	**Gross production required** (W2)	28,000	29,000	33,000	

		£	£	£
	Weekly labour cost	21,280	21,280	21,280
(ii)	**Cost of overtime** (W3)	–	–	5,200
	Total labour cost	21,280	21,280	26,480
	Cost of material (W4)	140,000	145,000	165,000
	Fixed production overhead (W5)	63,000	65,250	74,250
(iii)	**Cost of production**	224,280	231,530	265,730

Workings

1   Based on following week's sales

2   There is a 2% rejection rate and so production has to be greater than sales.
   ie 98% of production units = sales units
   ∴ 0.98 production = sales
   ∴ production = sales ÷ 0.98

3   (Units in excess of weekly capacity) × £2
   Week 1 – nil × £2
   Week 2 – nil × £2
   Week 3 – (33,000 – 30,400) units × £2 = £5,200

4   Gross production units × £5 per unit

5   Budgeted annual fixed overheads = £3,792,825

Estimated annual production = 1,685,700 units

∴   Budgeted fixed overhead absorption rate per unit
= £3,792,825/1,685,700 = £2.25 per unit

∴   Overheads absorbed per week = gross production volume × £2.25

(b)   (i)

	Week 1 Units	Week 2 Units	Week 3 Units
Gross production	28,000	29,000	33,000
Capacity	30,400	30,400	30,400
(Spare capacity)/overtime units	(2,400)	(1,400)	2,600
Additional production/(reduced production)	1,200	1,400	(2,600)
Revised production plan	29,200	30,400	30,400

Units will be made in week 2 before week 1 to minimise the financing costs.

(ii)   **Net savings if revised production plan accepted**

	£	£
Overtime costs saved (from task (a)(ii))		5,200
Financing costs : week 1 (1,200 × £0.20 × 2 wks)	480	
week 2 (1,400 × £0.20 × 1 wk)	280	
		(760)
Net saving		4,440

26 Pickerings Canning Company

Tutorial note. If there is 50% waste in production and the net amount of apples in 1,000 cans is 100kgs, 200kgs of apples are actually required to produce 1,000 cans.

(a)   (i)   **Materials purchases budget**

Apples required for 84,211 cans (W2)	16.8422 tonnes
Cost per tonne (basic)	× £200
Purchase cost	£3,368.44

(ii)   **Labour budget**

Production for September 20X7 **(W1)**	84,211 cans
Hours required per can	× 0.006
Labour hours required to produce 84,211 cans	505.266 hrs
Hours worked per month per employee **(W3)**	136.8 hrs
Number of employees required for September 20X7 (505.266 ÷ 136.8)	4 employees

(iii)   **Cost of materials purchased**

16.8422 tonnes at £208.33 per tonne (W4) = £3,508.74

Workings

1   **80,000 cans per month are required by customers. 5% of cans are damaged in the final stages of production, we therefore need to budget production of 84,211 cans (80,000 × $^{100}/_{95}$ = 84,211).**

2   Per (W1) 84,211 cans need to be produced

   1,000 cans require 100kg of apple (net) (or 0.1 tonnes)
   1,000 cans require 200kg of apple (gross) (or 0.2 tonnes)
   84,211 cans require 8.4211 tonnes of apple (net) or 16.8422 tonnes of apples (gross)

3   **Each employee works a 38 hour week. 10% absenteeism means that on average each employee will only work 38 hrs × 0.9 = 34.2 hours per week, or 136.8 hours (34.2 × 4) per month.**

4   £200 × $\dfrac{125}{120}$ = £208.33 per tonne

(b)

Memorandum

To:	C. Hathaway, Production Manager
From:	M. Greene, Assistant Cost Accountant
Date:	XX August 20X8
Subject:	**Short-term budget for September 20X8**

Internal index of apple prices

The **usefulness** of the materials price indices supplied by the buyer for budgeting the costs of materials will probably **depend on whether the crop of apples last year was similar to this year**. For example, a poor crop of apples may cause the price of apples to rise, whereas a bumper crop may cause the price of apples to be lowered so that they can all be sold. If the conditions in 20X7 were the same as in 20X8, and the supply and demand were similar then the internal index of apple prices may be a useful means of predicting prices.

Estimates based on **actual figures for last year are not likely to be very useful**, as costs are likely to have risen, even if only by the amount of **inflation**. Last year's costs will not include any increases due to inflation, and are therefore not likely to be very reliable.

An **alternative method** for predicting material prices might be to use a **special published index** such as the Retail Prices Index (**RPI**). The RPI is a measure of the change in the cost of living and its principal use is as a measure of inflation. It is a weighted index which is published every month and which has a base date of January 20X7. Since the cost of apples will be affected by inflation (wages of apple pickers, transport costs, storage costs) the RPI is a useful index for predicting costs of materials.

Wages

Wages costs are a significant part of the company's expenditure. It is important therefore that there is adequate control in this area. The type of information which should be supplied is summarised as follows.

On a **daily** basis, it would be useful to have a **log of absentees**, along with the reasons (sickness, holiday and so on). On a **weekly** basis it is important that **timesheets** are completed (showing hours worked per week by each employee).

On a **monthly** basis, **performance reports** should be prepared which compare actual results with budgets. For example, labour rate, efficiency and total variances should be calculated and any significant variances should be investigated. It would also be useful to supply an idle time report on a monthly basis with reasons of why these non-productive periods have occurred.

27 Northern Products Ltd

(a)

> **Tutorial note.** The calculations in part (a)(i) are necessary in order to complete the budgets in part (a)(ii). Don't forget to use them where appropriate, rather than wasting time calculating the information a second time!

(i) (1) Number of production days in quarter 1 = 12 weeks × 5 days = 60 days

(2) Quarter 1 closing finished goods stock:
Exe = 8 days × (930 ÷ 60 per day)   = 124 units
Wye = 9 days × (1,320 ÷ 60 per day)   = 198 units

(3) Quarter 1 labour hours available before overtime
= 12 weeks × 35 hours × 46 employees = 19,320 hours

(ii) (1) **Production budget for quarter 1, twelve weeks ending 24 March 20X0**

		Exe Units		Wye Units
Budgeted sales		930		1,320
Required closing stock (from (a))		124		198
		1,054		1,518
Less opening stock		(172)		(257)
Good production required		882		1,261
Failed product allowance (W)	(× 2/98)	18	(× 3/97)	39
Total production required		900		1,300

Working

Good production represents (100 – 2)% of total Exe production.

∴ 882 units = 98% of total production

∴ Total production = 882/98 × 100%

Alternatively, allowance = 2/98 of 882 = 2/98 × 882

(2) **Material purchases budget for quarter 1, twelve weeks ending 24 March 20X0**

		Litres
Material required for production:	Exe (900 units × 6 litres)	5,400
	Wye (1,300 units × 9 litres)	11,700
		17,100
Required closing stock	(5 days × (17,100/60) litres per day)	1,425
		18,525
Less opening stock		1,878
Material purchases required		16,647

Value of material purchases required (× £15)   £249,705

(3)   **Production labour budget for quarter 1, twelve weeks ending 24 March 20X0**

		Hours
Labour hours required for production:	Exe (900 units × 12 hours)	10,800
	Wye (1,300 units × 7 hours)	9,100
Total hours required		19,900
Labour hours available before overtime (from (a)(i)(3))		19,320
Overtime hours required		580

Cost of budgeted labour hours	£
Basic pay (19,900 hours × £6)	119,400
Overtime premium (580 hours × £1.80)	1,044
Total budgeted labour cost	120,444

(iii)

	Opening stock	Closing stock	Stock reduction	Storage cost per quarter £ per unit	Saving £
Product Exe	172 units	124 units	48 units	4	192
Product Wye	257 units	198 units	59 units	5	295
Raw material	1,878 litres	1,425 litres	453 litres	1	453
Savings arising from changes in required stock levels					940

(b)

> **Tutorial note.** You can guard against some arithmetical errors by checking that your total sales budget amounts to 20,000 units, after you have adjusted for seasonal variations.

(i)

	Quarter 1 Units	Quarter 2 Units	Quarter 3 Units	Quarter 4 Units
Quarterly sales before seasonal variations (20,000 ÷ 4)	5,000	5,000	5,000	5,000
Seasonal variations	(+20%) 1,000	(+30%) 1,500	(−10%) (500)	(−40%) (2,000)
Budgeted sales volume of Zed	6,000	6,500	4,500	3,000

(ii)

> **Tutorial note.** You will need to think carefully to determine the formulae in the spreadsheet. Effectively you are simply putting into formulae form the reasoning that you have applied in part (b)(i).

A	B	C	D	E	F
1	Unit selling price	£90			
2	Annual volume	20,000			
3	Seasonal variations	20%	30%	− 10%	− 40%
4		Quarter 1	Quarter 2	Quarter 3	Quarter 4
5	Seasonal variations (units)	= (C2/4) * C3	= (C2/4) * D3	= (C2/4) * E3	=(C2/4) * F3
6	Quarterly volume	= (C2/4)+C5	= (C2/4)+D5	= (C2/4)+E5	= (C2/4)+F5
7	Quarterly turnover	= C6 * C1	= D6 * C1	= E6 * C1	= F6 * C1

189

28 Sandwell Ltd

(a)

> **Tutorial note.** Remember that opening stock + production − closing stock = sales. Rearrange this to enable you to determine good production in (a)(i). Another point to note is that closing stock in one period (say period 1) becomes the opening stock in the next (period 2). If you have trouble dealing with scrap, have a look at Chapter 9 of the BPP Interactive Text.
>
> In (a)(ii), you need to rearrange opening stock + purchases − closing stock = material used in production.
>
> The assessor commented on four common errors in his report on candidates' performance in this assessment. Did you make these mistakes?
>
> - Closing finished stocks were sometimes based on the current period's sales volume rather than the following period's.
>
> - Rote learning of a previous central assessment task caused candidates to use an incorrect figure for the number of days in the period.
>
> - Many candidates could not account for the faulty production. Some used 3/100 instead of 3/97, some deducted faulty production from good production, some based it on sales volume, while others applied the 3/97 to material and labour as well as to production.
>
> - Some candidates ignored the guaranteed weekly wage in the labour budget.

(i) **Gross production budget**

	Period 1 Units	Period 2 Units	Period 3 Units	Period 4 Units
Sales	19,400	21,340	23,280	22,310
Opening stock	(3,880)	(4,268)	(4,656)	(4,462)
Closing stock (W1)	4,268	4,656	4,462	4,462
Good production	19,788	21,728	23,086	22,310
Faulty production (W2)	612	672	714	690
Gross production	20,400	22,400	23,800	23,000

Workings

1   There are 4 × 5 days in each period.

   Closing stock = 4 days' sales in the next period = 4/20 of next period's sales
   Closing stock in period 1 = 4/20 × 21,340 =   4,268
   Closing stock in period 2 = 4/20 × 23,280=   4,656
   Closing stock in period 3 = 4/20 × 22,310 =   4,462
   Closing stock in period 4 = 4/20 ×22,310 =   4,462

2   3% of gross production is scrapped. Good production therefore represents 97% (or 97/100) of gross production. Faulty production is 3% (or 3/100) of gross production and hence 3/97 of good production.

   ∴ Faulty production is 3/97 × good production.

(ii) Material purchases budget

	Period 1 Litres	Period 2 Litres	Period 3 Litres
Material used in production (W1)	61,200	67,200	71,400
Opening stock	(16,500)	(16,800)	(17,850)
Closing stock (W2)	16,800	17,850	17,250
Purchases	61,500	68,250	70,800

Workings

1   Each Gamma requires three litres of material.

∴   Material used in production = 3 × gross production (from (a)(i))

∴   Material used in production, period 1 = 3 × 20,400 = 61,200
Material used in production, period 2 = 3 × 22,400 = 67,200
Material used in production, period 3 = 3 × 23,800 = 71,400

2   • As we have already worked out, there are 20 days in each period.

   • Closing stock must equal five days' gross production in the next period.

   • Each Gamma requires three litres of material.

   • Closing stock in period 1 = 5/20 × 22,400 (from (a)(i)) × 3 = 16,800
     Closing stock in period 2 = 5/20 × 23,800 × 3 = 17,850
     Closing stock in period 3 = 5/20 × 23,000 × 3 = 17,250

(iii) Cost of material purchases

	Period 1	Period 2	Period 3
Material to be purchased (from (a)(ii))	61,500 litres	68,250 litres	70,800 litres
Cost per litre	× £8	× £8	× £8
Cost of material purchases	£492,000	£546,000	£566,400

(iv) Labour budget

	Period 1	Period 2	Period 3
Gross production (units) (from (a)(i))	20,400	22,400	23,800
Labour hrs required per unit	× 0.5	× 0.5	× 0.5
Labour hrs required	10,200	11,200	11,900
Basic labour hrs available *	11,200	11,200	11,200
Surplus hrs/(overtime hrs)	1,000	–	(700)

* 70 workers × 40 hrs per wk × 4 wks = 11,200

(v) Cost of labour budget

	Period 1 £	Period 2 £	Period 3 £
Labour cost per period (guaranteed) *	67,200	67,200	67,200
Cost of overtime (700 × £9)	–	–	6,300
Cost of labour	67,200	67,200	73,500

* 70 workers × £240 × 4 wks

(b)

> **Tutorial note.** You may have been slightly mystified as to what exactly you needed to do in (b)(i). The requirement actually meant that you needed to determine whether there was any way in which the need for overtime could be removed and the cost savings if it could. Given the guaranteed wage, the actual savings should be based on the full hourly rate for overtime, not just the premium.
>
> Keep to the point and answer the question set in (b)(iii). You were supposed to consider the advantages of sampling as a method of discovering the reasons for faulty production rather than the gains to be made from discovering the reasons for faulty production.
>
> Stratified sampling is the answer to (b)(v). If systematic sampling was applied, there is a possibility that every nth Gamma would be made by the same worker and so the sample would consist of the work of just one employee. Although it is less likely, the work of some employees could also be left out of the sample if simple random sampling were used.

Memo

To: Production director
From: Management accountant
Date: 17 May 20X1
Subject: **Budget 20X1 – overtime and faulty production**

I have investigated the points you raised about the budget for 20X1 and have set out my findings below.

(i) **The value of possible overtime savings**

In period 3, 700 hours of overtime are needed to produce the required number of units. There are 1,000 surplus labour hours available in period 1, however. If an **extra 1,400 units** (700 hrs ÷ 0.5 hrs) were **produced in period 1**, using 700 of the surplus hours available, the need for overtime in period 3 would be removed and **£6,300** (£9 overtime rate × 700 hrs) **saved**.

(ii) **Extra costs to achieve overtime savings**

The extra 1,400 units produced in period 1 are not needed until period 3 and so would need to be stored until then. This would incur additional **storage** costs.

The cost of the raw materials for the extra units produced in period 1 will not be covered by the sales revenue from the units until period 3 at the earliest. Additional financing may therefore be required to purchase this raw material, with the result that the company incurs **financing costs**.

(iii) **Advantages of using sampling to determine reasons for faulty production**

Instead of checking every Gamma produced to see whether or not it is faulty, a sample of Gammas can be inspected. This has a number of advantages.

(1) It is likely to be **cheaper** to inspect a sample of Gammas rather than all those produced.

(2) Inspection of all production would be extremely **time** consuming and would slow down the time between the start of production and the transfer to finished goods.

(3)   Inspection may sometimes require **destruction** of the item in question. For example, testing fireworks involves setting them off.

(iv)   **Differences between various methods of sampling**

   (1)   **Random sampling** involves selecting a sample (of Gammas in this instance) in such a way that every item in the population (ie all Gammas produced) has an equal chance of being included. Random samples are drawn up by listing all items in the population (sampling frame), numbering them and then selecting items using random number tables or random numbers generated by computer.

   (2)   **Systematic sampling** can provide a good approximation to random sampling. It works by selecting every nth item after a random start. For example, if it was decided to select a sample of 20 from a population of 800, then every 40th (800 ÷ 20) item after a random start in the first 40 should be selected. If (say) 23 was chosen, the sample would include the 23rd, 63rd, 103rd, 143rd, ..., 783rd items.

   (3)   **Stratified sampling** can often be the best method of choosing a sample (although it must be possible to divide the population into strata or categories for stratified sampling to be applied).

   Suppose we wanted to know whether the area of a particular country in which students live has any bearing on their success in the AAT assessments. If we took a random sample of all AAT students in the country, it is conceivable that the entire sample might consist of AAT students living in one particular region. Stratified sampling removes this possibility.

   If the country's population of AAT students is divided into categories depending on where they live, random samples of students can be taken from each area of the country, the number in each sample being proportional to the total number of students in each category. So if there are 50,000 AAT students in the country in total, and 5,000 live in the north-west area, 10% of the sample should be chosen (randomly) from those living in the north-west.

(v)   **The form of sampling appropriate for our company**

Given that the faulty Gammas are thought to be caused by poor work practices of some of the production workers, those production workers need to be identified. It is therefore important to sample the work of every employee. By dividing the population of Gammas into categories based on the production worker who manufactured them, and applying **stratified sampling**, work of every employee would be inspected.

Chapters 10 and 11 Budgetary control and further aspects of budgeting

29 Flexed budgets

> **Tutorial note**. In task (b) remember to check the unit cost rate at every level of activity in case the cost is semi-variable.

(a)   **Calculation of budgeted production** (units)

	Period 1	Period 2	Period 3	Period 4
Sales	15,000	20,000	16,500	21,000
Closing stock	2,500	3,300	2,500	3,000
	17,500	23,300	19,000	24,000
Less opening stock	4,000	2,500	3,300	2,500
Budgeted production	13,500	20,800	15,700	21,500

(b)   **Direct labour**

Production in period 4 will be above 18,000 units so we **need to know the bonus rate which applies** above that level.

Direct labour rate below 18,000 units	=	as periods 1 and 3 = £20 per unit
∴ Basic labour cost for period 2 production	=	£20 × 20,800 = £416,000
Actual labour cost	=	£444,000
∴ Bonus paid for extra 2,800 units (£444,000 − £416,000)	=	£28,000
∴ Bonus per unit above 18,000 units	=	£10

Direct materials

Constant rate per unit for all levels of output = $\dfrac{£108,000}{13,500}$ = £8

Production overhead

The rate per unit is not constant for all levels of output so this is a semi-variable cost. Using the **incremental method**:

	Units	£
Period 2	20,800	154,000
Period 1	13,500	117,500
Change	7,300	36,500

∴ Variable cost per unit   = $\dfrac{£36,500}{7,300}$ = £5

∴ Fixed cost   =   £154,000 − (£5 × 20,800) = £50,000

Administration overhead

Using the incremental method again:

	Units	£
Period 2	20,800	106,600
Period 1	13,500	92,000
Change	7,300	14,600

$\therefore$ Variable cost per unit $= \dfrac{£14,600}{7,300} = £2$

$\therefore$ Fixed cost $= £106,600 - (£2 \times 20,800) = £65,000$

Selling overhead

Using the **incremental method** again:

	Units	£
Period 2	20,000	65,000
Period 1	15,000	60,000
Change	5,000	5,000

$\therefore$ Variable cost per unit $=$ £1

$\therefore$ Fixed cost $=$ £65,000 − (£1 × 20,000) = £45,000

COST BUDGET FOR PERIOD 4
PRODUCTION VOLUME 21,500 UNITS

			£'000	£'000
Direct labour	– basic rate	21,500 × £20	430.0	
	– bonus	3,500 × £10	35.0	
				465.0
Direct materials		21,500 × £8		172.0
Production overhead	– variable	21,500 × £5	107.5	
	– fixed		50.0	
				157.5
Depreciation				40.0
Administration overhead	– variable	21,500 × £2	43.0	
	– fixed		65.0	
				108.0
Selling overhead	– variable	21,000 × £1	21.0	
	– fixed		45.0	
				66.0
Total budgeted cost				1,008.5

(c)   **Variance report for period 4**

	Budget £'000	Actual £'000	Variance £'000	
Direct labour	465.0	458	7.0	Favourable
Direct material	172.0	176	4.0	Adverse
Production overhead	157.5	181	23.5	Adverse
Depreciation	40.0	40	–	
Administration overhead	108.0	128	20.0	Adverse
Selling overhead	66.0	62	4.0	Favourable
	1,008.5	1,045	36.5	Adverse

30 Spreadsheets

Spreadsheet design to produce the labour requirements budget for August 20X9

The labour requirements budget for August would be **determined by the production budget**, which is **in turn dependent on the requirement for sales and stock**. Consequently, there would be a **'cascade' approach**.

Once the production requirement has been determined there would need to be an **adjustment for the 10% defect rate**. This would provide a figure for actual production required. This adjustment is complicated by the fact that whole units are required, and so a **correction to bring the output up to the next complete unit** may be necessary. This correction could be **dispensed with** in the interests of **simplicity**, however.

The next step would be to **convert** the actual production **into labour hours** by multiplying output by hours per unit. The hours per unit may well be contained in a data table to permit easy adjustment of the budget if production levels change.

The final step would be to **convert** the labour hours **into money** by reference to an hourly rate of pay. The hourly rate also could be located in the data table to permit easy amendment of the budget.

A **cell layout diagram** is set out below.

	A	B	C	D	E	F	G	H
1	**Labour budget**							
2	**Data table**							
3	Closing stock as a proportion of following month's sales						0.5	
4	Defect rate						0.1	
5	Labour hours per unit						10	
6	Labour wage rate per hour						£8	
7								
8	Month					August	September	
9	Budgeted sales units					300	600	
10	Opening stock					= F9 * G3		
11	Closing stock					= G9 * G3		
12	Good production required					= F9 – F10 + F11		
13	Actual production in units after adjustment for defect rate					= F12 /(1–G4)		
14	Labour hours budget					= F13 * G5		
15	Wages budget					= F14 * G6		

31 World History Museum

> **Tutorial note**. A useful check is to ensure that the difference between the total cost allowance at the actual level of activity and the total actual cost equals the total of the variances.

(a) and (b)

Analysis of budgeted costs

	Fixed cost £	Variable cost £	Variable cost per course* £
Speakers' fees	-	3,180	530
Hire of premises	-	1,500	250
Depreciation of equipment	180	-	-
Stationery	-	600	100
Catering	250	1,500	250
Insurance	100	720	120
Administration	1,620	–	–

*Variable cost per course = (Total variable cost)/6

Flexible budget control statement for April

Expenditure	Fixed cost allowance £	Variable cost allowance* £	Total cost allowance £	Actual cost £	Variance £
Speakers' fees	–	2,650	2,650	2,500	150 (F)
Hire of premises	–	1,250	1,250	1,500	250 (A)
Dep'n of equipment	180	–	180	200	20 (A)
Stationery	–	500	500	530	30 (A)
Catering	250	1,250	1,500	1,500	–
Insurance	100	600	700	700	–
Administration	1,620	–	1,620	1,650	30 (A)
	2,150	6,250	8,400	8,580	180 (A)

* Variable cost allowance = variable cost per course × 5

Note. (F) denotes a favourable variance, (A) an adverse variance.

(c)
Memorandum

To: Chris Brooks
From: Assistant management accountant
Date: Monday 13 June 20X1
Subject: **Participative budgeting**

As requested I enclose brief explanations of the advantages and disadvantages of participative budgeting.

Advantages

(i)   Managers are likely to be demotivated if budgets are imposed on them without any prior consultation. If they are consulted they are more likely to accept the budgets as realistic targets.

(ii)   If managers are consulted then the budgets are more likely to take account of their own aspiration levels. Aspiration levels are personal targets which individuals or departments set for themselves. If budget targets exceed aspiration levels then the budgets can have a negative motivational impact because they will be perceived as unachievable. However, if the targets fall too far below aspiration levels then the performance of the individuals or departments may be lower than might otherwise have been achieved.

(iii)   Managers who are consulted may be motivated by the feeling that their views are valuable to senior management.

(iv)   Managers who are closely involved with the day to day running of operations may be able to give very valuable input to the forecasting and planning process.

Disadvantages

(i)   If too many people are involved in budgetary planning it can make the process very slow and difficult to manage.

(ii)   Senior managers may need to overrule decisions made by local managers. This can be demotivating if it is not dealt with correctly.

(iii)   The participative process may not be genuine. Managers must feel that their participation is really valued by senior management. A false attempt to appear to be interested in their views can be even more demotivating than a system of imposed budgets.

(iv)   Managers may attempt to include excess expenditure in their budgets, due to 'empire building' or a desire to guard against unforeseen circumstances.

32 Parmod plc

Tutorial note. Task (b) was quite tricky. You had to realise that, because production volume would be greater than sales volume, there would be closing stocks of computers and so you had to calculate a unit cost for stock valuation purposes. What is more, you had to remember to value finished stocks on the basis of 80% activity.

(a) **Trygon Ltd**

Flexible budget at 75% activity

Activity level	80%	40%	Variable cost per unit	75%
Sales and production (units)	120,000	60,000		112,500
	£	£	£	£
Direct materials	24,000,000	12,000,000	200	22,500,000 (W1)
Direct labour	7,200,000	7,200,000		7,200,000 (W2)
Light, heat and power	4,000,000	2,200,000	30	3,775,000 (W3)
Production management salaries	1,500,000	1,500,000		1,500,000 (W2)
Factory rent, rates and insurance	9,400,000	9,400,000		9,400,000 (W4)
Depreciation of factory machinery	5,500,000	5,500,000		5,500,000 (W4)
National advertising	20,000,000	20,000,000		20,000,000 (W4)
Marketing and administration	2,300,000	2,300,000		2,300,000 (W4)
Delivery costs	2,400,000	1,200,000	20	2,250,000 (W5)
Total costs	76,300,000	61,300,000		74,425,000
Sales revenue	84,000,000	42,000,000		78,750,000 (W6)
Operating profit/(loss)	7,700,000	(19,300,000)		4,325,000

Workings

1   Direct material cost per unit = £24,000,000 ÷ 120,000 = £200

∴ Direct material cost at 75% activity level = £200 × 112,500 = £22,500,000

2   Production below 120,000 units pa

∴ No overtime and no bonus

3   Variable cost of (120,000 – 60,000) units = £(4,000,000 – 2,200,000)

∴ Variable cost per unit = £1,800,000 ÷ 60,000 = £30

∴ Variable cost at 75% activity level = £30 × 112,500 = £3,375,000

∴ Fixed cost = £4,000,000 – (120,000 × £30) = £400,000

∴ Total cost at 75% activity level = £(400,000 + 3,375,000) = £3,775,000

4   Part of factory fixed costs and therefore constant, whatever the actual activity level.

5   Variable cost of (120,000 – 60,000) units = £(2,400,000 – 1,200,000)

∴ Variable cost per unit = £20

∴ Fixed cost = £(2,400,000 – (120,000 × £20)) = £0

∴ Cost at 75% activity level = £20 × 112,500 = £2,250,000

6   Price per unit = £84,000,000 ÷ 120,000 = £700

∴ Sales revenue for 112,500 units = £700 × 112,500 = £78,750,000

(b)   **Report**

To: Board of Directors
From: Management Accountant
Date: 1 June 20X9
Subject: **Budgeting at Trygon Ltd**

In accordance with the instructions of the Managing Director, this **report contains**:

(i)   a recalculation of the flexible budget based on production at 95% capacity, assuming fixed overheads in finished stock are based on 80% activity;

(ii)   an explanation as to why the revised flexible budget differs from that circulated at the meeting on 23 May;

(iii)   answers to issues raised by Alan Williams at the aforementioned meeting;

(iv)   a discussion of budget preparation responsibilities.

        We will now look at these issues in detail.

(i)   **Trygon Ltd**

        Flexible budget at 75% sales activity/95% production activity

	£	£
Factory costs		
Direct materials (142,500 × £200)		28,500,000
Direct labour (£7,200,000 + (22,500 × £70))		8,775,000
Light, heat and power (£400,000 + (142,500 × £30))		4,675,000
Production management salaries (£1,500,000 + (22,500 × £15))		1,837,500
Factory rent, rates and insurance		9,400,000
Depreciation of factory machinery		5,500,000
		58,687,500
Less: closing stock ((142,500 – 112,500) × £430) (See Appendix 1)		(12,900,000)
Factory cost of sales		45,787,500
Non-production expenses		
National advertising	20,000,000	
Marketing and administration	2,300,000	
Delivery costs (112,500 × £20)	2,250,000	
		24,550,000
Cost of sales		70,337,500
Sales (112,500 × £700)		78,750,000
Operating profit		8,412,500

(ii)   If sales activity remains at 75% capacity but the production level is increased to 95% capacity, **budgeted profit increases** by £(8,412,500 – 4,325,000) = £4,087,500, despite the additional costs of overtime and bonus payments. This is mainly **due to the treatment of overheads**.

        When all the units produced in a period are sold, there are no closing stocks and so all fixed overheads are charged against the profit of the period in which they are incurred. If the number of units produced is greater than the number of units sold, however, the **fixed overhead included in the valuation of closing stock** will not be charged against the current period's profit but will be **carried forward and charged against the profit of a subsequent period.**

In Trygon Ltd's case, if production is greater than sales by 30,000 units, £140 (see Appendix 1 at the end of this report) × 30,000 = £4,200,000 of fixed overhead will be carried forward rather than being charged against profit.

The increase in profit is therefore the net result of the treatment of fixed overheads and the overtime/bonus payments.

(iii) **Fixed and flexible budgets**

The original budget prepared by Mike Barratt at the beginning of the budget period is known as a fixed budget. By the term 'fixed', we do not mean that the budget is kept unchanged. Revisions to a fixed master budget will be made if the situation so demands. The term **'fixed' means the following**.

(1) The budget is prepared on the basis of an estimated volume of production and an estimated volume of sales, but **no plans are made for the event that actual volumes of production and sales may differ from budgeted volumes**.

(2) When actual volumes of production and sales during a control period (possibly a month or four weeks) are achieved, a fixed budget is **not adjusted in retrospect to the new levels of activity.**

Fixed budgets are therefore used as a **starting point** for the on-going budgeting process. They provide a **plan or target** for where an organisation wants to be at the end of a budget period and, by integrating all the subsidiary budgets, a means of coordination which facilitates the identification of bottlenecks and their reduction before production and selling commences.

The budget which has been prepared is a **flexible budget**. Flexible budgets are designed to **change so as to relate to the actual volume of production and sales in a period**, and can be used in one of two ways. Firstly they can be used at the **planning** stage and help to show the likely results if conditions were to change (for example if 112,500 units are sold instead of 120,000). Secondly, they can be used **retrospectively**; the flexible budget identifies what the costs or revenues and profit *should have been* at the actual volume of activity and, by comparing it to the actual results, management can see how good or bad actual performance has been.

Note that **flexible budgets** are constructed around the **assumption** that **fixed costs remain unchanged** when activity levels change whereas **variable costs increase in proportion to increases in volume.**

Budgeting objectives

For a budget to have any value or meaning, the organisation must have a clear, unambiguous objective. If managers are unaware of the organisation's objective or there are a number of conflicting objectives, attempts to achieve the budget will be difficult. If some managers believe the maximisation of sales revenue to be the overall objective and some believe it to be the production of a quality product, it is unlikely that a budget based on the objective of, say, reducing costs will be achieved simply because managers are concentrating their efforts in the wrong places.

The manipulation of budget data

It is clear that we are unlikely to meet the budget target set at the beginning of the year. If Parmod plc is simply concerned with profits, however, we are able to meet the original profit target by manipulating the results. All we need to do is produce more computers. We do not have to actually sell the computers produced. Although variable costs will increase in proportion with the increase in production, fixed costs will remain at the same level and, because there will be more units in closing stocks, a greater proportion of those fixed costs will be carried forward in closing stock to be set against the sales revenue of another period rather than the current period. **By increasing production to an appropriate level, we will appear to have achieved our budgeted profit target**.

(iv) Turning to the issue raised by Anne Darcy, there is an **intuitive feeling** that **participation** by managers in the budgeting process will **improve** their **motivation** and so will **improve** the **quality of their decisions** and their **efforts to achieve their targets**. It would also seem **logical** that **budgets should be developed by lower level managers**, based on their perceptions of what is achievable and the associated necessary resources, rather than being developed by top management, with little or no input from operating personnel. The belief is that morale and motivation will be improved and that acceptance of and commitment to organisational goals and objectives by operational managers will increase. Moreover, it is argued that operating managers are the only ones with sufficiently detailed knowledge to develop a meaningful budget.

Unfortunately, it is **naïve to believe that participative approaches to budgeting are always more effective than more imposed or authoritative styles**. A budget should be drawn up so as to ensure that the goals or objectives of top management and the goals of other employees harmonise with the goals of the organisation as a whole. This is known as **goal congruence**. But because, as I explained in part (c) of this report, organisational objectives are sometimes not clearly defined (and one organisation is likely to have a number of different objectives anyway), different managers will perceive their objectives differently and so could have incompatible budget demands. There are other **disadvantages** to a participative approach to budgeting.

(1) It requires more time.

(2) Coordination of the various subsidiary budgets may be difficult

(3) It may cause managers to introduce budgetary slack.

(4) Managers may be ambivalent about participation or even unqualified to participate and hence the budget may be unachievable.

(5) It can support 'empire building' by subordinates.

(6) Managers may base future plans on past results instead of using the opportunity for formalised planning to look at alternative options and new ideas.

It is therefore unclear whether it is advisable for Anne Darcy to have been responsible for providing the original budget.

BPP

Appendix 1

As production volume will be greater than sales volume, there will be closing stocks of computers at 31 December 20X8. We therefore need to calculate a unit cost for stock valuation purposes.

Following the instructions of the Group Finance Director, **finished stocks are to be valued on the basis of 80% activity.**

Unit cost calculation

	£	£
Direct materials		200
Direct labour (£7,200,000 ÷ 120,000)*		60
Light, heat and power (variable element)		30
Fixed factory overheads*:		
Light, heat and power (fixed element)	400,000	
Production management salaries	1,500,000	
Factory rent, rates and insurance	9,400,000	
Depreciation of factory machinery	5,500,000	
	16,800,000	
÷ 120,000 units		140
		430

***Labour element and fixed factory overheads element always based on production level of 120,000 units.**

33 Happy Holidays Ltd

> **Tutorial note.** Try to provide examples related to the scenario when answering (b)(iii).

(a)   (i)   **y = 640 + 40x**

           In 20X9, x = 9 and so y (annual demand) = 640 + (40 × 9) = 1,000

           ∴ Weekly demand in 20X9 = 1,000 ÷ 25 = 40 holidays

   (ii)   **Weaknesses of the least squares regression formula in forecasting weekly demand for holidays**

       (1)   Use of the formula assumes a linear relationship between annual demand and time. This may not be true.

       (2)   It ignores any seasonal and cyclical variations which might exist. For example, weeks when children are at school might be more popular and during a recession demand may drop significantly.

       (3)   Its use assumes that the level of demand can be estimated on the basis of time. In reality, demand may depend on several other variables (such as the weather in the UK, whether the economy is booming or in recession, the relative popularity of short-haul and long-haul holidays, crime or political unrest in other holiday destinations, exchange rates, and/or changing tastes of holiday makers).

       (4)   It is only valid within the range of data used to determine the equation in the first place.

(5)   The data used to determine the equation may no longer be relevant. The holiday market in 20X9 is different to that in 20X1, with increased accessibility to long-haul destinations, the opening of the Channel Tunnel, improvements in facilities for those remaining in the UK for their holidays and so on.

(b)

Memo

To:	Financial Controller
From:	Accounting Technician
Date:	17 December 20X8
Subject:	**Revisions to cost statement for 10 days ended 27 November 20X8**

Following our recent meeting, I set out below the information you requested.

(i)   **Revised cost statement (prepared using flexible budgeting) for 10 days ended 27 November 20X8**

	Original budget £	Flexed budget £	Actual results £	Variances £
Aircraft seats	18,000	18,000 (W1)	18,600	600 (A)
Coach hire	5,000	5,000 (W2)	4,700	300 (F)
Hotel rooms	14,000	14,300 (W3)	14,200	100 (F)
Meals	4,800	4,560 (W4)	4,600	40 (A)
Tour guide	1,800	1,800 (W2)	1,700	100 (F)
Advertising	2,000	2,000 (W2)	1,800	200 (F)
	45,600	45,660	45,600	60 (F)

(F) denotes a favourable variance, (A) an adverse variance.

Workings

1   38 tourists travelled and so two blocks of 20 seats purchased for $2 \times 20 \times £450 = £18,000$
2   These are fixed costs and so do not change when the budget is flexed.
3   (4 single rooms $\times$ £60 $\times$ 10 days) + (17 double rooms $\times$ £70 $\times$ 10 days) = £14,300
4   £12 $\times$ 10 days $\times$ 38 tourists = £4,560

Note that the original budget was based on (using the cost of meals) (£4,800 ÷ £12)/10 days = 40 tourists.

(ii)   The revised cost statement is more useful for management control of costs. The original statement compares the actual costs incurred when 38 tourists travelled with the costs that should have been incurred when 40 tourists travelled. It is therefore meaningless to compare the two as one would expect variable costs such as the cost of meals and hotel rooms to vary.

The **flexible budget statement compares like with like**, however. The budget represents what costs should have been for the number of tourists who actually did travel. This is compared to the costs actually incurred. The flexible budget therefore provides a **more meaningful target** for managers to aim at, and **more meaningful variances** (the difference between what costs should have been and what costs were).

(iii) **Factors to take into account in deciding whether or not to investigate individual variances**

(1) **Materiality**. Because a standard cost is really only an average expected cost, small variations between actual and standard are bound to occur. Such variances should therefore not be investigated.

(2) **Controllability**. If there is nothing that management can do to control the occurrence of the variance (perhaps there has been a general worldwide increase in aircraft fuel prices), the standard should be changed rather than the variance investigated.

(3) **Variance trend.** Individual variances should not be looked at in isolation. They should be scrutinised for a number of successive periods because, although small variations in a single period are unlikely to be significant, small variations that occur consistently may need more attention.

(4) **Interrelationships between variances**. Individual variances should not be looked at in isolation. One variance might be interrelated with another, and much of it might have occurred only because the other variance occurred too. For example, if the actual proportion of total tourists who require a single room is greater than the budgeted proportion, there is likely to be an adverse variance on the cost of hotel rooms. However this will be more than offset by the increase in the cost of single tourists' holidays and the resulting selling price variance.

(5) **Control limits**. Control limits should be decided and only those variances which exceed such control limits should be investigated. Management might set an absolute control limit, such as £50, and any variance exceeding £50 will be investigated. Alternatively they might establish a rule that any variance should be investigated if it exceeds a certain percentage of standard, say 10%.

34 Professor Pauline Heath

Tutorial note. Hopefully you didn't waste your time in task (a)(i) by including figures. It was clearly set out in the task that you were not required to do so.

(a)   (i)   **Rearrangement of account headings**

	Actual this month £	Budget this month £	Variance this month £	Actual to date £	Budget to date £	Variance to date £	Annual budget £	Budget remaining £
Tuition fees								
Higher education grant								
Total revenue								
Full-time academic								
Part-time academic								
Teaching and research fees								
Total teaching costs								
Teaching and learning material								
Total non-teaching course costs								
Clerical and administrative								
Agency staff (clerical and admin)								
Total support costs								
External room hire								
Internal room hire								
Rental light and heat recharge								
Total accommodation costs								
Course advertising (press)								
Postage and telephone recharge								
Total other overheads								
Departmental contribution								
Central services recharge								
Departmental surplus/deficit								

(ii)   **Justification for rearrangement of account headings**

In its **original format**, the monthly management report showed information in the **order of what appears to be financial accounting codes**. It is unlikely that such an order is appropriate for Pauline Heath. Moreover it is possible that the way in which data is classified may be **unsuitable**. For example, the Professor is unlikely to be interested in whether part-time staff are on the payroll or invoice the university for their services. She is probably more interested in the total cost of part-time staff.

Within the constraints of the existing system, **accounts have been brought together by function**. This makes it clear the total expenditure on teaching, on support, on accommodation and so on and hence indicates the areas where costs are being incurred, with the result that they should be more easily controllable. It also highlights how favourable variances on one type of functional expense, such as the saving in staff costs resulting from the vacancies, are balanced by adverse variances on another type of the same functional expense, such as the cost of part-time academic staff.

The revised management report has **introduced monthly data**. In the original format, monthly information could only be derived by comparing the current month's year-to-date figures with those of the previous month. Moreover year-to-date variances offer management very little assistance in control since they hide monthly fluctuations about which it is vital management are aware.

The budget remaining figure has been retained. This represents the difference between the annual budget allowance and actual expenditure to date and hence shows the amount of further authorised expenditure possible under the various account headings.

In the variance column the **direction of the variance has been made clearer**. (A) should denote an adverse variance and (F) a favourable variance.

(b) **Strength of the current system**

The principal strength of the current system is that it identifies the amount of the budget allowance remaining under the various account headings, thereby showing the authorised expenditure remaining for each type of expense.

Weaknesses of the current system

As well as the weaknesses referred to in (a)(ii), the current system does have a number of other disadvantages.

(i) The annual budget has been divided into monthly control periods. It appears that the **monthly budget figure is simply one twelfth of the annual figure**. This does not reflect the way in which expenses are incurred. For example, course advertising is likely to be greatest towards the end of the academic year as courses are marketed for the subsequent year (hence a budget allowance of £25,400 remaining of the total allowance of £26,000). This has produced a favourable variance of £12,400 which does not mean that savings of £12,400 have been made because it is unlikely that any of the expenditure bar the £600 should have yet been incurred. Budget to date should therefore be built up of individual monthly budgets rather than various proportions of an overall budget.

(ii) The report **fails to provide any non-financial data** such as the number of students.

(iii) The **actual figures are not prepared on an accruals basis** and hence do not provide a meaningful figure for control purposes. In particular, the current report fails to accrue for part-time salaries.

Proposals to assist with management of the department

To effectively manage her department, Professor Heath needs to know where the department's income is coming from and where and why expenses are being incurred, information which is not provided by the current system.

At the moment, the university appears to view the department as having one activity whereas there are actually several activities going on in the department in the form of different courses. In the private sector these different courses would probably be called products. Effectively, therefore, the **department produces three products**: two degree courses and a diploma course. It is vital that the Professor knows the **contribution** to the departmental surplus made by each of these products and so the first priority in the improvement of the management accounting report is to **extend the coding and account heading system so as to facilitate the recording of revenue and expenses by course.** Some costs, such as teaching materials, can be directly allocated to individual courses whereas other costs, such as the cost of full-time academics, may have to be apportioned.

Consideration should also be given to the introduction of some form of **flexible budgeting** within the department, although this will be of only limited use because of the high proportion of fixed costs. Nevertheless, it would explain whether changes in revenue were due to an increase or decrease against budgeted student numbers or to a change in fees against those budgeted.

(c)

Course	Revenue £	Number of terms	Number of months	Income to date £
MBA	560,000	3	12	280,000 (W1)
MSc	256,000	3	12	128,000 (W2)
Diploma	120,000	2	8	90,000 (W3)
Total tuition fees				498,000
Government grant				375,000 (W4)
Revenue for 6 months to 28 February				873,000

Workings

1   £560,000 × 6/12 = £280,000
2   £256,000 × 6/12 = £128,000
3   £120,000 × 6/8 = £90,000
4   £750,000 × 6/12 = £375,000

35 Rivermede Ltd

Tutorial note. You will need to use the high-low method to analyse the costs in part (a)(i). Since you are repeating the same method three times, working in columns will result in a quicker and neater answer.

(a)   (i)   **Calculation of fixed costs and variable unit costs**

	Original budget	Revised budget	Difference		Variable cost per unit
Production and sales units	24,000	20,000	4,000		
	£	£	£		£
Variable costs					
Material	216,000	180,000	36,000	(÷ 4,000)	9
Labour	288,000	240,000	8,000	(÷ 4,000)	12
Semi-variable costs					
Heat, light and power	31,000	27,000	4,000	(÷ 4,000)	1

The fixed element of heat, light and power costs can now be determined using figures from the original budget.

	£
Total costs	31,000
Variable cost (24,000 units × £1)	24,000
∴ Fixed costs of heat, light and power	7,000

(ii) **Flexible budget comparison for the year ended 31 May 20X5**

		Flexible budget		Actual results	Variance
Fasta production and sales units		22,000		22,000	
		£		£	£
Variable costs					
Material	22,000 × £9	198,000	(£206,800 + £7,520)	214,320	16,320 (A)
Labour	22,000 × £12	264,000		255,200	8,800 (F)
Semi-variable costs					
Heat, light and power:	£				
variable 22,000 × £1	22,000				
fixed	7,000				
		29,000	(£33,400 − £7,520)	25,880	3,120 (F)
Fixed costs					
Rents, rates and depreciation		40,000		38,000	2,000 (F)
		531,000		533,400	2,400 (A)

Note. (A) denotes an adverse variance. (F) denotes a favourable variance.

(b)

> **Tutorial note.** Any valid reasons can be suggested for parts (ii) and (iii), as long as they are consistent with a favourable cost variance and increased sales volumes respectively.

Memorandum

To: Steven Jones, managing director
From: Management accountant
Date: 31 August 20X5
Subject: **Flexible budget statement for the year ended 31 May 20X5**

This memorandum deals with your queries regarding the latest flexible budget statement.

(i) **Why the flexible budgeting variances differ from those in the original statement**

The variances in the original statement were derived from a comparison of the budgeted costs for 20,000 units with the actual costs for 22,000 units. Since variable costs increase when output increases, the actual costs are almost certain to be higher than the budget costs, with consequent adverse variances.

The flexible budget statement compares like with like, by determining the budgeted costs for the actual volume of 22,000 units and comparing these with the actual results.

The resulting mixture of adverse and favourable variances is much more realistic. Your assertion that the large reduction in adverse variances is due to the introduction of participative budgeting is not necessarily true.

(ii) **Two reasons why a favourable cost variance may have arisen**

(1) **Managers may have included unrealistically high costs in the original budget.** This is a problem which can arise with participative budgeting; managers include extra cost allowances to ensure that they achieve their budgets. The submitted budgets therefore need careful checking, although this may be difficult because the managers themselves are the ones with the technical expertise.

(2) **Costs may have been lower than the level expected when the original budget was determined.** For example, an expected rise in rent or rates costs may not have occurred. Such savings are not necessarily the result of management control action.

(iii) **Two reasons why higher sales volume may not be the result of improved motivation**

(1) The **market** for Fastas may have **expanded** and Rivermede could have reaped the benefit of a general increase in the demand for this product. This general market increase is not necessarily the result of improved motivation of sales staff.

(2) The sales staff may have **submitted an unrealistically low sales target** for the budget, to ensure that they achieve the target. Thus the fact that the sales volume is higher than budget *may* be a result of participative budgeting, but it may be due to manipulation of the system rather than improved motivation.

36 Viking Smelting Company

Tutorial note. We suggest answering in turn the points raised at the management meeting in your report.

(a) **Viking Smelting Company**

Flexible budget report for the reclamation division May 20X8

Production budget

	Fixed budget	Flexible budget	Actual results	Variance
Production (tonnes)	250	200	200	
	£	£	£	£
Costs for which Reclamation Division are responsible				
Wages and social security costs (W1)	45,586	43,936	46,133	2,197 (A)
Fuel (W2)	18,750	15,000	15,500	500 (A)
Consumables (W3)	2,500	2,000	2,100	100 (A)
Power (W4)	1,750	1,500	1,590	90 (A)
	68,586	62,436	65,323	2,887 (A)
Costs for which Reclamation Division are not responsible				
Divisional overheads (W5)	20,000	20,000	21,000	1,000 (A)
Plant maintenance (W5)	5,950	5,950	6,900	950 (A)
Central services (W5)	6,850	6,850	7,300	450 (A)
	101,386	95,236	100,523	5,287 (A)

Workings

1   Number of employees = 4 × 6 = 24

Number of hours worked = 24 × 42 × 4 = 4,032 hours

Wages paid = 4,032 hours × £7.50 = £30,240

Social security and other employment costs = 40% of £30,240 = £12,096

Total wages = £30,240 + £12,096 = £42,336

Bonus = 200 tonnes × £8 per tonne = £1,600

Total wages including bonuses = £42,336 + £1,600 = £43,936

2   Fuel costs = 200 × £75 = £15,000

3   Consumables = 200 × £10 = £2,000

4   Power = fixed charge + variable charge = £500 + (200 × £5) = £500 + £1,000 = £1,500

5   Overheads directly attributable to the division, plant maintenance and central services costs are all fixed costs. These costs are therefore not the direct responsibility of the reclamation division.

(b)   **Memorandum**

To: The management of the reclamation division

From: D Ross, deputy financial controller, reclamation division

Date: XX June 20X8

Subject: **Revised flexible budget report**

Following my meeting with Sharon Houghton, it has become clear that there is some confusion about the performance reports which you have recently been presented with. Sharon has passed on to me the queries which were raised by the team at the management meeting when the original report was presented. I hope that the following will help to answer your queries.

Answer to Question 1

The budget figures are based on two-year old data taken from the original proposal. The main reason for this is because the original data provides a plan which shows how we should like the reclamation division to be performing in the future. For this reason we base our budgets on the **two-year old data**, and we are provided with a **target** of where we are aiming to be in the future.

Answer to Question 2

The **budget data should be based on what we are proposing to do, rather than what we actually did**. As mentioned above, the company should always have a target to aim for. In this case, our proposals show where we are aiming for as these were drawn up at the planning stage. It is important to always keep them in mind when looking at the actual results on a monthly basis.

Answer to Question 3

The initial performance report that you were presented with for May 20X8 simply compared actual results of 200 tonnes of production with a budget of 250 tonnes of production. In such cases, it is likely that the lower the production, the more favourable the variances will be, since the costs involved with making lower than budgeted production, are likely to be less than budgeted costs. The **revised performance report takes into account the actual level of production**, and the flexible budget is based upon the actual activity level. The revised performance report therefore compares actual costs of 200 tonnes of production with a budget based on 200 tonnes of production (as opposed to 250 tonnes of production).

Answer to Question 4

Plant maintenance is essential in all divisions of a manufacturing company, and in Viking Smelting it is **apportioned to each division on the basis of capital values**. The **reclamation division** was established in April 20X6, at which time there was a large amount of expenditure on **capital equipment**. This equipment has a **higher value** than the equipment in other divisions because it has not yet been depreciated to any great extent. This means that a **greater proportion of the maintenance department's costs** are apportioned to the reclamation division.

The maintenance department is a service department. Almost all of the costs that they incur are due to the work they are doing for other divisions. For this reason, the costs of running the maintenance department should be apportioned to the divisions who use the services of this department.

Answer to Question 5

The comments which explain the variances could, and shall be improved by giving an explanation of why the variance has occurred. When variances are investigated, and satisfactory explanations obtained, these comments should be noted in the performance report. These comments will add value to the reports and management should be able to see at a glance why variances have occurred.

Answer to Question 6

It is best to investigate all material variances on a performance report, whether they are adverse or favourable. However, it is fairly essential that **all adverse variances can be explained**. **Favourable variances should not be ignored**, since they may indicate that a manager has contributed to the performance of the division, and managers should be held responsible for favourable variances as well as those which are adverse.

Answer to Question 7

Showing the costs of central services on the divisional performance report may help to control these costs to some extent since central services, like the maintenance department are a service department. If the divisions within the company are more efficient, then this may have an effect on the costs of the central services department. These costs may therefore be controlled to some extent by the Divisional Managers. This in turn may have a motivational effect on the managers.

Main objective of revised report

The main objective of the revised performance report is to compare the actual costs for May 20X8 with a flexible budget which takes into account the actual production for the month. The flexible budget shows costs which would be expected for 200 tonnes of production, and this is compared with the actual results for 200 tonnes of production to give more meaningful variances than those calculated when comparing with a budget for 250 tonnes of production.

Advantages of revised report

The revised performance report has a number of **advantages** over the original report.

Firstly, it divides the costs into controllable and uncontrollable, thereby showing clearly the variances which have occurred in the areas for which divisional managers are responsible. Secondly, they are less demotivating for divisional managers since actual results are compared against a more meaningful budget. Managers may be not keen to increase production if variances are going to be unfavourable. With flexible budgeting, managers will not be put off increasing production, since the flexible budget will be amended to reflect the increased activity levels.

37 Parkside Manufacturing Ltd

(a)

> **Tutorial note**. The assessor commented that the most common error in this task was to treat the production labour as a variable cost, rather than a step cost. In order to determine the number of employees expected to achieve an output of 125,000 units, you will need to divide the output volume by the number of units that can be produced by one employee (10,000 units). This comes to 12.5 employees, but half a person cannot be employed! The number of production employees in a flexible budget for 125,000 units would therefore be 13.

(i)   (1)   Budgeted cost of material per Delta = $\dfrac{£600,000}{100,000 \text{ units}}$ = £6 per unit

      (2)

	Budgeted cost £
Total budgeted cost of light, heat and power for 100,000 units	200,000
Budgeted fixed cost of light, heat and power	40,000
Budgeted variable cost of light, heat and power for 100,000 units	160,000

         ∴ Budgeted variable cost of light, heat and power per unit = £160,000/100,000 = £1.60 per unit

      (3)   Number of production employees in budget

          = $\dfrac{£120,000}{£12,000 \text{ wages per employee}}$ = 10 employees

(ii)   **Flexible budget statement for the year ended 30 November 20X0**

	Flexible budget	Actual results	Variances	
Volume (units of Delta)	125,000	125,000	–	
	£'000	£'000	£'000	
Turnover (125/100 × £2,000,000)	2,500	2,250	250	(A)
Material (£6 (a)(i)(1) × 125,000)	750	800	50	(A)
Light, heat and power (note 1)	240	265	25	(A)
Production labour (note 2)	156	156	–	
Rent, rates and depreciation (fixed cost)	140	175	35	(A)
Administrative expenses (fixed cost)	110	110	–	
	1,396	1,506	110	(A)
Profit	1,104	744	360	(A)

Key. (A) is an adverse variance.

Notes		£
1	Budgeted fixed cost of light, heat and power	40,000
	Variable cost of light, heat and power (125,000 × £1.60)	200,000
		240,000

2   Number of employees required   = 125,000 units/10,000 units per employee
                                              = 13 employees

       Wages at £12,000 per employee   = £156,000

(b)

> **Tutorial note**. Try to relate your answer to the task scenario, rather than producing memorised lists, for example of the factors to be taken into account before investigating variances. The assessor commented that memorised lists are inconsistent with the spirit of competencies.
>
> According to the assessor, some candidates who sat this assessment lacked even the most basic of presentation skills and answered all three parts of this task as a single paragraph, with no clue as to where one part ended and the next began.

REPORT

To: Judith Green, production director
From: Management accountant
Subject: **Flexible budgets, variances and forecasting**
Date: 7 January 20X1

This report deals with the aspects of budgeting, variances and forecasting that you wish to discuss at your forthcoming board meeting.

(i)   **Fixed budgets and flexible budgets**

Two types of budgets are used within Parkside Manufacturing Ltd.

The **fixed budget** prepared by the previous management accountant is a **planning device**. It is **prepared in advance** of the period to provide a **single target level** of activity and shows associated budgeted costs and revenues. This single target ensures that all functions are **co-ordinated** towards the achievement of a single activity level.

If the **actual** activity level turns out to be **different from the budgeted activity level**, however (as happened last year), this can cause **difficulties** from a **control** point of view. The existence of **variable costs**, such as material cost and the variable element of light, heat and power costs, means that **extra costs will be incurred when activity increases**. It is therefore difficult to achieve control by comparing the actual costs for 125,000 units of Delta with the original budgeted cost for 100,000 units.

The flexible budget is designed to **flex the variable elements** of revenue and cost, to derive a **realistic target for control purposes** in the light of the actual activity achieved. The resulting variances are then more meaningful for control purposes.

(ii) **Factors to consider in deciding whether or not to investigate variances**

Not all variances are worthy of investigation. The **overriding factor** to consider is whether the **cost of an investigation will outweigh any benefits received** as a result. Three **general factors** should be considered.

(1) **Materiality**

Small variations of cost are usually expected each period and so a limit might be set beyond which a variance could be considered worthy of investigation.

The limit could be an **absolute amount** for a cost variance of, say, £50,000. This would mean that the material cost variance for last year should be investigated.

Alternatively a **percentage limit** could be set of, say, ten percent of standard cost. In this case the material cost variance would not be investigated since it is only seven percent of standard cost ((£50,000/£750,000) × 100%).

(2) **Controllability**

Some variances are, by their nature, less controllable than others. For example the £35,000 adverse variance on rent, rates and depreciation may be due to a rent increase which is outside the control of management.

A detailed investigation into this type of variance would not be worthwhile.

(3) **Variance trend**

Individual variances should not be looked at in isolation. Variances should be monitored for a number of periods to appreciate their full significance.

If there is a continuing trend in variances then a investigation might be worthwhile since the variance is probably not due to random causes.

Furthermore, the variance for an individual period may not be significant, but if the variance is allowed to continue unchecked for several periods, the absolute amount of overspending could be very high.

(iii) **Limitations in the use of linear regression in sales forecasting**

The use of linear regression may help to improve sales forecasting of Deltas but it does have a number of limitations.

(1) It **assumes a linear relationship** between sales of Deltas and the time period. In fact, demand for Deltas might follow a curvilinear pattern.

(2) It **assumes that demand for Deltas can be predicted from the period of time**, so that there are no other factors affecting demand other than the period of time in question. In fact many other factors could influence demand, including economic factors and changes in tastes and fashion.

(3) It **assumes that past events will provide a reliable guide to the future**. Changes such as inflation or a new competitor entering the market can mean that historical data is no longer a reliable basis for forecasting, however.

38 HFD plc

(a)

> **Tutorial note**. You will need a sound understanding of the difference between cost of sales and cost of production. The **actual** cost incurred in the period is the cost of **production.** This is then adjusted for the movement in stocks to determine the cost of sales.

(i) (1) Budgeted selling price = £960,000 turnover ÷ 20,000 units = £48 per unit

(2) Budgeted material cost = £240,000 material cost ÷ 20,000 units = £12 per unit

(3) Total budgeted marginal cost of light, heat and power

= £68,000 − fixed cost £20,000 = £48,000

Budgeted marginal cost of light, heat and power per unit

= £48,000 ÷ 20,000 = £2.40 per unit

(4) Actual marginal cost of light, heat and power

= £74,500 production cost − fixed costs £12,000 = £62,500

Actual marginal cost of light, heat and power per unit

= £62,500 ÷ 25,000 units produced = £2.50 per unit

(ii)

> **Tutorial note.** A flexible budget prepared using a marginal costing approach should show a separate analysis of fixed and variable costs. The variable cost of sales is determined by multiplying the **sales volume** by the unit marginal cost. The fixed overheads, however, are not based on units. All of the fixed overhead incurred is written off in the period as a period cost. You therefore need to determine the **production** cost of fixed overhead, and charge this amount against the sales value for the period. The assessor noted that a particular area of weakness was flexible budgeting.

HFD Processes Ltd

Flexible budget statement for year ended 30 November 20X1

Sales units	Flexible budget 22,000 units		Actual results 22,000 units		Variance
	£	£	£	£	£
Turnover (22,000 × £48 (from (a)(i)(1)))		1,056,000		1,012,000	44,000 (A)
Variable costs					
Material (22,000 × £12)	264,000		261,800		2,200 (F)
Light, heat and power					
(22,000 × £2.40)	52,800		55,000*		2,200 (A)
		316,800		316,800	
Contribution		739,200		695,200	
Fixed costs					
Production labour	260,000		273,000		13,000 (A)
Light, heat and power	20,000		12,000		8,000 (F)
Fixed overheads	400,000		430,000		30,000 (A)
		680,000		715,000	
Operating profit/(loss)		59,200		(19,800)	79,000 (A)

Note. (A) denotes an adverse variance; (F) denotes a favourable variance.

*Variable cost of light, heat and power = £2.50 (from (a)) × 22,000 = £55,000

(b)   **Memorandum**

To: Chief executive of HFD plc
From: Management accountant
Date: 8 December 20X1
Subject: **Flexible budget statement for year ended 30 November 20X1**

This memorandum addresses your concerns regarding the results shown in the flexible budget statement.

(i)   **Why the flexible budget operating statement shows different results from the original operating results**

   (1)   The flexible budget is prepared on a marginal cost basis whereas the original budget and actual results were prepared on an absorption cost basis. Since production was higher than sales, some fixed overhead was carried forward in stock with absorption costing. With marginal costing, however, all of the fixed overheads are charged as period costs against the sales for the period, resulting in a lower reported profit figure.

   (2)   The flexible budget is a realistic target for costs and revenues for the actual activity level of 22,000 units sold. The 2,000 units sold in excess of the original budgeted amount would be expected to increase both revenue and variable costs. The flexible budget makes allowances for these increases caused by the change in volume.

217

(ii) **Why the flexible budget operating statement might be a better measure of management performance**

The flexible budget statement compares like with like. When the activity level changes, the expected revenue and variable costs also change. It is therefore logical to alter the budget to allow for these changes. The resulting variances will provide a better measure for management performance.

Furthermore the profit shown in the original statement, which was prepared on an absorption costing basis, can be distorted by increases or decreases in stock, as fixed overheads are carried forward in, or 'released from', stock. The use of marginal costing, however, avoids such profit distortions.

39 Hall Ltd

(a)

> **Tutorial note.** An alternative approach to finding selling price or variable unit cost is to use the **incremental** approach. This can only be used when there are two budget statements, however. The selling price or variable cost per unit = difference in budget values ÷ difference in budget volumes.
>
> In (a)(i)(6) you can use the percentage you derived in (a)(i)(5) to find the cost of sales of each of material, labour and light, heat and power. The fixed element must be deducted from the total cost of light, heat and power before the percentage is applied, however.
>
> Parts (a)(i)(6) and (7) then provide the basis for the actual figures in the budget statement required in (a)(ii).
>
> A flexible budget statement prepared using variable or marginal costing shows variable costs, contribution and total fixed costs.

(i) (1) **Budgeted selling price per Omega**

Turnover ÷ sales volume = selling price
∴ £1,440,000 ÷ 36,000 = selling price
∴ £40 = selling price

(2) **Budgeted material cost per Omega**

Material is a variable cost and so total material cost ÷ sales volume * = material cost per unit
∴ £432,000 ÷ 36,000 = material cost per unit
∴ £12 = material cost per unit

* Production equals sales and so material cost of production is the same as material cost of sales.

(3) **Budgeted labour cost per Omega**

Labour is a variable cost and so total material cost ÷ sales volume = labour cost per unit

∴ £216,000 ÷ 36,000 = labour cost per unit
∴ £6 = labour cost per unit

(4) **Budgeted variable cost of light, heat and power per Omega**

	£
Total budgeted cost	92,000
Fixed element	20,000
Variable element	72,000

$\therefore$ Variable cost per unit = £72,000/36,000 = £2

(5)   **% of cost of production carried forward in closing stock**

Cost of production = £1,318,000

Closing stock = £164,750

Closing stock as a % of the cost of production = (164,750/1,318,000) $\times$ 100% = 12.5%

(6)

> **Tutorial note.** As there is no opening stock, variable production costs (100%) are split between the cost of closing stock (12.5%) and the cost of sales (100% − 12.5%).

Material cost of sales = 87.5% $\times$ £500,000 = 87.5/100 $\times$ £500,000   = £437,500

Labour cost of sales = 87.5% $\times$ £232,000 = 87.5/100 $\times$ £232,000   = £203,000

Variable production cost of light, heat and power = £(96,000 − 12,000) = £84,000

Variable cost of sales of light, heat and power = 87.5% $\times$ £84,000 = 87.5/100 $\times$ £84,000 = £73,500

Actual variable cost of sales

	£'000
Material	437.5
Labour	203.0
Light, heat and power	73.5
	714.0

(7)   **Total actual fixed costs**

	£'000
Light, heat and power	12.0
Deprecation	70.0
Other fixed overheads	420.0
	502.0

(ii)   **Hall Ltd − Flexible budget statement for year ended 30 November 20X1**

> **Tutorial note.** The assessor reported that an alternative approach that gained significant credit was to base actual and budgeted production on 40,000 units and to include a one line adjustment for 5,000 units in closing stock valued on a marginal costing basis.

	Original budget	Flexed budget		Actual results		Variances	
Sales volume (units)	36,000	35,000		35,000		–	
	£	£		£		£	
Turnover	1,440,000	1,400,000	(W1)	1,365,000		35,000	(A)
Variable costs							
Material	432,000	420,000	(W2)	437,500	(from (vi))	17,500	(A)
Labour	216,000	210,000	(W3)	203,000	(from (vi))	7,000	(F)
Light, heat, power	72,000	70,000	(W4)	73,500	(from (vi))	3,500	(A)
	720,000	700,000		714,000		14,000	(A)
Contribution	720,000	700,000		651,000		49,000	(A)
Fixed costs							
Light, heat, power	20,000	20,000		12,000		8,000	(F)
Depreciation	100,000	100,000		70,000		30,000	(F)
Other fixed overheads	400,000	400,000		420,000		20,000	(A)
	520,000	520,000		502,000		18,000	(F)
Profit	200,000	180,000		149,000		31,000	(A)

Workings

1 35,000 × £40 = £1,400,000
2 35,000 × £12 = £420,000
3 35,000 × £6 = £210,000
4 35,000 × £2 = £70,000

(b)

> **Tutorial note.** The requirement of task (b)(i)(2) is unclear. Does it refer to budget or actual results? Given that (1) refers to budget we can only assume that (2) refers to actual results.

Memo

To: Harry Easton, Chief executive
From: Assistant management accountant
Date: 20 December 20X1
Subject: **Hall Ltd – Flexible budget statement for year ended 30 November 20X1**

This memorandum addresses your concerns regarding the results shown in the flexible budget.

(i)   (1)   **Why there is a difference between the original budget and the flexible budget**

The original budget was for planning purposes and was based on sales and production volumes of 36,000 units. It provided a target at which management should have aimed. The flexible budget is based on sales and production volumes of 35,000 units. It is for control purposes and shows what costs and revenues should have been given actual sales and production volumes. The revenue and variable costs in the flexible budget will therefore be less than those in the original budget given the different volumes, although the fixed costs are the same.

(2) **Why there is a difference between the original actual operating profit and the flexible budget actual operating profit**

The original actual results were prepared using absorption costing, which involves matching all costs (including fixed costs) against revenue. Units in closing stock are therefore valued at full cost so that all costs including fixed costs can be matched against the revenue from the units when they are eventually sold in a later period. So not all fixed costs are charged in the period. Marginal costing, on the other hand, which was used to prepare the flexible budget, requires that all fixed costs are written off in the period in which they are incurred.

(ii) **Why the actual operating profit was greater than the budgeted operating profit, despite a lower sales volume**

(1) Because the actual level of production was greater than the actual level of sales, the use of absorption costing means that some of the fixed overhead is carried forward in the closing stock valuation to be charged against next year's profit.

(2) The actual contribution per unit was higher than the budgeted contribution per unit, and actual fixed costs were lower than budgeted fixed costs.

Chapters 12 and 13 Measurement of performance

40 Melsoven Ltd

(a) **Performance indicators for Melsoven Ltd for quarter 4**

(i)	Quarterly return on capital employed	$(352/8,111) \times 100\%$	4.3%
(ii)	Operating profit margin	$(352/4,759) \times 100\%$	7.4%
(iii)	Quarterly asset turnover	$4,759/8,111$	0.59 times
(iv)	Average age of period-end debtors in days	$(2,040/4,759) \times 91$	39 days
(v)	Average age of period-end trade creditors in days	$[2,362/(1,583 + 43)] \times 91$	132 days
(vi)	Average age of period end materials stocks in days	$(305/1,583) \times 91$	18 days
(vii)	Average age of period-end finished goods stocks in days	$(1,326/3,980) \times 91$	30 days

(b) (i) **Performance indicators for Melsoven Ltd for Quarters 1 to 4**

	Q1	Q2	Q3	Q4
Return on capital employed	4.3%	1.2%	2.8%	4.3%
Operating profit margin	9.0%	2.6%	5.3%	7.4%
Quarterly asset turnover	0.54	0.55	0.52	0.59
Age of debtors in days	39	38	44	39
Age of trade creditors in days	192	167	158	132
Age of materials stocks in days	29	24	18	18
Age of finished goods stocks in days	51	41	28	30

(ii)   **Briefing note**

To: Louise Simpson
From: Financial analyst
Date: xx/xx/xx
Subject: **Performance of Melsoven Ltd in Quarters 1 to 4**

The above financial performance ratios expose a sharp drop in performance between quarter 1 and quarter 2. Quarters 3 and 4 showed an improvement and the key ratios (return on capital employed, operating profit margin and asset turnover) are returning to the levels achieved in Quarter 1.

(1)   **Return on capital employed**. This ratio dropped from 4.3% to 1.2%. Between quarters 1 and 2, but has now returned to its earliest level.

(2)   **Operating profit margin**. This fell in quarter 2 and, although it improved in quarters 3 and 4, is not yet back to the level of quarter 1. The drop in profit margin in quarter 4 was the reason for the fall in ROCE.

(3)   **Quarterly asset turnover**. This was higher in quarter 4 than in any of the earlier quarters and is the reason that the return on capital employed is back to 4.3% in quarter 4 despite the profit margin being lower than in quarter 1.

(4)   **Age of debtors in days**. This ratio has remained comparatively stable during the year, and at 39 days is not excessively high.

(5)   **Age of trade creditors in days**. At the end of quarter 1 Melsoven was taking an average of 192 days (more than six months) to pay its trade creditors, which seems excessive. This figure has been progressively reduced during the year to 132 days (still more than 4 months, however) by the end of quarter 4.

(6)   **Age of materials stocks in days**. Material stocks have fallen from 29 days at the end of quarter 1 to stabilise at 18 days in quarters 3 and 4.

(7)   **Age of finished goods stocks in days**. Finished goods stocks have dropped from 51 days sales at the end of quarter 1 to 30 days at the end of the year. This is a significant improvement.

41 Chain of hotels

Tutorial note. The measures of performance which should be used to monitor the performance of managers in a hotel chain should be:

- measures which are within managers' control;
- measures which are a valid measure of performance;
- measures for which the data is readily available.

Examples include the following.

(a)   Net profit percentage
(b)   Cost per bed per night
(c)   Contribution per bed per night
(d)   Percentage occupancy of rooms
(e)   Contribution per meal served in restaurant
(f)   Number of days stock held
(g)   Contribution per employee
(h)   Value added per employee
(i)   Staff turnover
(j)   Breakages and losses as a percentage of turnover
(k)   Contribution per conference

42 Regent Hotel

Tutorial note. Remember that if you are bringing costs 'up to date' you must multiply by $\dfrac{\text{more 'up to date' index number}}{\text{older index number}}$

(a)   **Wages inflated by increase in index of average weekly earnings**

$$= £195 \times \frac{191.2}{173.4} = £215$$

(b)   **Memorandum**

To:	Manager, Regent Hotel
From:	Assistant to the Management Accountant
Date:	XX June 20X8
Subject:	**Earnings of full-time employees**

Following our recent meeting, I have **investigated the rate of increase in the weekly earnings of full-time employees compared with the industry average** and I set out my findings below.

(i)   If the average weekly earnings of the hotel's full-time employees had increased at the same rate as average earnings in the hotel and catering industry, in 20X7 the employees would be earning £215 per week. The average earnings have, however, increased to only £208 per week and so the average weekly earnings of the hotel's full-time employees have indeed fallen behind the industry average.

(ii)   You should bear in mind, however, that the mix of skills and experience of the Regent Hotel's full-time employees is different to the national average and that the rate of pay in our local area may not have risen at the same rate as the national average, thus limiting the usefulness of a comparison between the hotel's employees' earnings and the average for the hotel and catering industry.

(iii)   In the past, pay rises have always been based approximately on the annual increase in the Retail Prices Index (RPI).

The RPI measures the monthly change in the cost of living in the UK. Its principal use is as a measure of inflation. The index measures the changes, month by month, in the average level of prices of 'a representative basket of goods' purchased by the great majority of households in the UK. The items in the basket are weighted to take account of their relative importance and prices are collected from all over the UK. The main groups of the basket are food and catering, alcohol and tobacco, housing and household expenditure, personal expenditure and travel and leisure. Certain items such as mortgage payments and money spent on gambling are not included in the RPI but the items and their weights are continually reviewed to ensure that they remain as representative as possible. The base date of the RPI is January 1987 and the increases in prices are measured as weighted averages since that date.

The RPI was probably used by the previous manager as the basis for wage rate increases because he was trying to ensure that full-time employees' earnings kept pace with the rate of inflation.

I hope this information is useful. If I can be of any further assistance please do not hesitate to contact me.

43 Traders plc

Tutorial note. Don't forget to illustrate your answer to task (b) part (i) with data from the question.

According to the assessor, candidates had difficulty in task (b). In general, they produced poor answers when identifying the strengths and weaknesses of the company under review, with some stating the obvious while others made unwarranted conclusions. Few identified interrelationships between the ratios and many were unable to calculate a simple index.

(a) **ROCE**

$$= \frac{£2,906,000}{£7,265,000} \times 100\% = 40\%$$

Gross profit margin

$$= \frac{£7,236,000}{£26,800,000} \times 100\% = 27\%$$

Net margin

$$= \frac{£2,906,000}{£26,800,000} \times 100\% = 10.84\%$$

Asset turnover

$$= \frac{£26,800,000}{£7,265,000} = 3.69 \text{ times}$$

Turnover per employee

$$= \frac{£26,800,000}{200} = £134,000$$

Average age of working capital

$$= \frac{£1,995,000}{£19,564,000} \times 365 = 37 \text{ days}$$

Comparative performance ratios – year ended 30 June 20X8

	Traders plc	Sellars plc
Return on capital employed	33.33%	40%
Gross profit margin	25%	27%
Net margin	8.08%	10.84%
Asset turnover	4.12 times	3.69 times
Turnover per employee	£141,176	£134,000
Average age of working capital	30 days	37 days

(b)

Briefing paper
Performance of Traders plc
year ended 30 June 20X8

This paper explains in outline the meaning and limitations of the performance ratios in Appendix 1 (see Task (a)) and considers the strengths and weaknesses of Traders plc as highlighted by the analysis. It also details the growth in sales volume since last year.

(i)/(ii) **Meaning and limitation of ratios and Traders' strengths and weaknesses**

(1) The **return on capital employed (ROCE)** is an overall measure which shows how well the managers of the organisation have used the resources under their control to generate profit. Profits alone do not show whether the return made is sufficient for the volume of resources committed but ROCE is a relative measure and takes volume of resources into account.

Sellars plc appears to have the more efficient management since they are able to generate 40p of profit from every £1 of resources. This compares with only 33.33p per £1 by the management of Traders plc.

However, the accuracy of the ROCE relies on the figure used for capital or resources employed. For example, the depreciation policy used by an organisation will affect the valuation of capital employed. Traders plc is depreciating its fixtures and fittings and motor vehicles at 20% and 25% respectively, compared with the 10% and 20% used by Sellars plc. Moreover the year-end value of assets used in the ratio may not be representative of assets employed during the accounting period and hence will affect the accuracy of the ROCE as a measure of performance.

(2) The **gross profit margin** is a measure of the profitability of sales. The absolute gross profit is calculated as sales revenue less the cost of goods sold and hence it focuses on a company's trading and manufacturing activities.

Because the ratio takes account of the cost of goods sold it is affected by the stock valuation method used. Moreover, the ratio fails to take account of differences in organisations' cost structures.

For every pound of sales, Sellars is able to generate 27p of gross profit whereas Traders is only able to generate 25p. If both companies have similar pricing policies and similar ranges of goods, the rates might suggest that Sellars' management are more efficient in negotiating terms with suppliers. On the other hand, it might be that the suppliers' terms are very similar but that Traders' management has set low selling prices as part of its marketing strategy.

(3) The **sales margin (or net margin)** shows the operating profit as a percentage of sales. The operating profit is calculated before interest and tax and is the profit over which operational management can exercise day to day control. It is the amount left after all direct costs and overheads have been deducted from sales revenue. The principal disadvantage of the ratio is that it is affected by different stock valuation and depreciation policies.

The return on capital employed is influenced by two factors: the intensity with which assets have been used (the asset turnover ratio (see (4)) and the margin achieved on sales (sales margin ratio). Either increasing the sales margin (by charging higher prices or reducing costs) or obtaining more sales from the same asset base will improve the overall ROCE. Care needs to be taken when interpreting the two ratios since they may be interdependent; an increase in prices (and hence the sales margin) may lead to a fall in sales volume and hence a reduction in the asset turnover.

Sellars has a higher sales margin than Traders, indicating that it is able to squeeze more profit out of each pound of sales.

(4) The **asset turnover** ratio shows sales per pound of assets and demonstrates how effectively the assets of a business are being used to generate sales. Because of the interrelationship between asset turnover and ROCE, they both suffer from the same limitation: the valuation of capital employed can have a significant effect on the ratio reported. Moreover, as noted earlier, the asset turnover ratio might be interrelated with the sales margin. Traders appears to be able to use its assets more effectively than Sellars.

(5) The **turnover per employee** is a measure of how effectively resources are being used. A particular advantage of this ratio is that it is less influenced by accounting conventions and other distortions than, for example, asset turnover. Traders plc appears to be the more successful of the two companies, achieving turnover of £141,176 per employee compared with £134,000 for Sellars plc. Management of Traders plc should ensure that customer service and quality are not suffering as a result of low staffing levels, however, a factor which is not revealed by this ratio. Moreover, care is required when comparing the ratios of the two companies as they may be operating in different segments of the market, those segments requiring different levels of service.

(6) Working capital control is concerned with minimising funds tied up in net current assets while ensuring that sufficient stock, cash and credit facilities are in place to enable trading to take place. Some insight into working capital control can be gained by calculating the **average age of working capital**, which identifies how long it takes to convert the purchase of stocks into cash from sales. There are a number of limitations in the use of this ratio: it is based on the working capital level on one particular day which may not, of course, be representative of working capital levels throughout the entire accounting period; working capital includes a figure for stocks which is a subjective valuation.

Traders have a significantly lower ratio than Sellars; Traders' management therefore appear to have greater control over its working capital (they control debtors, keep stock levels at an acceptable level and make efficient use of credit facilities).

Care needs to be taken when determining the ideal ratio. Reduce it too low and there may be insufficient stock and other current assets to sustain the volume of trade but taking too much credit from suppliers may jeopardise relationships and/or cause suppliers to increase prices.

If the ratios are compared, consideration must be given to the wider reasons for differences. In our example, Sellars might be deliberately allowing credit to customers in order to generate sales although it is, of course, possible that it is paying creditors early to gain discounts.

(iii) **Percentage growth in Traders' sales volume**

Last year's sales at this year's prices $= £23,000,000 \times \dfrac{237.90}{224.50} = £24,372,829$

This year's sales $= £24,000,000$

Growth in current terms $= £(24,000,000 - 24,372,829) = £(372,829)$

Percentage growth $= \dfrac{£(372,829)}{£24,372,829} \times 100\% = -1.53\%$

(iv)   **The accuracy of the sales growth figure**

There are a number of reasons why the estimate of sales growth calculated above might not be accurate.

(1)   The calculation assumes that prices have remained constant. Traders could well have lowered prices in order to increase market share. Sales *revenue* may have fallen but sales *volume* may have increased.

(2)   The use of the trade association's index assumes that Traders' product range is typical of all organisation's in the industry. If this is not the case the index used may not be entirely appropriate since it may not reflect Traders' circumstances.

(3)   The trade association index may be a simple average for the whole year whereas much of Traders' sales might be seasonal.

44 Middle plc

> **Tutorial note**. It is always a good idea to set out how a ratio is calculated (for example, ROCE = operating profit ÷ net assets) in case you inadvertently use the incorrect figures.

(a)   To: Angela Wade
      From: A Technician
      Date: XX December 20X8
      Subject: **West Ltd and East Ltd – Performance Report**

(i)   **Return on capital employed (ROCE)**

The ROCE is a key financial ratio which shows the amount of profit which has been made in relation to the amount of resources invested. It also gives some idea of how efficiently the company has been operating.

$$ROCE = \frac{Operating\,profit}{Net\,assets}$$

$$ROCE\,(West\,Ltd) = \frac{3,068}{15,340} = 0.2 \times 100\% = 20\%$$

$$ROCE\,(East\,Ltd) = \frac{2,795}{6,500} = 0.43 \times 100\% = 43\%$$

(ii)   **Asset turnover**

The asset turnover is one of the main balance sheet ratios, and is a measure of how well the assets of a business are being used to generate sales.

$$Asset\,turnover = \frac{Net\,turnover}{Net\,assets}$$

$$Asset\,turnover\,(West\,Ltd) = \frac{17,910}{15,340} = 1.17\,times$$

$$\text{Asset turnover (East Ltd)} = \frac{17,424}{6,500} = 2.68 \text{ times}$$

(iii) **Sales margin**

The sales margin ratio is a measure of overall profitability and it provides a measure of performance for management. Unsatisfactory sales margins are investigated by management, and are generally followed by control action. Increasing selling prices and reducing costs will have a direct effect on this ratio.

$$\text{Sales margin} = \frac{\text{Operating profit}}{\text{Net turnover}}$$

$$\text{Sales margin (West Ltd)} = \frac{3,068}{17,910} = 0.171 \times 100\% = 17.1\%$$

$$\text{Sales margin (East Ltd)} = \frac{2,795}{17,424} = 0.16 \times 100\% = 16\%$$

(b) **Measure of customer service : faulty sales**

The percentage of faulty sales as a measure of the level of customer service is calculated as :

$$\frac{\text{Returns}}{\text{Gross sales}}$$

$$\text{West Ltd} = \frac{100}{20,000} = 0.005\% \times 100\% = 0.5\%$$

$$\text{East Ltd} = \frac{220}{22,000} = 0.01\% \times 100\% = 1\%$$

(c) **Further measure of customer service**

Another possible measure of the level of customer service which could be derived from the accounting data is the number of days between order and delivery of goods.

This can be calculated as follows.

Time between order and delivery $= \dfrac{\text{Orders received in year} - \text{net sales}}{\text{Net Sales}} \times 365 \text{ days (in '000 litres)}$

$$\text{West Ltd} = \frac{20,173 - 19,900}{19,900} \times 365 \text{ days} = 5 \text{ days}$$

$$\text{East Ltd} = \frac{22,854 - 21,780}{21,780} \times 365 \text{ days} = 18 \text{ days}$$

The amount of money which the subsidiaries invest in research and development, and training could also provide a measure of customer service.

(d)   **Limitations of financial ratios**

Financial ratios as a measure of performance are **only concerned with the data recorded in the accounts**. For example, East Ltd appears to be a much more efficient company than West Ltd based on its ROCE and asset turnover ratios. However, when calculations are made to measure customer service, West Ltd has far fewer days between order and delivery of goods, and half as many faulty sales (as a percentage of gross sales).

The financial ratios also treat **research and development, and training costs as expenses** which are written off to the profit and loss account. These expenses are likely to have an impact on the future profitability of the company, and **are more of an investment than expense**.

Both West Ltd and East Ltd use plant of similar size and technology. There is however, a large difference in the net book values of the plant, and hence a large **difference in the net assets** of each company.

East Ltd purchased its plant before West Ltd, and has a lower cost, and a higher depreciation to date than West Ltd. These differences arise mainly due to the fact that the accounts are prepared using historical cost accounting. The fact that East Ltd's net assets are so much lower than those of West Ltd, means that the ROCE of East Ltd will be much higher than that of West Ltd.

45 Grand Hotel

> **Tutorial note**. If the occupancy rate increases from 70% to 80% then the revised turnover is calculated at $8/7 \times$ turnover.

(a)

Maximum occupancy	=	number of days in year × number of bedrooms
	=	365 × 80 = 29,200
Occupancy rate	=	annual total of rooms let per night as percentage of maximum occupancy (where annual total of rooms let per night = **accommodation** turnover ÷ charge per night = £1,635,200/£80= 20,440)
	=	$\dfrac{20,440}{29,200} \times 100\% = 70\%$
Gross margin: accommodation	=	contribution from accommodation ÷ accommodation turnover
	=	$\dfrac{£327,040}{£1,635,200} \times 100\% = 20\%$
Gross margin: restaurant	=	contribution from restaurant ÷ restaurant turnover
	=	$\dfrac{£157,680}{£630,720} \times 100\% = 25\%$
Operating profit: hotel	=	profit before interest but after all other expenses
	=	£33,296 + £80,000 = £113,296
Sales margin: hotel	=	operating profit ÷ total turnover
	=	$\dfrac{£113,296}{£2,265,920} \times 100\% = 5\%$
ROCE: hotel	=	operating profit ÷ net assets
	=	$\dfrac{£113,296}{£1,416,200} \times 100\% = 8\%$
Asset turnover: hotel	=	turnover ÷ net assets
	=	£2,265,920 ÷ £1,416,200 = 1.6 times

(b)

GREEN AND CO
AUDITORS

Ms C Hill
Manager
Grand Hotel

10 December 20X8

Dear Ms Hill

Thank you for your recent letter setting out your proposals for increasing the hotel's return on capital employed. I have evaluated these proposals and I set out my comments below.

(i)   **Operating profit required on existing capital employed to give 20% return**

The operating profit required will be 20% of £1,416,200, which is £283,240.

(ii) **Revised profit if proposals achieved**

	£	£
Increase in occupancy rate		
Revised contribution (80/70 × £327,040)	373,760	
Existing contribution	327,040	
Increase in contribution		46,720
Change in restaurant prices/costs		
Increase in turnover (5% × £630,720)	31,536	
Decreases in costs (5% × £473,040)	23,652	
Increase in contribution		55,188
Total increase in contribution		101,908
Current profit		113,296
Revised operating profit		215,204

(iii) **Revised performance in indicators**

(1)   Return on capital employed $= \dfrac{\text{revised operating profit}}{\text{current net assets}} \times 100\%$

$= \dfrac{£215,204}{£1,416,200} \times 100\% = 15.2\%$

(2)   Asset turnover = revised turnover/net assets × 100%

To calculate revised turnover:

	£
from accommodation (8/7 × £1,635,200) =	1,868,800
from restaurant (105% × £630,720) =	662,256
	2,531,056

∴ Asset turnover = £2,531,056/1,416,200 = 1.79 times

(3)   Sales margin   =   revised operating profit/revised turnover × 100%
                    =   £215,204/£2,531,056 × 100% = 8.5%

(iv) **Suggestions**

If both of your proposals are implemented and achieved operating profit will increase to £215,204, thereby almost doubling ROCE to 15.2% and increasing the sales margin from 5% to 8.5% but having very little impact on asset turnover (from 1.6 times to 1.79 times). All three measures are, however, below those of hotels in similar categories and locations.

(1) Of the planned increase in profits of £101,908, 45.8% is due to the increased occupancy rate and hence a more intensive use of assets while 54.2% is due to the restaurant's pricing and costing structure (that is, improved sales margins).

(2) Even before the proposed changes to the restaurant's pricing and costing structure, the restaurant's gross margin was better than the industry average. Once the proposals are implemented it is therefore most unlikely that additional profit can be derived from the restaurant.

The proposed occupancy rate is the same as the industry average and so it may be extremely difficult to increase this further. The gross margin on accommodation is, at 20%, below the industry average and hence some improvement may be possible here. It may be possible to raise prices, which would support the asset turnover and the sales margin, or it may be possible to reduce variable costs. Alternatively there may be scope for reducing the level of fixed costs. Cheaper insurance may be available and it is quite likely that cost savings could be made within the administration function. A reduction in fixed costs would increase profits and improve both the hotel's sales margin and ROCE.

I hope that my comments have been useful. If I can be of any further assistance please do not hesitate to contact me.

Your sincerely

A Technician

46 Student Housing Society

> **Tutorial note.** The revised cash/bank balance in (b)(ii) is made up of the decrease in debtors, the increase in contribution (the difference between the original operating surplus and the revised operating surplus) and the existing cash balance.

(a) (i) **Return on net assets**
= (operating surplus/net assets) × 100%
= (£12,000/£600,000) × 100% = 2%

(ii) **Operating surplus as a % of rents receivable**
= (£12,000/£192,000) × 100% = 6.25%

(iii) **Occupancy rate**
= (number of rooms occupied/maximum number of rooms) × 100%
= ((£192,000/£2,400)/100) × 100% = 80%

(iv) **Average age of rent arrears in months** = (rent arrears/rents receivable) × 12
= (£48,000/£192,000) × 12 = 3 months

(v) **Number of months expenses could be paid from the cash and bank balance**
= (cash available/expenses involving cash) × 12
= (£4,500/£(180,000 − 14,000)) × 12 = 0.325 months

(b)
Memo

To: Helen Brown, General Manager
From: Accounting Technician
Date: 30 June 20X8
Subject: **Meeting and objectives**

Further to our recent discussions, I set out below the information you requested. Workings are in the attached appendix.

(i)   If a 95% occupancy rate had been achieved, turnover would have been £228,000 and an operating surplus of £42,000 would have been achieved.

(ii)   The increased turnover and a reduction in the average age of rent arrears to one month would have caused debtors to fall to £19,000 and the cash/bank balance to increase to £63,500.

(iii)   Given the revisions to the occupancy rate and the average age of rent arrears, performance indicators would have been as follows.
        (1)   Return on net assets: 6.67%
        (2)   Operating surplus as a % of rents receivable: 18.42%
        (3)   Cash available to pay cash-based expenses: 4.4 months

(iv)   (1)   **Efficiency** is the relationship between an organisation's inputs and its outputs.

        (2)   **Effectiveness** is the relationship between an organisation's outputs and its objectives (ie the degree to which the objectives are met).

        (3)   Commercial organisations generally have profit maximisation as the objective which guides the process of managing resources economically, efficiently and effectively. **Charities** do not generally have such an objective, however, and so **cannot be satisfactorily judged by return on net assets**, the measure often used to assess profit-making organisations.

               The **objective** of our housing society is to provide for the accommodation needs of students. By following this objective we are unable to follow more profitable objectives, such as using the accommodation as a hotel. The fact that resources are not being used to maximise profit means that return on net assets may not be an adequate measure of the efficiency of the housing society.

Appendix

Workings

(i) **Revised operating surplus if 95% occupancy rate achieved**

Revenue and variable costs will have to increase by a factor of 95%/80% = 0.95/0.8 = 1.1875.

	£	£
Rent receivable (£192,000 × 1.1875)		228,000
Variable expenses		
Cleaning (£16,000 × 1.1875)	19,000	
Lighting and heating (£4,800 × 1.1875)	5,700	
Maintenance (£11,200 × 1.1875)	13,300	
		38,000
Contribution		190,000
Fixed expenses		
Rates payable	76,000	
Amortisation	14,000	
Administration costs	58,000	
		148,000
Revised operating surplus		42,000

(ii) **Revised value of debtors**   =   (revised rent receivable/12) × revised average age of debtors
                                     =   (£228,000/12) × 1 month = £19,000

Revised cash balance

	£
Decrease in debtors (£(48,000 – 19,000))	29,000
Increase in contribution*	30,000
Existing cash balance	4,500
	63,500

* This is the difference between the original operating surplus (£12,000) and the operating surplus calculated in (i)(£42,000).

(iii) (1) **Revised net assets**

	£
Fixed assets	564,000
Debtors	19,000
Cash	63,500
Creditors*	(16,500)
	630,000

* Does not change as relates to fixed costs, which are unaffected by the change in occupancy rate.

∴ **Revised return on net assets**   = (£42,000/£630,000) × 100% = 6.67%

(2) **Revised operating surplus as a % of rents receivable** = (£42,000/£228,000) × 100% = 18.42%

(3) **Number of months expenses could be paid from the revised cash/bank balance**

= (revised cash/bank balance ÷ cash expenses) × 12

= (£63,500/(£(38,000 + 76,000 + 58,000)) × 12 = (£63,500/£172,000) × 12
= 4.4 months

47 Micro Circuits Ltd

Tutorial note. To find the average delay in fulfilling orders in (b)(iii), you need to find the difference between orders and turnover (= unfilled orders) and then you need to calculate the delay on this difference as a proportion of turnover, multiplied by 12.

(a)   (i)   **Return on capital employed**
= (operating profit ÷ net assets) × 100%
= (£975,000/£4,875,000) × 100% = 20%

(ii)   **Asset turnover**
= turnover/net assets = £3,900,000/£4,875,000 = 0.8

(iii)   **Sales (operating profit) margin**
= (operating profit/turnover) × 100%
= (£975,000/£3,900,000 × 100%
= 25%

(iv)   **Average age of debtors (in months)**
= (debtors/turnover) × 12
= (£325,000/£3,900,000) × 12
= 1 month

(v)   **Average age of finished stock (in months)**
= (finished goods stock/cost of sales) × 12
= (£140,000/£840,000) × 12 = 2 months

(b)   **Briefing notes on the usefulness of performance indicators**

Prepared for Angela Frear
Prepared by Financial Analyst
Dated: 14 December 20X8

(i)   **Return on capital employed**

The return on capital employed can be misleading.

(1)   Profits should be related to average capital employed but we compute the ratio using year-end assets. Using year-end figures can distort trends and comparisons. If a new investment is undertaken near to a year end and financed, for example, by an issue of shares, the capital employed will rise by the finance raised but profits will only have a month or two of the new investment's contribution.

(2)   The ROCE would be higher if costs such as marketing, research and development and training were not treated as revenue expenditure but were viewed as investment for the future and were capitalised.

(ii)   **Sales (operating profit) margin**

The sales (or operating profit) margin can be manipulated in a number of ways. The following activities would result in short-term improvements in the margin, but probably at the expense of the organisation's long-term viability.

(1)   Reducing expenditure on discretionary cost items such as research and development
(2)   Depreciating assets over a longer period of time, so that the depreciation charge is less
(3)   Choosing an alternative stock valuation method to increase the value of closing stock

(iii) **Average delay in fulfilling orders**

	£
Orders during the year	4,550,000
Turnover during the year	3,900,000
Unfulfilled orders	650,000

Average delay = (£650,000/£3,900,000) × 12 months = 2 months

(iv) **Measures of customer satisfaction**

As well as the delay in fulfilling orders, other measures of customer satisfaction include the following.

- Repeat business ((£3,120,000/£3,900,000) × 100% = 80%)
- Cost of customer support per £ of turnover (£400,000/£3,900,000 = 10p)
- Cost of customer support per customer (information not available)

(v) **Measuring performance from an internal perspective**

A number of indicators may help to measure performance from an internal perspective.

- Training costs as a percentage of production costs ((£140,000/£930,000) × 100% = 15.05%)
- Reworked faulty production as a percentage of total production ((£37,200/ £930,000) × 100% = 4%)
- Returns as a percentage of sales ((£100,000/£4m) × 100% = 2.5%)

The first indicator should be relatively high, the second and third as low as possible.

(vi) **Measuring the innovation and learning perspective**

The innovation and learning perspective could be measured with one of the following indicators.

- Turnover from new products as a percentage of total turnover ((£1.56m/£3.9m) × 100% = 40%)

- Research and development expenditure as a percentage of cost of production ((£750,000/£930,000) × 100% = 81%)

- Research and development expenditure as a percentage of turnover ((£750,000/£3.9m) × 100% = 19.2%)

48 ALV Ltd

> **Tutorial note**. Always show the formulae you are using when calculating performance measures. This makes it clearer for you and the marker, and if you make mistakes in your calculations you will still receive full credit for your workings.

(a) **Performance indicators for ALV (West) Ltd**

(i) **Asset turnover** = turnover/capital employed
= 2,520/2,100 = 1.2 times

(ii) **Net profit margin** = (operating profit/sales) × 100%
= (378/2,520) × 100% = 15%

(iii) **Return on capital employed** = (operating profit/capital employed) × 100%
= (378/2,100) × 100% = 18%

    (iv)   **Wages per employee**   = production labour cost/number of employees
                                        = £260,000/20 = £13,000

    (v)   **Production labour cost per unit** = production labour cost/units produced
                                          = £260,000/30,000 = £8.67

    (vi)   **Output per employee**   = units produced/number of employees
                                          = 30,000/20 = 1,500 units

    (vii) **Added value per employee** = added value/number of employees
                                          = £(2,520,000 − £1,020,000)/20 = £75,000

    (viii) **Profit per employee**   = profit/number of employees
                                          = £378,000/20 = £18,900

(b)

Report

To: Jill Morgan, chief executive ALV Ltd
From: Accounting technician
Date: 13 June 20X3
Subject: **The efficiency and productivity of ALV (East) and ALV (West)**

This report deals with issues surrounding the productivity and efficiency of ALV (East) and ALV (West).

    (i)   **What is meant by productivity and efficiency**

        (1)   **Productivity** is a measure of the quantity of product produced (output) in relation to the resources put in (input).

        (2)   The measurement of **efficiency** tends to focus on the financial **value** generated by the outputs.

        An organisation can be highly **productive** in terms of producing a high level of output in relation to the measured input of resources. If, however, the output has low value or cannot be sold profitably, profitability is reduced. There may therefore be a more **efficient** way to use these resources.

    (ii)   **Two performance indicators used to measure efficiency**

        A major measurement of efficiency is **return on capital employed**. In this case, the **value** generated by the output is the profit earned, and this is related to the input used to earn this profit, the capital employed. The ratio is therefore measuring the **efficiency** with which the capital has been used to generate the profit (the **value** of the output).

        A second measurement of efficiency is provided by the **net profit margin**.

	ALV (West)	ALV (East)
	%	%
Return on capital employed	18	42
Net profit margin	15	20

        Both of these performance measures indicate that ALV (East) has the most efficient operations.

    (iii) **Two performance indicators to measure productivity**

        Major indicators to measure productivity include **output per employee** and **added value per employee** (or alternatively the **profit per employee**).

        These are both relative measures which relate the outputs generated to the inputs used to generate them.

	ALV (West)	ALV (East)
Output per employee (units)	1,500	556
Added value per employee	£75,000	£27,778

Both of these performance measures indicate that ALV (West) has the higher productivity.

(iv) **Using net fixed assets to measure productivity**

The fixed asset turnover ratio may be used to monitor productivity.

	ALV (West)	ALV (East)
Turnover	£2,520,000	£840,000
Net book value of fixed assets	÷ £2,100,000	÷ £360,000
Fixed asset turnover	1.2 times	2.3 times

This performance measure appears to indicate that ALV (East) is making more productive use of fixed assets, in terms of generating sales. The value of the ratio is affected by the age of the fixed assets and their value, however, as discussed below.

(v) **Different rankings given by the performance measures**

One reason why the productivity and efficiency measures might give different rankings is **the differences in the fixed asset base of the two companies.**

ALV (West) has a net book value of plant and machinery of £720,000 compared with £60,000 for ALV (East). Furthermore the average age of ALV (West)'s plant and machinery is much lower, as shown by the following calculation.

Proportion of original cost depreciated:

ALV (West) (£180,000 ÷ £900,000) = 20%
ALV (East)   (£240,000 ÷ £300,000) = 80%

Both the 'newness' of its fixed assets, combined with its **larger asset base**, are likely to help the employees in ALV (West) achieve higher productivity in terms of the number of units output per employee and the added value per employee.

The value and age of the fixed assets also impacts upon efficiency when it is measured in terms of return on capital employed. A **higher value attached to fixed assets** would tend to **increase capital employed**, and may **decrease profit** as a result of **a higher depreciation charge.** These two factors would combine to reduce ROCE, and so may well have impacted on the calculation of ALV (West)'s ROCE.

49 Cam Car Company

> **Tutorial note**. If you are unsure how to calculate an indicator requested, use the information provided on the car division to see how that division's indicators have been determined.

(a)

	Van Division	Car Division
Return on capital employed (ROCE)	40%	2.53%
Asset turnover	1.5 times	0.6 times
Wages per employee	£11,000	£11,500
Production labour cost per unit	£2,200	£1,643
Profit margin	26.67%	4.21%
Profit per employee	£11,200	£4,000
Output per employee	5 vehicles	7 vehicles
Added value per employee	£32,500	£29,167

Workings

1 ROCE = $\dfrac{\text{Profit}}{\text{Net assets}} = \dfrac{112}{280} \times 100\% = 40\%$

2 Asset turnover = $\dfrac{\text{Turnover}}{\text{Net assets}} = \dfrac{420}{280} = 1.5$ times

3 Wages per employee = $\dfrac{\text{Production labour}}{\text{Number of production employees}} = \dfrac{£110,000,000}{10,000} = £11,000$

4 Production cost per unit = $\dfrac{\text{Production labour}}{\text{Vehicles produced}} = \dfrac{£110,000,000}{50,000} = £2,200$

5 Profit margin = $\dfrac{\text{Profit}}{\text{Turnover}} = \dfrac{112m}{420m} \times 100\% = 26.67\%$

6 Profit per employee = $\dfrac{\text{Profit}}{\text{Number of production employees}} = \dfrac{£112m}{10,000} = £11,200$

7 Output per employee = $\dfrac{\text{Vehicles produced}}{\text{Number of production employees}} = \dfrac{50,000}{10,000} = 5$ vehicles

8 Added value per employee = $\dfrac{\text{Turnover} - \text{Materials and bought-in-components}}{\text{Number of production employees}} = \dfrac{£(420m - 95m)}{10,000}$

= £32,500

(b)

Memorandum

To: Peter Ross, Management team
From: Management Accountant, Cam Car Company
Date: XX July 20X8
Subject: **Performance indicators for the car and van divisions**

(i)   (1)   **Productivity**

Productivity defines how efficiently resources are being used. In the Cam Car Company, productivity would indicate the number of vans or cars produced in relation to the resources put in (the materials and bought-in-components).

(2)   **Added value**

Added value gives an indication of how much value has been added to a product by altering its form, location or availability. In the Cam Car Company, the turnover less the cost of materials and bought-in-components represents the added value, ie the amount by which the value of the bought-in-components and materials have increased by converting them into cars and vans.

(ii)   (1)   **The profitability of the van division**

The van division may wish to justify their claims in terms of profitability by looking at the following performance indicators.

- Profit margin
- Profit per employee

The profit margin for the van division is 26.67%, compared to 4.21% for the car division.

The profit per employee is £11,200 for the van division, whereas it is only £4,000 for the car division.

These two performance indicators do certainly indicate that the van division is indeed more profitable than the car division.

(2)   **The productivity of the van division**

The van division may wish to look at the following performance indicators in order to justify their claims in terms of productivity.

- Return on capital employed (ROCE)
- Added value per employee
- Asset turnover

The van division has a ROCE of 40%, compared to 2.53% for the car division.

The van division has an added value per employee of £32,500 which is marginally higher than the £29,167 for the car division.

The asset turnover for the van division is 1.5 times, as compared to 0.6 times for the car division.

In conclusion, the van division appears to have performance indicators which indicate that it is more productive than the car division.

(iii) **Output per employee**

The performance indicator 'output per employee' shows that the car division makes 7 vehicles per employee, whereas the van division only makes 5 vehicles per employee. This performance indicator could be used to counter the claims of higher productivity and profitability in the van division.

The main limitation of this performance indicator is that the van and car divisions make different products, and the different products cannot really be compared with each other (the time that it takes to manufacture one car and one van, and the methods used may be very different). It is also important to note that the number of vehicles produced in the van division is only 50,000 whereas in the car division it is 84,000, and there are 12,000 production employees in the car division whereas there are only 10,000 in the van division.

By looking at the output per employee as a performance indicator, it appears that the car division is more productive/profitable than the van division, and these could most certainly be used to counter the claims of the van division.

(iv) **Overstatement of performance indicators**

The performance ratios calculated in task (a) may be overstated because the van division has fairly low net assets, and the ratio of materials and bought-in-components to turnover is small when compared to the car division.

The ROCE increases as the net assets decrease (if the profit remains constant). The net assets of the van division are low, probably due to the low value of stocks held at the end of the period, and also because the cash balance is overdrawn. These factors affect the net assets of the company and, in turn could cause the ROCE to be overstated.

The added value per employee could be overstated if the materials and bought-in-components are understated. The figure given in the accounts is very low, especially when compared to the car division. It would be useful to check last year's accounts to see whether the ratio of materials and bought-in-components to turnover is similar.

50 Travel Bus Ltd

(a)

> **Tutorial note**. You can use a short cut when it comes to calculating the total cost (part (f)). Instead of laboriously adding up all of the individual costs, you can simply calculate the difference between the turnover and the net profit. Much quicker, and less prone to error!
>
> According to the assessor's report, the overwhelming majority of candidates prepared faultless answers to this task.

(i)   Gross profit margin $= \dfrac{£221{,}760}{£633{,}600} \times 100\%$ $= 35\%$

(ii)   Net profit margin $= \dfrac{£76{,}032}{£633{,}600} \times 100\%$ $= 12\%$

(iii)   Return on capital employed $= \dfrac{£76{,}032}{£95{,}040} \times 100\%$ $= 80\%$

(iv)   Asset turnover $= \dfrac{£633{,}600}{£95{,}040}$ $= 6.7$ times

(v)   No. of passengers in the year $= \dfrac{\text{turnover}}{\text{fare per passenger}}$ $= \dfrac{£633{,}600}{£1} = 633{,}600$ passengers

(vi)   Total cost per mile $= \dfrac{£633{,}600 - £76{,}032}{356{,}400}$ $= £1.56$

(vii)   No. of journeys in the year $= \dfrac{356{,}400\ \text{miles}}{18\ \text{miles per journey}}$ $= 19{,}800$ journeys

         No. of journeys per day $= \dfrac{19{,}800}{360}$ $= 55$ journeys

(viii)   Maintenance cost per mile $= \dfrac{£28{,}512}{356{,}400}$ $= £0.08$

(ix)   Passengers per day $= \dfrac{633{,}600\ (\text{from}(v))}{360}$ $= 1{,}760$ passengers

(x)   Passengers per journey $= \dfrac{1{,}760\ (\text{from}(ix))}{55\ (\text{from}(vii))}$ $= 32$ passengers

(xi)   Number of drivers $= \dfrac{\text{wages paid}}{\text{wages per driver}}$ $= \dfrac{£142{,}000}{£14{,}200} = 10$ drivers

(b)

> **Tutorial note**. Once again, it is important to relate your answer to the task data. Don't be tempted to rely on memorised lists of performance indicators. You need to demonstrate that you can apply your knowledge and understanding to the simulated workplace issues within the case scenario.

Memo

To: Chief executive
From: Management accountant
Date: 6 January 20X1
Subject: **Performance of Travel Bus Ltd for the year to 30 November 20X0**

This memo addresses a number of issues concerning the productivity and profitability of Travel Bus Ltd.

(i)   **Productivity and profitability**

Productivity is the quantity of service produced (**output**) in relation to the resources put in (**input**). It measures **how efficiently resources are being used**.

An **increase in productivity does not always lead to increased profitability**. For example the number of passengers carried per driver, a measure of productivity, could increase. The extra passengers may have been attracted by offering substantial fare reductions, however, and this could lead to reduced profitability.

Another example might be an increase in productivity in terms of the number of journeys per bus. This increase in 'output' arising from the increase in productivity may not be saleable: the buses may be running empty. The revenue gained might be less than the additional costs incurred, leading to reduced profitability.

(ii)   **Driver productivity**

A possible measure of driver productivity is the **number of miles per driver**.

	20W9	20X0
Miles per driver	$\dfrac{324,000}{8} = 40,500$	$\dfrac{356,400}{10} = 35,640$

The number of miles per driver has **decreased** between 20W9 and 20X0 and so, in terms of this measure of productivity, the **drivers' claim** that their productivity has increased is **incorrect**.

Even if the productivity had increased the drivers might still be unable to claim that this had resulted in improved profitability. As discussed above, the extra miles might have been travelled with too few fare-paying passengers, so profitability would not necessarily have improved.

> **Tutorial note**. Alternatively you might have calculated the number of passengers carried per driver in 20W9 and 20X0. This measure shows a decrease but even if it had increased, any resulting increase in profitability would have arisen because the fixed cost per bus was being spread across more passengers, rather than because of extra effort by the drivers.

(iii) **Reason for improved profitability**

A major reason for the improved profitability was the **Council's decision not to charge for parking**. This reduced the overall cost of using the service for passengers, and demand therefore increased considerably. Since many of the costs incurred by Travel Bus Ltd are fixed, costs did not increase at the same rate as turnover, and profitability improved.

(iv) **Performance indicators to measure the satisfaction of passenger needs**

(1) The satisfaction of passenger needs could be monitored by the number of passengers per journey.

	20W9	20X0
Number of passengers per journey	30	32

Depending on the size of the buses, passenger needs may have been less satisfied during 20X0 because of more crowding or the need to stand because no seats were available.

Another measure of the satisfaction of passenger needs is the number of journeys per day.

	20W9	20X0
Number of journeys per day	50	55

This increase probably led to reduced waiting times and so passenger needs may have been better satisfied in 20X0.

(2) A measure of the satisfaction of customer needs that cannot be derived from the existing data is cleanliness of the buses.

Monitoring the cleaning cost per day or per bus might give some indication of the effort put into keeping the buses clean.

Another measure of the satisfaction of customer needs **is punctuality** of the buses and their **adherence to published** timetables.

Monitoring the percentage of buses arriving and departing within five minutes of their published time would give an indication of performance in this area.

(v) **Monitoring the safety aspect of Travel Bus's operations**

(1) The safety aspect of Travel Bus's operations could be monitored by the maintenance cost per mile.

	20W9	20X0
Maintenance cost per mile	£0.10	£0.08

This has reduced, which may **indicate a reduction in attention to safety**, especially as maintenance costs are likely to increase as **buses become older**. No new buses have been added to the fleet (cost value of buses has remained at £240,000); the buses are older and likely to require more maintenance.

On the other hand, some of this reduction in the cost per mile may have been caused by the **spreading of the fixed element of maintenance costs over a higher number of miles** in the year 20X0.

Another indicator of attention to the safety aspect might be the **average age of the buses**. The depreciation charge for the year 20X0 was £12,000 (£180,000 – £168,000). On a cost value of £240,000, assuming straight line depreciation and no residual value, this suggests a useful life of 20 years. Accumulated depreciation of £180,000 means that the buses were on average 15 years old by the end of 20X0, and thus nearing the end of their useful lives.

(2) A measure of the safety aspect that cannot be derived from the existing data is the number of accidents per year.

Another measure could be the **percentage of maintenance cost that is incurred to prevent faults compared with the percentage incurred to correct faults**. This would indicate whether faults were being prevented before they occurred, or whether maintenance was being carried out 'after the event', which could compromise safety.

51 Bon Repose

Tutorial note. This task was straightforward and should have caused you little problem except possibly part (a)(vii). The task does not make it 100% clear what 'expenses' are. If you used just variable costs (breakfast and laundry) this is understandable.

The assessor, in his report, stressed the importance of showing your workings. It is not possible to give credit for what might be partially correct answers if workings are not shown.

(a)   (i)   **Gross (or contribution) margin**

= (contribution/turnover) × 100%
= (£385,440/£560,640) × 100% = 68.75%

     (ii)   **Net profit (or sales) margin**

= (net profit/sales) × 100%
= (£42,048/£560,640) × 100% = 7.5%

     (iii)   **Return on capital employed**

= (net profit/net assets) × 100%
= (£42,048/£700,800) × 100% = 6%

     (iv)   **Asset turnover**

= turnover/net assets
= £560,640/£700,800 = 0.8

     (v)   **Average age of debtors** in months

= (debtors/turnover) × 12
= (£35,040/£560,640) × 12 = 0.75 months

     (vi)   **Average age of creditors** in months

= (creditors/variable costs) × 12
= (£14,600/£175,200) × 12 = 1 month

     (vii)   **Number of months that expenses could be paid from the cash balance**

Expenses per month = £(175,200 + 343,392)/12 = £43,216

Cash balance = £10,804

∴ Expenses could be paid for £10,804/£43,216 = 0.25 months

     (viii)   **Maximum capacity of hotel**

= number of rooms × number of days open
= 80 × 365 = 29,200 room-nights

     (ix)   **% room-night occupancy rate**

= (actual number of room nights sold/maximum capacity) × 100%
= (17,520/29,200) ×100% = 60%

(b)

Tutorial note. You may have wondered what cash balance to include in the statement in (ii). The correct figure was simply £3,000 (as given in the task), the remaining cash having been transferred to head office.

Memo

To: Helene de la Tour
From: Management accountant
Date: 17 December 20X1
Subject: **Performance of Bon Repose UK Hotel**

Further to our recent conversation, I have investigated the reasons for the poor profits of the UK hotel and set out below the relevant information.

(i)   **Effect of discounting**

  (1)   Had there been no discounts, turnover would have been £700,800. This is based on a price of £40 for each of the 17,520 room-nights sold.

  (2)   The discount given by the hotel manager was therefore £(700,800 – 560,640) = £140,160.

  (3)   Rooms can be discounted by £20 to £20 and so the number of discounted room nights was £140,160/£20 = 7,008.

  (4)   The percentage of room-nights discounted was therefore (7,008/17,520) × 100% = 40%.

(ii) **Revised statements**

If the company's policies had been met but no discounts offered, the operating statement and net asset statement would appear as follows.

Revised operating statement year ended 30 November 20X1

	£	£
Turnover		700,800
Variable costs		
Breakfast and laundry		175,200
Contribution		525,600
Fixed costs		
Labour	133,865	
Light and heat	89,045	
Rates, insurance, maintenance	120,482	
		343,392
Net profit		182,208

Revised statement of net assets at 30 November 20X1

	£	£
Fixed assets		669,556
Net current assets		
Debtors (W1)	29,200	
Cash (given)	3,000	
	32,200	
Creditors (W2)	(29,200)	
		3,000
Net assets		672,556

Workings

1   If the average age of debtors is 0.5 months, then on the basis of the revised turnover figure, debtors = (£700,800/12) × 0.5 = £29,200

2   The average age of creditors should be 2 × 1 month = 2 months. Variable costs are £175,200 and so creditors should be (£175,200/12) × 2 = £29,200.

(iii)   **Revised performance indicators**

Revised performance indicators based on the statements above can now be calculated.

(1)   **Revised gross (or contribution) margin**

= (revised contribution/revised turnover) × 100%
= (£525,600/£700,800) × 100% = 75%

(2)   **Revised net profit (or sales) margin**

= (revised net profit/revised turnover) × 100%
= (£182,208/£700,800) × 100% = 26%

(3)   **Revised return on capital employed**

= (revised net profit/revised net assets) × 100%
= (£182,208/£672,556) × 100% = 27.09%

(iv)   **Discounting and profitability**

The revised operating statement shows that if all rooms could have been sold at full price, profit would have increased by £140,160. Discounting is therefore one of the reasons for the reduced profit.

The hotel type is new to the UK, however, and so demand is bound to be relatively low until customers become aware of its existence. This could explain the 60% occupancy rate. It is possible that profit could have been even less in the first year if discounting had not been used, as it may have encouraged guests to try the hotel rather than an established competitor.

If maximum capacity had been achieved with the same proportion of room nights discounted, revenue would have been £560,640/60% = £934,400. Variable costs would have increased to £175,200/60% = £292,000 but fixed costs (by definition) would have remained unchanged.

The resulting net profit would have been £(934,400 – 292,000 – 343,392) = £299,008, an increase of £(299,008 – 42,048) = £256,960.

The low occupancy rate is therefore of more significance than discounting as a reason for the reduced profits.

I trust this information is useful. If I can be of further assistance please do not hesitate to get in touch.

Chapters 14 and 15 Cost management

52 Fill in the table

(a)

Activity	Total ovh'd £	(i) Total cost driver units Units	(i) Ovh'd per cost Driver Unit £	Cost driver units per product X Units	Cost driver units per product Y Units	Cost driver units per product Z Units	(ii) Total overhead per product per activity X £	(ii) Total overhead per product per activity Y £	(ii) Total overhead per product per activity Z £
Machinery set-ups	32,000	320	100	140	80	100	14,000	8,000	10,000
Materials handling	16,000	40	400	12	14	14	4,800	5,600	5,600
Quality control	25,800	200	129	75	55	70	9,675	7,095	9,030
Supervision	7,400	50	148	10	15	25	1,480	2,220	3,700
Maintenance	6,585	15	439	4	6	5	1,756	2,634	2,195
							31,711	25,549	30,525
			Number of units produced				1,250	500	550
			(iii) Cost per item				£25.37	£51.10	£55.50

(b) A cost driver is an activity which generates cost, such as number of quality inspections, or number of deliveries. The cost driver unit, therefore, is one inspection, one delivery and so forth. Hours or weight may also be cost driver units, depending upon the cost driver in question.

Examples for each of the activities in the table are as follows.

Activity	Possible cost driver unit
Machinery set-ups	Number of set-ups
Materials handling	Kilograms of materials handled
Quality control	Inspection hours
Supervision	Number of work teams
Maintenance	Maintenance staff hours

53 Charleroi Aircon Ltd

(a)

	HMG/012 £	CFG/013 £
Equipment cost	175,000	120,000
Direct labour cost	130,000	66,000
Total direct cost	305,000	186,000
Gross profit percentage	50%	50%
Price	£457,500	£279,000

(b) **Calculation of cost per unit of cost driver**

Activity	Budgeted cost pool £	Cost driver	Cost driver units pa	Cost per unit of cost driver £
Design department	675,000	Design hours	25,000	27.00
Site engineers	370,000	Miles travelled	185,000	2.00
Purchasing department	105,000	Items purchased	15,000	7.00
Payroll department	75,000	Direct hours	300,000	0.25
Site management	750,000	Direct hours	300,000	2.50
Post-installation inspection	80,000	Items purchased	20,000	4.00

Schedule of activity-based overhead costs

		HMG/012		CFG/013	
Activity	Cost per unit of cost driver £	Cost driver units	ABC cost £	Cost driver units	ABC cost £
Design department	27.00	1,280	34,560	620	16,740
Site engineers	2.00	9,600*	19,200	900*	1,800
Purchasing department	7.00	650	4,550	410	2,870
Payroll department	0.25	10,000	2,500	6,000	1,500
Site management	2.50	10,000	25,000	6,000	15,000
Post installation inspection	4.00	650	2,600	410	1,640
Activity-based overhead			88,410		39,550

* Miles travelled = distance × visits

(c)

Memo

To: Alice Devereaux
From: Accounts assistant
Cc: Mark Langton
Date: xx/xx/xx
Subject: **Profitability of jobs HMG/012 and CFG/013**

As requested, I have investigated jobs HMG/012 and CFG/013. Set out below is a statement which contains the **projected profit** for those two jobs.

	HMG/012 £	CFG/013 £
Price	457,500	279,000
Equipment cost	175,000	120,000
Direct labour cost	130,000	66,000
Total direct cost	305,000	186,000
Gross profit	152,500	93,000
Activity-based overhead	88,410	39,550
Projected profit	64,090	53,450
Profit as a % of selling price	14.0%	19.2%
Profit as a % of total cost	16.3%	23.7%

Both jobs would be profitable at the suggested prices. The **government contract** is **less profitable** than the furniture store, however, because it **is carrying a higher overhead cost**. This higher overhead cost is **caused by** the **extra complexity** of the government contract and the **distance** of the government offices from our offices. It may therefore be necessary to increase the quoted price for the government contract to provide an adequate level of profit.

Please contact me if you require further information.

54 Benefits of ABC

Tutorial note. Try to use the situation given in the question as the basis for your answer. The organisation is a law firm and so before you begin to write you will need to think about the type of activity that they might undertake.

Activity based costing (ABC)

A paper prepared for Lucy Thomson

Introduction

This paper will describe both how ABC works (illustrating the methodology with a simple illustration) and the advantages of ABC.

ABC arose from a dissatisfaction with the information that was provided by traditional overhead absorption methods. For example, in our firm we have always recovered our overhead costs on an hourly rate per client. ABC recognises that this may not be the most suitable basis for recovering overheads. An **ABC** system **looks more carefully at what actually causes overhead costs** and **attempts to allocate overheads more realistically** to the products produced/services provided.

How ABC works

The first step in an ABC exercise is to **analyse the activities** (rather than departments as required by absorption costing) that are undertaken in an organisation. Our activities include consulting with clients, maintaining client accounts, ordering stationery supplies and so on. All staff would therefore need to provide a description of exactly what they do and the way in which they do it.

Once the activities are identified the next step is to **determine the cost driver for the activity**. A cost driver causes the costs of the activity to alter. For example, the cost driver for maintaining client accounts might be the number of clients currently on our books. A client who simply requires a basic will to be drawn up may place as much burden on our resources for maintaining client accounts as one who requires detailed advice in a divorce case.

Each activity is treated as a cost pool and the costs are collected in much the same way as with a traditional cost centre system. Each total cost pool is then divided by the appropriate number of cost drivers to find the **cost per cost driver**. The number of cost drivers a product (or service) causes is then identified (which is equivalent to the degree by which the product/service has caused the costs of the activity to change). The cost per cost driver is then multiplied by the appropriate number of cost drivers to determine the share of the activity's cost the product/service must bear.

Illustration

For purposes of illustration assume that our organisation has two activities and that the relevant cost drivers are as follows.

Activity	Cost of activity during period £	Cost driver	Cost per unit of cost driver
Consulting with clients	20,000	250 consultant hours	£80 per hour
Client account maintenance	4,000	400 clients	£10 per client

The costing system would therefore charge each client £80 per consultant hour for consulting time, and £10 per period for account maintenance regardless of the number of hours they have spent with our legal consultants.

The benefits of ABC

The benefits of ABC include the following.

(a)   Staff will have a better understanding of the firm's overhead costs and what causes them, instead of simply assuming that all overhead costs are incurred at an hourly rate.

(b)   Clients will be charged an appropriate amount which more closely relates to the burden that they have placed on the firm's resources.

(c)   The process of describing activities will provide a focus for cost reduction exercises, forcing all of the firm's employees to look more closely at the way that they do things.

(d)   A better understanding of overhead costs will improve budgeting and planning in the future.

(e)   A carefully determined cost driver rate can provide the basis for improved cost control and perhaps some form of performance assessment.

(f)   A client profitability exercise may be carried out, resulting in more of an idea of what it is costing to service each type of client. This may provide the basis for a reassessment of fees charged and may even lead to a decision to discontinue a particular type of business.

55 BeePee plc

(a)   **Prevention costs** are the costs of any action taken to investigate, prevent or reduce defects and failures.

Appraisal costs are the costs of assessing the quality achieved.

Internal failure costs are the costs arising within the organisation of failing to achieve the required level of quality.

External failure costs are the costs arising outside the organisation of failing to achieve the required level of quality (after transfer of ownership to the customer).

(b)   **Examples of each category appropriate to a manufacturing environment**

(i)   Examples of **prevention costs** include the following.

(1)   Cost of training personnel in quality control

(2)   Cost of designing, developing and maintaining quality control and inspection equipment

(ii) Examples of **appraisal costs** include the following.

    (1)   Cost of the inspection of finished products or services and other checking procedures and supplier vetting

    (2)   Cost of the inspection of goods inwards

(iii) Examples of **internal failure costs** include the following.

    (1)   Cost of material scrapped due to inefficiencies in goods receiving procedures and stores control

    (2)   Cost of material lost or wasted during production

    (3)   Cost of units rejected during inspection processes

    (4)   Losses due to lower selling prices for sub-quality goods

    (5)   Cost of reviewing product specifications after failures

(iv) Examples of **external failure costs** include the following.

    (1)   Cost of product liability claims from customers

    (2)   Cost of repairing products returned from customers

    (3)   Cost of providing replacement items due to sub-standard products

    (4)   Cost of delivering returned units

    (5)   Cost of administration of customer services section

    (6)   Cost of customer services section

Note. Only one example was required for each cost classification.

(c) **Examples of each category appropriate to management accounting**

(i) Examples **of prevention costs** include the following.

    (1)   Cost of staff training programmes

    (2)   Cost of introducing computers to perform tasks previously performed manually

(ii) Examples of **appraisal costs** include the following.

    (1)   Cost of batch input controls to check the validity of processed data

    (2)   Cost of performing computer audits to confirm the reliability of computer software

(iii) Examples of **internal failure costs** include the following.

    (1)   Cost of reprocessing data input to the system incorrectly

    (2)   Cost of reproducing incorrect reports

(iv) Examples of **external failure costs** include the following.

    (1)   Cost to other functions in the organisation of incorrect decisions made on the basis of inaccurate or untimely information provided by the management accounting function (such as quoting uneconomical prices for jobs on the basis of incorrect information about labour, material and overhead)

    (2)   Cost of dealing with external audit queries

56 Local Engineering Ltd

> **Tutorial note**. What the assessor was looking for in task (a)(iii) were the four types of quality-related costs set out in BS 6143. The word 'activities' in the question therefore refers to the types of activity giving rise to the costs.

(a)

Background paper for meeting on 7 July 20X8

To:	Jane Greenwood, Management Accountant
From:	Assistant Management Accountant
Subject:	**Total quality management and the cost of quality**
Date:	30 June 20X8

(i) **The meaning of Total Quality Management**

Total Quality Management (TQM) is a philosophy that guides every activity within a business. It is concerned with **developing and sustaining a culture of continuous improvement which focuses on meeting customers' expectations.**

One of the basic principles of TQM is therefore a dissatisfaction with the *status quo:* the belief that it is always possible to improve and so the aim should be to **'get it more right next time'**. This involves the development of a commitment to quality by all staff and a programme of continuous learning throughout the entire organisation, possibly by **empowering employees** and making them responsible for the quality of production or by introducing **quality circles.**

The customer-centred approach of TQM hinges upon identifying the 'customers', focusing attention on them and then meeting their needs in terms of price, quality and timing. Organisations must therefore be **customer orientated** rather than, as is traditionally the case, production orientated.

One of the goals of TQM is to get it right first time. By continuously improving towards **zero defects**, the quality of the product delivered to the customer is improved. The quality of output depends on the quality of materials input, however, and so either extensive **quality control procedures** are needed at the point where goods are accepted and inspected or quality assurance schemes, whereby the supplier guarantees the quality of the goods supplied, must be in place.

A small proportion of mistakes are inevitable in any organisation but more often than not those mistakes have been 'designed' into the production process. Because TQM aims to get it right first time, however, quality and not faults must be designed into an organisation's products and operations from the outset. Quality control must therefore happen at the production design and production engineering stages of a product's life, as well as actually during production.

In summary, TQM involves getting it right first time and **improving continuously**.

(ii) **Failure of the current accounting system to highlight the cost of quality**

Traditionally, the costs of scrapped units, wasted materials and reworking have been **subsumed within the costs of production** by assigning the costs of an expected level of loss (a normal loss) to the costs of good production, while accounting for **other costs of poor quality** within **production or marketing overheads**. Such costs are therefore not only considered as **inevitable** but are not **highlighted** for management attention. Moreover, traditional accounting reports tend to **ignore the hidden but real**

costs of excessive stock levels (held to enable faulty material to be replaced without hindering production) and the facilities necessary for storing that stock.

(iii)/(iv) **Explicit costs of quality**

There are four recognised categories of cost identifiable within an accounting system which make up the cost of quality.

(1) **Prevention costs** are the costs of any action taken to investigate, prevent or reduce the production of faulty output. Included within this category are the costs of training in quality control and the cost of the design/development and maintenance of quality control and inspection equipment.

(2) **Appraisal costs** are the costs of assessing the actual quality achieved. Examples include the cost of the inspection of goods delivered and the cost of inspecting production during the manufacturing process.

(3) **Internal failure costs** are the costs incurred by the organisation when production fails to meet the level of quality required. Such costs include losses due to lower selling prices for sub-quality goods, the costs of reviewing product specifications after failures and losses arising from the failure of purchased items.

(4) **External failure costs** are the costs which arise outside the organisation (after the customer has received the product) due to failure to achieve the required level of quality. Included within this category are the costs of repairing products returned from customers, the cost of providing replacement items due to sub-standard products or marketing errors and the costs of a customer service department.

(v) **Quality costs not identified by the accounting system**

Quality costs which are not identified by the accounting system tend to be of two forms.

(1) Opportunity costs such as the loss of future sales to a customer dissatisfied with faulty goods.

(2) Costs which tend to be subsumed within other account headings such as those costs which result from the disruption caused by stockouts due to faulty purchases.

(b) (i) **Explicit cost of quality**

	£
Reworking (labour cost)	13,500
Customer support (contractors)	24,300
Store inspection costs	10,000
Cost of returns	4,500
	52,300

(ii) **Cost of quality not reported in the accounting records**

Opportunity cost (lost contribution from 100 X4s due to faulty circuit board) = £795 (W1) × 100 = £79,500.

Workings

		£
1	Labour (W2)	200
	Printed circuit board (£120,000 ÷ 1,000)	120
	Other material (£121,500 ÷ 900)	135
	Marginal cost	455
	Selling price	(1,250)
	Contribution	795

		£
2	Total labour cost	193,500
	Less: cost of reworking	(13,500)
		180,000

∴ Unit cost per good unit = £180,000 ÷ 900 = £200

Answers to Full Assessments

UNIT 8 FULL ASSESSMENT 1 (JUNE 2002)

NVQ/SVQ in ACCOUNTING, LEVEL 4

UNIT 8

CONTRIBUTING to the MANAGEMENT of PERFORMANCE and the ENHANCEMENT of VALUE (PEV)

SUGGESTED ANSWERS

UNIT 8 (PEV) Full Assessment 1 : mapping against Standards

Performance Criteria / Range Statement	Task 1.1	Task 1.2	Task 2.1	Task 2.2	Task 2.3
8.1 Collect, analyse cost information					
A Identify relevant information	✓	✓			
B Monitor and analyse trends					✓
C Compare trends and identify implications					✓
D Compare standard and actual costs and analyse variances	✓				
E Analyse accounting policies on reported costs	✓	✓			
F Consult staff re trends and variances					
G Reports summarising data, presentation and trends	✓	✓			✓
8.1 Range Statement					
Information	✓				
Methods of summarising data					✓
Methods of presenting information in reports		✓			✓
Variance analysis	✓				
Build-up of costs	✓	✓			
8.2 Monitor performance/ recommendations					
A Analyse routine cost reports, implications			✓		
B Prepare/ monitor performance indicators, improvements			✓	✓	
C Consult specialists, identify reduction of costs, value					✓
D Exception reports					✓
E Make recommendations					
8.2 Range statement					
Performance indicators			✓	✓	
Recommendations					

SECTION 1

Tutorial note. Task 1.1 was similar to tasks in the June and December 2001 assessments, and presented you with a standard cost card and actual results. Most candidates had no difficulty with part (a), according to the assessor. As in past assessments you needed to be able to rearrange equations and carry out calculations efficiently. Look in Chapter 4 of the 2003 edition of the BPP Interactive Text for Units 8 and 9 if you struggled with this part of the task.

The first major problem you could have encountered may have been in the calculation of the price and usage variances for telephone calls in task 1.1(b). These variances should relate to the telephone cost expense (and so should be based on units used), but you may have based them on the total cost of a telephone call (as did a number of candidates sitting the assessment, according to the assessor).

The fixed overhead volume variance is another tricky one. You need to value the difference between actual and budgeted number of calls at the **fixed overhead absorbed per call,** as the volume variance measures the under or over absorption of fixed overhead due to a difference between budgeted and actual volumes of activity. The capacity and efficiency variances, on the other hand, are valued at the fixed overhead absorbed per hour.

Don't forget that you should either include the fixed overhead volume variance or the fixed overhead capacity and efficiency variances, but not both, as the former is the sum of the latter two.

The assessor was very pleased with the high quality of answers to task 1.1, a significant number of candidates providing perfect answers.

In his report, the assessor stressed the importance of clear workings, noting that 'Even where errors occurred, many candidates were able to gain significant credit for process by including easily identifiable workings. All too often, however, candidates assessed as not yet competent showed no logic to their answers and no clear audit trail to their workings.'

According to the assessor, ' The overwhelming majority of candidates produced good answers' to task 1.2. Common errors included not answering part (b) and writing extensively about ABC versus traditional fixed overhead costing, which was not required. Again, it was important to lay out your workings clearly, so as to ensure the logic of your thought processes was evident.

Task 1.1

(a) (i)   Actual cost of a telephone unit = total actual cost ÷ total actual units = £79,200 ÷ 1,200,000 = £0.066

     (ii) Actual hourly wage rate of operators = actual total cost of operators' wages ÷ actual hours worked = £478,800 ÷ 114,000 hours = £4.20

     (iii) Standard number of operator hours per call = 6 mins = 0.1 hr

           ∴ Standard number of operator hours for 1,000,000 calls = 0.1 hr × 1,000,000 = 100,000 hours

(iv)   Fixed overheads are based on budgeted operator hours.

Budgeted number of calls   = 900,000

Budgeted number of operator hours   = 900,000 × 0.1 hour = 90,000

Fixed overhead absorption rate   = £6.50 per hour

∴ Budgeted cost of fixed overheads   = 90,000 hours × £6.50 per hour
                                        = £585,000

(v)   See (iv) above

(vi)   Standard cost of actual operations = actual number of calls × standard cost per call = 1,000,000 × £1.07 = £1,070,000

(b)   (i)   **Price variance for telephone calls**

	£
1,200,000 units should have cost (× £0.07)	84,000
but did cost	79,200
	4,800 (F)

(ii)   **Usage variance for telephone calls**

1,000,000 calls should have used (× 1 unit)	1,000,000 units
but did use	1,200,000 units
Variance in units	200,000 units (A)
× standard rate per unit	× £0.07
	£14,000 (A)

(iii)   **Labour rate variance for the telephone operators**

	£
114,000 hours should have cost (× £3.50)	399,000
but did cost	478,800
	79,800 (A)

(iv)   **Labour efficiency variance for the telephone operators**

1,000,000 calls should have taken (from (a)(iii))	100,000 hrs
but did take	114,000 hrs
Variance in hours	14,000 hrs (A)
× standard rate per hour	× £3.50
	£49,000 (A)

(v)   **Fixed overhead expenditure variance**

	£
Budgeted expenditure (from (a)(iv))	585,000
Actual expenditure	540,400
	44,600 (F)

(vi) Fixed overhead volume variance

Budgeted number of calls	900,000
Actual number of calls	1,000,000
Variance in calls	100,000 (F)
× standard fixed overhead per call	× £0.65
	£65,000 (F)

(vii) Fixed overhead capacity variance

Budgeted operator hours (from (a)(v))	90,000 hrs
Actual operator hours	114,000 hrs
Variance in units	24,000 hrs (F)
× standard absorption rate per hour	× £6.50
	£156,000 (F)

(viii) Fixed overhead capacity variance

Labour efficiency variance (as overheads are absorbed on a labour hour basis)(from (b)(iv))	14,000 hrs (A)
× standard absorption rate per hour	× £6.50
	£91,000 (A)

(c) Reconciliation statement – 3 months ended 31 May 20X2

	£ (F)	£ (A)	£
Standard cost of actual operations (from(a)(vi))			1,070,000
Variances			
Price for telephone calls	4,800		
Usage for telephone calls		14,000	
Labour rate		79,800	
Labour efficiency		49,000	
Fixed overhead expenditure	44,600		
Fixed overhead capacity	156,000		
Fixed overhead efficiency		91,000	
	205,400	233,800	28,400 (A)
Actual cost of actual operations			1,098,400

Task 1.2

File note

To: Drampton's finance director
From: Financial analyst
Date: 17 June 20X2
Subject: **Little Ltd – treatment of fixed overheads**

Following our recent discussions, I set out below calculations showing the reclassification of fixed overheads between the two computer models manufactured by Little Ltd, using activity based costing.

(a) **Reallocation of Little Ltd's budgeted total fixed annual overheads between mainframe and desktop production**

Step 1. Calculation of cost per cost driver

	Budgeted total annual overheads £	Cost driver	Number of cost drivers	Cost per cost driver £
Set-up costs	10,000	Number of set-ups	5	2,000.00
Rent and power (production area)	120,000	Number of wks' production	50	2,400.00
Rent (stores area)	50,000	Floor area of stores (m²)	800	62.50
Salaries of store issue staff	40,000	No of issues of stock	10,000	4.00
	220,000			

Step 2. Reallocation of overheads based on costs per cost driver

Mainframe	(i) Number of cost drivers	(ii) Cost per cost driver £	(i) × (ii) Allocated overheads
Set-up costs	5	2,000.00	10,000.00
Rent and power (production area)	10	2,400.00	24,000.00
Rent (stores area)	400	62.50	25,000.00
Salaries of store issue staff	2,000	4.00	8,000.00
			67,000.00

Desktop	(i) Number of cost drivers	(ii) Cost per cost driver £	(i) × (ii) Allocated overheads
Set-up costs	0	2,000.00	–
Rent and power (production area)	40	2,400.00	96,000
Rent (stores area)	400	62.50	25,000
Salaries of store issue staff	8,000	4.00	32,000
			153,000

(b) **Revised unit fixed overheads for each of the two types of computer**

Type of computer	Allocated overheads £'000	Annual budgeted volume Units	Unit fixed overheads £
Mainframe	67	5	13,400.00
Desktop	153	5,000	30.60

SECTION 2

Tutorial note. Gross sales includes the computers actually returned. .

You should have had no problems in dealing with parts (a) to (i) of task 2.1. Identical and/ or very similar tasks have appeared in previous assessments included in this Kit. You should have based the gross and net sales margins on net sales, not gross, as the returns cannot contribute to profitability.

The calculation of the average delay in supplying an order was slightly more difficult (although it had been required in the December 1998 assessment).

Task 2.2 was straightforward. You were only required to name one perspective for each indicator: we have identified more for completeness.

According to the assessor, task 2.3 was, in general, poorly answered. The trickiest part of part (b) was probably dealing with sales correctly. Gross sales includes the free replacements, net sales of 20,000 units is the volume for which revenue is earned.

Task 2.1

(a) **Gross profit margin**
= (gross profit / turnover) × 100%
= (£2,250,000 / £6,000,000) × 100%
= 37.5%

(b) **Net profit (or sales) margin**
= (net profit/ turnover) × 100%
= (£240,000 / £6,000,000) × 100%
= 4%

(c) **Return on capital employed**
= net profit/ net assets × 100%
= (£240,000/ £3,000,000) × 100%
= 8%

(d) **Asset turnover**
= revenue/ net assets
= £6,000,000/ £3,000,000
= 2 times

(e) **Average age of debtors** (in months)
= (debtors/ turnover) × 12 months
= (£1,500,000 / £6,000,000) × 12 months
= 3 months

(f) **Research and development as a percentage of the cost of production**
= (research and development expenditure/ cost of production) × 100%
= (£768,000 / £4,800,000) × 100%
= 16%

(g) **Training as a percentage of the cost of production**
= (cost of training/cost of production) × 100%
= (£576,000/ £4,800,000) × 100%
= 12%

(h) **Customer support as a percentage of turnover**

$$= \text{(cost of customer support/ turnover)} \times 100\%$$
$$= (£240,000/ £6,000,000) \times 100\%$$
$$= 4\%$$

(i) **Returns as a percentage of turnover** $= \text{(sales returns/ turnover)} \times 100\%$
$$= (£300,000/ £6,000,000) \times 100\%$$
$$= 5\%$$

(j) **Average delay in months between placing an order and receiving a fault-free hand-held computer**

$$= \text{((orders placed – sales of fault-free computers)/sales of fault-free computers)} \times 12 \text{ months}$$
$$= ((26,000 - 20,000)/20,000) \times 12 \text{ months}$$
$$= 3.6 \text{ months}$$

Task 2.2

Indicator	Balanced scorecard perspective being measured
(a) Gross profit margin	Financial or internal (unit cost measurement)
(b) Net profit (or sales) margin	Financial or internal (unit cost measurement)
(c) ROCE	Financial or internal
(d) Asset turnover	Internal
(e) Average age of debtors in months	Financial or customer
(f) R & D as a % of cost of production	Innovation and learning
(g) Training as a % of cost of production	Innovation and learning
(h) Customer support as a % of turnover	Customer
(i) Returns as a % of turnover	Internal or customer
(j) Average delay in months between placing an order and receiving a fault-free computer	Internal or customer

Task 2.3

Memo

To: Finance director
From: Financial analyst
Date :   23 July 20X2
Subject: **Hand Power Systems Ltd – accounting policies and forecast data**

(a)   **Accounting policies and their effects on profit**

(i)   **Stock valuation**

Closing stock of finished goods is valued on a last-in, first-out basis, which means that the items in stock at the year end are valued on the basis of earlier rather than more recent material purchases. As material prices are falling, closing stock is possibly overvalued. This means that profit could be overstated.

(ii)   **Depreciation**

Hand Power Systems Ltd's fixed assets originally cost £5 million. Given depreciation for the year of £1 million, and assuming a straight-line basis and no residual value, fixed assets are being depreciated over five years. Similar fixed assets in other companies have an average life of ten years. Hand Power Systems Ltd's depreciation policy could be deemed overly prudent, reducing profit by £500,000 per annum (based on current fixed assets).

(b)   (i)   Current selling price   = £300,000/1,000 = £300
              Forecast selling price   = £300 × (forecast index/current index)
                                              = £300 × (100/120) = £250

(ii)   Gross sales volume of 21,000 includes the 1,000 free replacements.

∴ If there had been no faults, gross sales volume would have been 20,000.

With the introduction of TQM, there will be no returns and so forecast gross sales volume should be based on 20,000 units.

Forecast sales volume = 20,000 × (130/100) = 26,000

(iii) **Forecast sales turnover** = forecasting selling price (from (i)) × forecast sales volume (from (ii)) = £250 × 26,000 = £6,500,000

(iv)   Current unit material cost = total material costs / units produced = £3,360,000/24,000 = £140

Forecast material cost per hand-held computer = £140 × (forecast index/current index)

= £140 × (140/175) = £112

(v)   Current unit labour cost = total labour cost/ units produced = £960,000/24,000 = £40

Forecast labour cost per hand-held computer = £40 × 75% (to allow for saving due to new machinery and equipment) = £30

(vi)   Computers will be made to order and so there will be no closing stock.

∴ Forecast production volume = forecast sales volume – forecast opening stock

Forecast opening stock = closing stock at 31 May 20X2 = 5,000

∴ **Forecast production volume** = 26,000 (from (ii)) – 5,000 = 21,000

(vii)

	£
Forecast material costs (£112 (from (iv)) × 21,000 (from (vi)))	2,352,000
Forecast labour costs (£30 (from (v)) × 21,000 (from (vi)))	630,000
Forecast production fixed overheads (W)	320,000
Forecast cost of production	3,302,000

Working

	£
Current production fixed overheads	480,000
Savings	160,000
Forecast production fixed overheads	320,000

(viii)   Cost of sales = opening stock value + production costs – closing stock value

Closing stock is forecast to be nil.

Opening stock is closing stock at 31 May 20X2.

	£
Opening stock	1,350,000
Forecast cost of production (from(vii))	3,302,000
Forecast cost of sales	4,652,000

(ix)   Gross profit = sales turnover – cost of sales

∴ **Forecast gross profit** = £(6,500,000 (from (iii)) – 4,652,000 (from (viii)) = £1,848,000

UNIT 8 FULL ASSESSMENT 2 (DECEMBER 2002)

NVQ/SVQ in ACCOUNTING, LEVEL 4

UNIT 8

CONTRIBUTING to the MANAGEMENT of PERFORMANCE and the ENHANCEMENT of VALUE (PEV)

SUGGESTED ANSWERS

UNIT 8 (PEV) Full Assessment 2 : mapping against Standards

Performance Criteria / Range Statement		Task 1.1	Task 1.2	Task 2.1	Task 2.2	Task 2.3
8.1 Collect, analyse cost information						
A	Identify relevant information	✓	✓			
B	Monitor and analyse trends		✓			
C	Compare trends and identify implications		✓			
D	Compare standard and actual costs and analyse variances	✓	✓			
E	Analyse accounting policies on reported costs					
F	Consult staff re trends and variances		✓			
G	Reports summarising data, presentation and trends	✓	✓			✓
8.1 Range Statement						
Information		✓				
Methods of summarising data			✓			
Methods of presenting information in reports			✓			✓
Variance analysis		✓	✓			
Build-up of costs		✓				
8.2 Monitor performance/ recommendations						
A	Analyse routine cost reports, implications				✓	
B	Prepare/ monitor performance indicators, improvements				✓	✓	✓
C	Consult specialists, identify reduction of costs, value					
D	Exception reports					✓	
E	Make recommendations					✓	✓
8.2 Range statement						
Performance indicators				✓	✓	✓
Recommendations					✓	✓

Tutorial note. In his report the assessor set out the principal reasons why candidates were deemed not yet competent.

- Clear gaps in their knowledge and understanding

- Practically no knowledge and understanding required for this unit

- Rote learning answers to previous examinations and reproducing these, no matter how irrelevant they might be to the specific task requirements

- Three unsound failings: no workings and no audit trail to workings; very poor presentation skills; simple numerical errors that might otherwise have been condoned

'Candidates have been told many times that a failure to provide clear and clearly signposted workings is a high-risk strategy. With no workings – or extensive and contradictory workings along with extensive crossings out – it is often impossible to follow the candidate's thought processes. As a result, it is not possible to award process marks when an answer is incorrect.'

Section 1

Tutorial note. Task 1.1(a) was straightforward and should have presented you with few problems as very similar tasks have been asked before and are reproduced in this Kit. The only part that may have stopped you in your tracks is part (viii). You weren't required to calculate the standard fixed overhead per barrel but the standard full cost (ie including absorbed fixed overheads) per barrel.

Variance calculations always appear in the Unit 8 exam and so you must be able to deal with them. You should have noted that the fixed overheads were absorbed on the basis of machine hours rather than labour hours.

The reconciliation statement required in (c) should reconcile the standard absorption cost of actual operations to the actual absorption cost of actual operations. The actual absorption cost of actual operations is straightforward – it is simply the actual costs total provided in the task data. But what about the standard absorption cost of actual operations? This is the standard absorption cost per barrel (calculated in (a)(viii)) × actual level of production. In other words you are reconciling what operations should have cost with what operations did cost.

You might have struggled with part (a)(i) of task 1.2. The key was noting the information in the task data that production volume varies during the year. If you can't see the significance of this let's consider a simple example. Suppose the price of item X is £10 in week 1 and £20 in week 2. A simple average price would be £15. But if you purchased 10 items at £10 and 190 at £20, the average price you paid for the 200 items would not have been £15. It must be far closer to £20 as you purchased far more at that price. To find the average price paid you need to weight by the quantities purchased (average price = ((£10×10)+(£20×190))/(10+190) = £19.50). You do not have volume data to calculate a weighted average trend price in (b), so the revised standard cost should be based on the trend values given and the seasonal variations.

Subdivision of variances tasks extremely similar to that in part (c) have been asked on numerous occasions before and will be asked again so you must be able to deal with them. Because you are subdividing the price variance, the quantity you use in all the calculations is the one upon which the original price variance is based – the actual quantity of material.

Task 1.1

(a)   (i)   **Standard price of material per litre**

= standard cost for 12,500 litres ÷ 12,500 litres

= £106,250 ÷ 12,500 = £8.50

      (ii)   **Actual price of material per litre**

= actual cost for 11,520 litres ÷ 11,520 litres

= £99,072 ÷11,520 = £8.60

      (iii)   **Standard litres of material per barrel**

= standard litres for 2,500 barrels ÷ 2,500 barrels

= 12,500 litres ÷ 2,500 = 5

      (iv)   **Standard labour rate per hour**

= standard cost for 10,000 labour hours ÷ 10,000 labour hours

= £60,000 ÷ 10,000 = £6

      (v)   **Standard labour hours per barrel**

= standard labour hours for 2,500 barrels ÷ 2,500 barrels

= 10,000 labour hours ÷ 2,500 = 4

      (vi)   **Standard machine hours per barrel**

= standard machine hours for 2,500 barrels ÷ 2,500 barrels

= 20,000 machine hours ÷ 2,500 = 8

      (vii)   **Budgeted fixed overheads per budgeted machine hour**

= budgeted fixed overheads for 20,000 machine hours ÷ 20,000 machine hours

= £200,000 ÷ 20,000 = £10

      (viii)   **Standard absorption cost per barrel**

= standard absorption cost for 2,500 barrels ÷ 2,500 barrels

= £366,250 ÷ 2,500 = £146.50

(b) **(i)**

	£
11,520 litres should have cost (× £8.50 per (a)(i))	97,920
but did cost	99,072
Material price variance	1,152 (A)

(ii)

2,400 barrels should have used (× 5 litres per (a)(iii))	12,000 litres
but did use	11,520 litres
Usage variance in litres	480 litres (F)
× standard cost per litre	× £8.50
Material usage variance	£ 4,080 (F)

(iii)

	£
10,080 labour hours should have cost (× £6 per (a)(iv))	60,480
but did cost	61,488
Labour rate variance	1,008 (A)

(iv)

2,400 barrels should have taken (× 4 hours per (a)(v))	9,600 hrs
but did take	10,080 hrs
Efficiency variance in hours	480 hrs(A)
× standard rate per hour	× £6
Labour efficiency variance	£2,880 (A)

(v)

	£
Budgeted fixed overhead expenditure	200,000
Actual fixed overhead expenditure	185,808
Fixed overhead expenditure variance	14,192 (F)

(vi)

Budgeted production	2,500 barrels
Actual production	2,400 barrels
Volume variance in barrels	100 barrels (A)
× standard fixed overhead absorption rate per barrel*	× £80
Fixed overhead volume variance	£8,000 (A)

* = budgeted fixed overheads ÷ budgeted production = £200,000 ÷ 2,500 = £80

(vii)

Budgeted machine hours	20,000 hrs
Actual machine hours	18,960 hrs
Capacity variance in hours	1,040 hrs (A)
× standard fixed overhead absorption rate per machine hour (per (a)(vii))	× £10
Fixed overhead capacity variance	£10,400 (A)

(viii)

2,400 barrels should have taken (× 8 hrs per (a)(vi))	19,200 hrs
but did take	18,960 hrs
Efficiency variance in hours	240 hrs (F)
× standard fixed overhead absorption rate per machine hour	× £10
Fixed overhead efficiency variance	£2,400 (F)

(c) **Standard costing reconciliation statement week ended 30 November 20X2**

Standard absorption cost of actual operations (£146.50 (per (a)(viii))× 2,400)

	£ (A)	£ (F)	£ 351,600
Variances			
Material price	1,152		
Material usage		4,080	
Labour rate	1,008		
Labour efficiency	2,880		
Fixed overhead expenditure		14,192	
Fixed overhead capacity	10,400		
Fixed overhead efficiency		2,400	
	15,440	20,672	5,232 (F)
Actual absorption cost of actual operations			346,368

Task 1.2

Memo

To: Anthony Bush, financial controller

From: Trainee accounting technician

Date 17 December 20X2

Subject: **Standard material prices**

(a) (i) **Calculation of forecast average trend price**

The way in which the average trend price is **currently calculated** produces what is known as a **simple average**. This would be a **valid** average trend price if the **same quantities of material were purchased in each quarter**. Given that **production volume varies** throughout the year, however, more material will be purchased at some prices than at other prices. The **trend prices** therefore need to be **weighted** by the quantities purchased per quarter in order to derive a valid average trend price.

(ii) **Inclusion of seasonal variations in standard prices**

If variance analysis is to provide **valid control information** for management, standards need to be as **accurate** and as **up-to-date** as possible. Standards based on a trend value alone are not as accurate as those which also incorporate any seasonal variation in price that exists. Given that the **seasonal variations** are a **significant 20%** of the trend value at certain points in the year, an **adverse variance** could well be **reported**, say, simply **because the standard was inaccurate** rather than because of inefficiencies in purchasing.

(b) **Revised standard cost of material per litre**

Forecast trend value per litre for week ended 30 November 20X2	£10
Seasonal variation = + 20% = 20% × £10	£2
Revised standard cost per litre	£12

(c) **Subdivision of the material price variance**

	£	£
11,520 litres were expected to have cost (at the original standard of £8.50)	97,920	
but should then have been expected to cost (at the revised standard of £12)	138,240	
Variance due to difference between original and revised standards		40,320 (A)
11,520 litres should have cost, if the revised standard of £12 had been used	138,240	
but did cost	99,072	
Variance due to difference between the actual cost and revised standard cost		39,168 (F)
Total material price variance		1,152 (A)

SECTION 2

Tutorial note. Some of the performance indicators you were asked to calculate in task 2.1, such as average age of debtors, could relate to any number of scenarios, while others were specific to the type of scenario, such as number of teachers in the school. Points to note include:

- Return on net assets is the same as return on capital employed. 'Net assets and capital employed describe the same phenomenon but from different sides of the balance sheet.' (Assessor's report)

- Parts (g) and (h) could alternatively be calculated by dividing the number of children in the school (from (e)) by the staff to pupil ratio.

- The average age of creditors should be based on power and housekeeping costs only.

Part (e) was probably the most problematic in task 2.2. Over the year the cash balance would increase by the cash received and decrease by the expenses paid. The cash received during the year 31/08/X3 would include the opening debtors and the year's fee income less the closing debtors. This is effectively the fee income plus the difference between opening and closing debtors.

Likewise the cash paid is the total expenses in the operating statement less the non-cash expense of depreciation and adjusted by the difference between opening and closing creditors.

In his report on task 2.3, the assessor confirmed that candidates were not penalised if the figures used from previous tasks were incorrect.

It is vital that you know the essential difference between productivity and efficiency, and that you can identify appropriate measures. Not only are the concepts central to Unit 8, but they have been assessed on several occasions already.

Task 2.1

(a) **Operating surplus as a percentage of fee income**

= (£35,200 ÷ £1,760,000) × 100% = 2%

(b) **Return on net assets** = operating surplus ÷ net assets

= (£35,200 ÷ £7,040,000) × 100% = 0.5%

(c) **Average age of debtors in months** = (debtors ÷ fee income) × 12 months

= (£440,000 ÷ £1,760,000) × 12 = 3 months

(d) **Average age of creditors in months** = (creditors ÷ cost of power and housekeeping) × 12 months

= (£96,000 ÷ £(128,000 + 160,000)) × 12 = 4 months

(e) **Number of children in the school** = fee income ÷ fee per child

= £1,760,000 ÷ £22,000 = 80

BPP
PROFESSIONAL EDUCATION

(f)   **Occupancy rate of the school** = (number of children in the school ÷ maximum number) × 100%

= (80 ÷ 100) × 100% = 80%

(g)   **Number of teachers in the school** = total cost of teachers' salaries ÷ average salary per teacher

= £600,000 ÷ £30,000 = 20

(h)   **Number of nursing and support staff in the school** = total cost of nursing and support staff salaries ÷ average salary per member of staff

= £480,000 ÷ £12,000 = 40

(i)   **Total of cash-based expenses** = total expenses − depreciation

= (£1,724,800 − £236,800) = £1,488,000

(j)   **Number of months that cash-based expenses could be paid from the cash balance** = cash balance ÷ average monthly cash-based expenses

= £62,000 ÷ (£1,488,000 ÷ 12) = £62,000 ÷ £124,000 = 0.5 month

Task 2.2

(a)   **Forecast operating statement – year to 31 August 20X3**

	£	£
Fee income (W1)		1,936,000
Teacher salaries (W2)	660,000	
Nursing and support staff salaries (W3)	528,000	
Administrative expenses (W4)	120,000	
Power (W4)	128,000	
Housekeeping (W4)	160,000	
Depreciation (W4)	236,800	
Total expenses		1,832,800
Operating surplus		103,200

Workings

1   Number of children increased by 10% × original fee per child = 80 × 110% × £22,000 = £1,936,000

2   (Revised number of children/staff to student ratio) × average salary per teacher = ((80 × 110%)/4) × £30,000 = £660,000

3   (Revised number of children/staff to student ratio) × average salary − ((80 × 110%)/2) × £12,000 = £528,000

4   No change

(b)   **Year-end debtors**

At the year end, fees from the last 1.5 months of the year will be outstanding (as debtors will be allowed 1.5 months to pay). This represents 1.5/12 of revised annual fee income = 1.5/12 × £1,936,000 = £242,000.

(c)   **Year-end creditors**

At the year end, power and housekeeping costs incurred in the last two months of the year will not have been paid (as the average of creditors will be two months). This represents 2/12 of power and housekeeping expenditure = 2/12 × £(128,000 + 160,000) = £48,000.

(d)

	£
NBV of fixed assets 31.8.X2	6,634,000
Depreciation for year to 31.8.X3	(236,800)
NBV of fixed assets 31.8.X3	6,397,200

(e)

	£
Cash balance 31.8.X3	62,000
Add: operating surplus (see (a))	103,200
depreciation (non cash)	236,800
change in debtors (£(440,000 – 242,000))	198,000
Less: change in creditors (£(96,000 – 48,000))	(48,000)
Cash balance at 31.8.X3	552,000

(f)

	£
NBV of fixed assets	6,397,200
Debtors	242,000
Cash	552,000
Creditors	(48,000)
Net assets 31.8.X3	7,143,200

Task 2.3

Memo

To: Carol Jones, chief executive of Care4

From: Management accountant

Date   23 September 20X2

Subject: **Action plan and targets**

(a)   **Forecast information for year ended 31 August 20X3 assuming the action plan is achieved**

(i)   **Operating surplus as a percentage of fee income** (from task 2.2 (a)) = (£103,200 ÷ £1,936,000) × 100% = 5.33%

(ii)   **Return on net assets** = (operating surplus ÷ net assets (from task 2.2 (f)) × 100% = (£103,200 ÷ £7,143,200) × 100% = 1.44%

(iii)   **Cash available after buying the new equipment**

	£
Forecast cash balance at 31.8.X3 (task 2.2 (e))	552,000
Purchase of new equipment	(400,000)
Forecast cash balance after buying new equipment	152,000

(iv) **Number of months that cash-based expenses could be paid from the cash balance after allowing for buying the new equipment**

= forecast cash balance after buying new equipment ÷ forecast average monthly cash-based expenses

= £152,000 ÷ (forecast total expenses – depreciation) /12)

= £152,000 ÷ (£(1,832,800 (from task 2.2(a)) – 236,800)/12)

= £152,000 ÷ £133,000 = 1.14 months

(b) **Does the action plan achieve the proposed targets?**

Target	Actual results Year to 31.8.X2	Forecast results following action plan Year to 31.8.X3	Target achieved?
• Operating surplus as a % of fee income to double	2%	5.33%	Yes
• Return on net assets to double	0.5%	1.44%	Yes
• Sufficient cash to pay for new equipment			Yes (Surplus of £152,000)
• Cash balance equivalent to one month's cash –based expenses		1.14 months	Yes

The action plan **achieves all** four of the proposed **targets**.

(c) **The difference between productivity and efficiency**

Productivity is a measure of **output relative** to some form of **input**.

- The **output** might be widgets produced in a factory, meals served in a restaurant or telephone calls answered in a call centre.

- The **input** might be the workforce, raw materials or machinery.

Efficiency also looks at **output relative to input but** it is not the same as productivity because the **output** is considered **in terms of financial gain or value** to the organisation.

In many organisations the **value** generated is normally some kind of **profit**.

(d) **Increased productivity as a result of implementing the action plan**

The action plan has no effect on the value of land and buildings (output) but the number of children is set to increase (input). The school's land and buildings will therefore be used more intensively.

UNIT 9 FULL ASSESSMENT 1 (JUNE 2002)

NVQ/SVQ in ACCOUNTING, LEVEL 4

UNIT 9

CONTRIBUTING to the PLANNING and CONTROL of RESOURCES (PCR)

SUGGESTED ANSWERS

UNIT 9 (PCR) Full Assessment 1 : mapping against Standards

Performance Criteria / Range Statement	Task 1.1	Task 1.2	Task 2.1	Task 2.2
9.1 Prepare forecasts of income/expenditure				
A Identify relevant data for projections				✓
B Communicate with individuals				✓
C Prepare forecasts, clear format, assumptions etc				
D Review/revise validity of forecasts in light of changes				✓
9.1 Range Statement				
Data				✓
Forecasts				
Projections				✓
9.2 Prepare draft budget proposals				
A Present clear draft budget proposals	✓	✓		
B Verify consistency, relevant data and assumptions	✓	✓		
C Break down budgets into periods				
D Communicate with budget holders				
9.2 Range statement				
Types of budget	✓	✓		
Data	✓	✓		
9.3 Monitor performance against budgets				
A Check and reconcile budget figures			✓	
B Code/allocate to responsibility centres				
C Identify variances/prepare relevant reports			✓	
D Discuss significant variances/help managers take action				
9.3 Range statement				
Types of budget			✓	
Responsibility centres				
Variances			✓	

Section 1

> **Tutorial note.** Task 1.1 (a), the preparation of production budgets, contained two common features of Unit 9 budget preparation tasks: finished goods stock given in terms of numbers of days' sales, and wastage. We have provided a detailed working for the first wastage calculation as this is an area many students find tricky. It is also covered in some depth in the BPP Interactive Text for Units 8 and 9.
>
> The cost of labour budget (task 1.1 (e)) should not be based on budgeted labour hours as the employees receive a guaranteed weekly wage irrespective of the hours worked.
>
> While the majority of candidates prepared well-written, perfect answers to task 1.1, the assessor listed a number of errors made by some candidates in his report.
>
> - Closing stocks were sometimes deducted from sales volumes and opening stocks added [in the preparation of the production budget]. The correct approach is to add closing stocks and deduct opening stocks.
>
> - Stocks were sometimes totally ignored.
>
> - Faulty production was sometimes deducted from good production to derive gross production. Of course, it should be added.
>
> - Material requirements were unnecessarily worked out for each product. This isn't an error, merely a waste of time. Adjusting both workings for given levels of opening and closing stocks is a double-counting error, however.
>
> - Labour requirements were sometimes based on sales volume rather than production volume.
>
> In task 1.2 (a) you had to check the implications of both constraints and work out which was the one that effectively limited production. The quickest way to do part (b) was simply to add the additional purchases to the purchases budget you had derived in task 1.1.

Task 1.1

(a)   Production = sales + closing stock – opening stock.

Production budget for Antelopes for the four weeks ending 26 July 20X2

	Units
Sales	141,120
Closing stock (W1)	42,336
Opening stock	(30,576)
Good production required	152,880
Faulty production (W2)	3,120
Gross production	156,000

Workings

1.   Demand in period 9 = 141,120 × 150% = 211,680
        Number of days in period 9 = 4 × 5 = 20
        Closing stock in period 8 = 4 days' sales in period 9
                                = 4/20 × 211,680 = 42,336

2.   Faulty production = 2% (or 2/100) of gross production
        ∴ 100/2 × faulty production = gross production   (1)

        98% of gross production is good
        ∴ good production = 98% (or 98/100) of gross production
        ∴ 100/98 × good production = gross production   (2)

        Equating (1) and (2):

        100/2 × faulty production = 100/98 × good production
        ∴ Faulty production = 2/98 × good production
                            = 2/98 × 152,880 = 3,120

Production budget for Bears for the four weeks ending 26 July 20X2

	Units
Sales	95,000
Closing stock (W1)	30,875
Opening stock	(25,175)
Good production required	100,700
Faulty production (W2)	5,300
Gross production	106,000

Workings

1.   Demand in period 9 = 95,000 × 130% = 123,500
        Closing stock in period 8 = 5 days' sales in period 9
                              = 5/20 × 123,500 = 30,875

2.   Faulty production = 5/95 × good production
                         = 5/95 × 100,700 = 5,300

(b)   Material purchases = materials used in production + closing stock – opening stock

Material purchases budget for the four weeks ending 26 July 20X2

	Kgs
Materials used in production	
Antelopes: 156,000 (from (a)) × 0.75 kgs	117,000
Bears: 106,000 (from (a)) × 0.50 kgs	53,000
	170,000
Closing stock	40,000
Opening stock	(30,000)
Material purchases	180,000

(c)   **Cost of material purchases budget for the four weeks ending 26 July 20X2**   = 180,000 kgs × £8
                                                               = £1,440,000

(d) **Labour budget in hours for the four weeks ending 26 July 20X2**

	Hrs
Hours for Antelope production: 156,000 × 0.1 hrs	15,600
Hours for Bear production: 106,000 × 0.05 hrs	5,300
	20,900

(e) **Cost of labour budget for the four weeks ending 26 July 20X2**

= 140 employees × 4 weeks × guaranteed weekly wage of £228 = £127,680

Task 1.2

(a) **Labour**

Number of available labour hours in period 8 = 140 employees × 4 weeks × 38 hours = 21,280

Budgeted labour hours required in period 8 (from task 1.1 (d)) = 20,900

Spare labour hours in period 8 = 21,280 – 20,900 = 380

In 380 hours, an extra 380/0.1 = 3,800 Antelopes could be produced.

Powdered rock

3,000 extra kgs of powdered rock could be purchased in period 8.

3,000/0.75 = 4,000 Antelopes would be made from this extra material.

Limiting factor

Extra production is therefore limited by the availability of labour to 3,800 Antelopes.

2% of production is faulty, however.

∴ 3,800 × 98% = 3,724 fault-free Antelopes could be produced.

(b) **Revised material purchases budget for the four weeks ending 26 July 20X2**

	Kgs
Original budgeted material purchases (from task 1.1 (c))	180,000
Additional material purchases required for 3,800 Antelopes (3,800 × 0.75 kgs)	2,850
	182,850

Section 2

Tutorial note. Task 2.1 was straightforward – there were no hidden complexities. The vast majority of candidates, according to the assessor, therefore produced excellent answers. Just because the assessor has introduced complexities into previous assessment tasks on flexible budgeting, it does not follow that these will always be present. You should use previous tasks for revision purposes, not just for question-spotting purposes.

It was vital to read the requirements of task 2.2. For (a) we have provided more than four techniques for completeness purposes. Don't write everything you know about forecasting, just answer the task.

Task 2.1

(a)   (i)   Budgeted variable cost per drum of material A = £240,000/80,000 = £3

       (ii)   Budgeted variable cost per drum of material B = £480,000/80,000 = £6

       (iii)   Budgeted variable cost per drum of material C = £320,000/80,000 = £4

       (iv)   Budgeted variable cost per drum of power = (£270,000 – fixed cost element of £110,000)/80,000 = £2

       (v)   Budgeted variable cost per drum of water = £(122,000 – fixed cost element of £90,000)/80,000 = £0.40

(b)   **Alderford Ltd**

Flexible budget statement for 12 months ended 31 May 20X2

	Flexed budget	Actual results	Variances
Number of drums produced and sold	125,000	125,000	-
	£'000	£'000	£'000
Turnover	3,750 (W1)	4,000	250 (F)
Variable costs			
Material A	375 (W2)	425	50 (A)
Material B	750 (W3)	680	70 (F)
Material C	500 (W4)	500	-
Semi-variable costs			
Power	360 (W5)	440	80 (A)
Water	140 (W6)	200	60 (A)
Stepped costs			
Supervision	260 (W7)	258	2 (F)
Fixed costs			
Rent and rates	250 (W8)	250	-
Lighting and heating	120 (W8)	118	2 (F)
Administrative expenses	200 (W8)	240	40 (A)
	2,955	3,111	156 (A)
Operating profit	795	889	94 (F)

Workings

1   Budgeted selling price per drum = £2,400,000/80,000 = £30
       Budget for sales of 125,000 drums = £30 × 125,000 = £3,750,000
       Alternatively: Flexed budget = 125/80 × £2,400,000 = £3,750,000

2   Budget for production of 125,000 drums = £3 (from (a)(i)) × 125,000 = £375,000
       Alternatively: Flexed budget = 125/80 × £240,000 = £375,000

3   Budget for production of 125,000 drums = £6 (from (a)(ii)) × 125,000 = £750,000
       Alternatively: Flexed budget = 125/80 × £480,000 = £750,000

4   Budget for production 125,000 drums = £4 (from (a)(iii)) × 125,000 = £500,000
       Alternatively: Flexed budget = 125/80 × £320,000 = £500,000

5   Budget for production of 125,000 drums = fixed cost of £110,000 + variable cost for 125,000 drums
       = £(110,000 + (£2 (from (a)(iv)) × 125,000) = £360,000

6   Budget for production of 125,000 drums = fixed cost of £90,000 + variable cost for 125,000 drums
       = £(90,000 + (£0.40 (from (a)(v)) × 125,000) = £140,000

7   Production of 125,000 drums requires 125,000/10,000 = 12.5 supervisors. Thirteen supervisors will
       therefore be required.

       Original budget based on 80,000/10,000 = 8 supervisors

       ∴ Budgeted cost per supervisor = £160,000/8 = £20,000

       ∴ Budget for production of 125,000 drums = 13 × £20,000 = £260,000

       Alternatively: Flexed budget = 13/8 × £160,000 = £260,000

8   Fixed costs remain the same regardless of the budgeted level of output.

Task 2.2

Memo

To: James Alexander, managing director of Alderford Ltd
From: Accounting technician
Date: 31 July 20X2
Subject: **Sales forecasting**

Following our recent meeting, I set out below the information you requested.

(a)   **Forecasting techniques that Alderford Ltd could currently use**

     (i)   **Sales personnel** could be asked to provide forecasts. The sales team should have up-to-date first hand knowledge of current sales patterns and will have a 'feel for the market'.

     (ii)   **Survey/market research methods** could be used (especially to gain information about development of new markets). Information could be obtained from the building industry about anticipated levels of new building, for example.

     (iii)   **Secondary sources of data** for the industry and/or for other industries could be investigated, although the data will have been collected for another purpose and so its limitations will not be known.

     (iv)   **Customers** could be consulted about their anticipated requirements in the next 12 months. This can be particularly helpful if there are just a small number of customers.

     (v)   Demand could be considered in terms of the **product life cycle**. This gives some indication of likely sales volumes given the stage of the product's sales history.

     (vi)   By following what is happening to a **leading indicator**, a variable which anticipates the trend of another variable, information about likely demand for Alderford Ltd's product may be provided. For example, a rapid rise in house prices might indicate an increased demand for new houses, in which Alderford Ltd's chemical could be used.

(b)   **Forecasting techniques Alderford Ltd is currently unable to use**

Because the company has only been operating for just over a year, there is insufficient past sales data available upon which to base forecasts. Techniques such as linear regression analysis and time series analysis which involve extrapolating a trend based on past data could therefore provide misleading results.

(c)   **Most appropriate forecasting techniques for the three sales strategies**

     (i)   **More sales to existing customers**. The most accurate forecasts would probably be based on information from the customers themselves or the sales team.

     (ii)   **Sales to new customers in the building industry**. The new customers need to be identified before forecasting can take place, so some form of market research could be used to determine who they might be.

     (iii)   **Development of new markets**. Again some form of market research could prove more useful. Focus groups could be used to determine the acceptability of the product in any new market, while surveys could provide information on the potential size of markets.

UNIT 9 FULL ASSESSMENT 2 (DECEMBER 2002)

NVQ/SVQ in ACCOUNTING, LEVEL 4

UNIT 9

CONTRIBUTING to the PLANNING and CONTROL of RESOURCES (PCR)

SUGGESTED ANSWERS

UNIT 9 (PCR) Full Assessment 2: mapping against Standards

Performance Criteria / Range Statement		Task 1.1	Task 1.2	Task 2.1	Task 2.2
9.1 Prepare forecasts of income/expenditure					
A	Identify relevant data for projections				
B	Communicate with individuals				
C	Prepare forecasts, clear format, assumptions etc				
D	Review/revise validity of forecasts in light of changes				
9.1 Range Statement					
Data					
Forecasts					
Projections					
9.2 Prepare draft budget proposals					
A	Present clear draft budget proposals	✓	✓		
B	Verify consistency, relevant data and assumptions	✓	✓		
C	Break down budgets into periods	✓	✓		
D	Communicate with budget holders		✓		
9.2 Range statement					
Types of budget		✓	✓		
Data		✓	✓		
9.3 Monitor performance against budgets					
A	Check and reconcile budget figures			✓	✓
B	Code/allocate to responsibility centres				
C	Identify variances/prepare relevant reports			✓	✓
D	Discuss significant variances/help managers take action				
9.3 Range statement					
Types of budget				✓	✓
Responsibility centres					
Variances				✓	

Tutorial note. Take very careful note of the following comment made by the assessor in his report on this exam.

' ... lack of appropriate workings to answers and how this was a high risk strategy. Despite this warning having been given on many previous occasions, some candidates are still ignoring the advice. On the evidence of this and other PAR [now PCR] examinations, it is the weaker candidate who often omits workings – the very candidate who needs to accumulate credit for valid processes. Without workings, and with imperfect answers, there is often no evidence. And without evidence, it is not possible to award credit.'

So take a look at the level of detail in our workings. You need to strike a happy medium between none at all and too much – so that you don't waste time writing out details that are unnecessary.

Section 1

Tutorial note. Do you still have problems accounting for wastage? It comes up so often in assessments that you **must** be able to deal with it. Look back to Chapter 9 of the BPP Interactive Text for Units 8 and 9 for a full explanation of what to do if you are unsure of the technique.

Don't forget that the employees are on a guaranteed wage for 240 hours work each per period and so your labour budget needs to show the overtime hours required.

According to the assessor, a common error in task 1.1 was to prepare budgets for the aggregate of the four periods. Always read the task requirements carefully as this was specifically not required. Candidates who did this lost substantial credit.

Task 1.1

(a) **Production budget in Zetas**

	Period 1 Zetas	Period 2 Zetas	Period 3 Zetas	Period 4 Zetas
Sales	14,400	15,000	15,600	16,800
Closing stocks (W)	6,000	6,240	6,720	6,720
Opening stocks	(5,760)	(6,000)	(6,240)	(6,720)
Production	14,640	15,240	16,080	16,800

Working

There are 5 days × 6 weeks = 30 working days in each period.

Closing stocks must therefore be 12/30 of the sales volume of the next period.

Sample: in period 1, closing stocks = 12/30 × 15,000 = 6,000 Zetas.

(b) **Purchases budget in litres**

	Period 1 Litres	Period 2 Litres	Period 3 Litres	Period 4 Litres
Required for good production (W1)	117,120	121,920	128,640	134,400
Plus: wastage (W2)	4,880	5,080	5,360	5,600
Required for gross production	122,000	127,000	134,000	140,000
Purchased under contract	122,000	127,000	130,000	130,000
Purchased on open market	–	–	4,000	10,000
	122,000	127,000	134,000	140,000

Workings

1 Production level × 8 litres

2 4/96 × litres required for good production

(c) **Cost of purchases budget**

	Period 1 £'000	Period 2 £'000	Period 3 £'000	Period 4 £'000
Purchases under contract at £7 per litre	854	889	910	910
Purchases on open market at £12 per litre	–	–	48	120
	854	889	958	1,030

(d) **Labour hours required for budgeted production**

	Period 1	Period 2	Period 3	Period 4
Gross production levels (units)	14,640	15,240	16,080	16,800
× two labour hrs per unit	× 2	× 2	× 2	× 2
Labour hours required	29,280	30,480	32,160	33,600
Guaranteed hours (W)	31,200	31,200	31,200	31,200
Overtime hours required	–	–	960	2,400

Working

130 employees × 6 weeks × 40 hrs per week

(e) **Cost of labour budget**

	Period 1 £	Period 2 £	Period 3 £	Period 4 £
Guaranteed wages (W1)	187,200	187,200	187,200	187,200
Overtime (W2)	–	–	6,720	16,800
	187,200	187,200	193,920	204,000

Workings

1 130 employees × 6 weeks × £240 = £187,200

2 Overtime hours from (d) × £7

Task 1.2

Tutorial note. Task 1.2 is quite tricky. Starting with the material purchases budget you need to optimise the purchasing so that, if possible, the maximum amount of material is purchased under contract. Raw material has to be used in the period in which it is purchased and so the production budget has to be based on the material available each period (per the purchases budget). Don't forget to take account of wastage. This time you are starting with the **total** material available (including that which will be wasted), and so the wastage is 4% of the total.

(a)　(i)　**Purchases budget in litres**

	Period 1 Litres	Period 2 Litres	Period 3 Litres	Period 4 Litres
Material required (task 1.1(b))	122,000	127,000	134,000	140,000
Material available	130,000	130,000	130,000	130,000
Surplus/(shortage)	8,000	3,000	(4,000)	(10,000)
Transfers to period 1	(8,000)	–	4,000	4,000
Transfers to period 2	–	(3,000)	–	3,000
Surplus/(shortage) against maximum	–			
Available	–	–	–	(3,000)
Revised requirement	130,000	130,000	130,000	133,000
Purchases under contract	130,000	130,000	130,000	130,000
Purchases on open market	–	–	–	3,000

(ii)　**Cost of purchases budget**

	Period 1 £'000	Period 2 £'000	Period 3 £'000	Period 4 £'000
Purchases under contract at £7 per Litre	910	910	910	910
Purchases on open market at £12 per Litre	–	–	–	36
	910	910	910	946

(iii)　**Production budget in Zetas**

	Period 1 Litres	Period 2 Litres	Period 3 Litres	Period 4 Litres
Revised material available	130,000	130,000	130,000	133,000
Less: wastage (W1)	(5,200)	(5,200)	(5,200)	(5,320)
Material available for production	124,800	124,800	124,800	127,680
Production in Zetas (W2)	15,600	15,600	15,600	15,960

Workings

1　Wastage is 4% of total material available

2　Material available ÷ 8 litres per Zeta

(iv) **Labour hours required for the revised budgeted production**

	Period 1	Period 2	Period 3	Period 4
Budgeted production (Zetas)	15,600	15,600	15,600	15,960
× two hours per Zeta	× 2	× 2	× 2	× 2
Hours required	31,200	31,200	31,200	31,920
	Hrs	Hrs	Hrs	Hrs
Guaranteed hours (from 1.1 (d))	31,200	31,200	31,200	31,200
Overtime hours	–	–	–	720
	31,200	31,200	31,200	31,920

(v) **Cost of labour budget**

	Period 1	Period 2	Period 3	Period 4
	£	£	£	£
Guaranteed wages (from 1.1 (e))	187,200	187,200	187,200	187,200
Overtime (at £7 per hour)	–	–	–	5,040
	187,200	187,200	187,200	192,240

(b) **Memo**

To: Production director
From: Management accountant
Date: 20 December 20X2
Subject: **Revised budgets for periods 1 to 4**

As a result of our conversation concerning amendments to the organisation's policy on finished goods, I have prepared revised budgets.

(i) **Total cost savings possible from revising the budgets**

Savings in material costs

Relaxing the policy on finished goods stocks means that the maximum amount of material can be purchased at the contracted price of £7 per litre and a reduced amount purchased at the open market price of £12 per litre.

	£
Original budgeted cost of purchases (W1)	3,731,000
Revised budgeted cost of purchases (W2)	3,676,000
Saving	55,000

Savings in labour costs

Given the revised production budget which follows as a result of the rescheduling of purchases, the hours paid under guaranteed wages can be used more effectively, with the result that fewer overtime hours are needed.

	£
Original budgeted overtime cost (W3)	23,520
Revised budgeted overtime cost (W4)	5,040
Saving	18,480

Total saving = £(55,000 + 18,480) = £73,480

Workings

1   Per task 1.1 (c)   £'000 (854 + 889 + 958 + 1,030)

2   Per task 1.2 (a)(ii)   £'000 (910 + 910 + 910 + 946)

3   Per task 1.1 (e)   £(6,720 + 16,800)

4   Per task 1.2 (a)(v)

(ii)   **Possible costs necessary to achieve the savings**

The revised budgets require additional Zetas to be produced in periods 1 and 2 and fewer in periods 3 and 4. This might incur additional **storage costs**.

The company might also incur additional **financing costs** as a result of producing in excess of demand in periods 1 and 2.

Section 2

Task 2.1

(a) (i) **Budgeted selling price per Omicron** = original budgeted turnover ÷ original budgeted sales volume

= £6,400,000 ÷ 400,000 = £16

(ii) **Budgeted variable cost of material per Omicron** = original budgeted material expenditure ÷ original budgeted production volume

= £1,600,000 ÷ 400,000 = £4

(iii) **Budgeted variable cost of labour per Omicron** = original budgeted labour expenditure ÷ original budgeted production volume

= £2,000,000 ÷ 400,000 = £5

(iv) **Budgeted variable cost of electricity per Omicron**

Using the **incremental method**

Incremental volume (440,000 − 400,000)	40,000 units
Incremental cost (£'000 (960 − 880))	£80,000
Variable cost per unit (£80,000 ÷ 40,000 units)	£2

(v) **Budgeted fixed cost of electricity**

Variable cost for 400,000 units	=	400,000 × £2 (from (iv)) = £800,000
Total cost for 400,000 units	=	£880,000
∴ Fixed cost = total cost − variable cost	=	£80,000

(b) (i) **Actual variable cost of material per Omicron** = actual material expenditure ÷ actual production volume = £2,520,000 ÷ 600,000 = £4.20

(ii) **Actual variable cost of labour per Omicron** = actual labour expenditure ÷ actual production volume = £3,180,000 ÷ 600,000 = £5.30

(iii) **Actual variable cost of electricity per Omicron** = actual electricity expenditure ÷ actual production volume = £1,200,000 ÷ 600,000 = £2

(c) **Actual expenses: year ended 30 November 20X2**

	£'000	£'000
Variable costs		
Material (450,000 × £4.20)	1,890	
Labour (450,000 × 5.30)	2,385	
Electricity (450,000 × £2)	900	
		5,175
Fixed costs		
Electricity	-	
Depreciation	300	
Maintenance	200	
Other fixed costs	800	
		1,300
		6,475

(d) **Flexible budget statement**

Year ended 30 November 20X2

	Flexed budget £'000	Actual result £'000	Variances £'000
Turnover	7,200 (W1)	6,840	360 (A)
Variable costs			
Material	1,800 (W2)	1,890	90 (A)
Labour	2,250 (W3)	2,385	135 (A)
Electricity	900 (W4)	900	–
	4,950	5,175	225 (A)
Contribution	2,250	1,665	585 (A)
Fixed costs			
Electricity	80 (W5)		80 (F)
Depreciation	500 (W6)	300	200 (F)
Maintenance	300 (W6)	200	100 (F)
Other fixed costs	700 (W6)	800	100 (A)
	1,580	1,300	280 (F)
Profit	670	365	305 (A)

Workings

1 £16 ((a)(i)) × 450,000 = £7,200,000

2 £4 ((a)(ii)) × 450,000 = £1,800,000

3 £5 ((a)(iii)) × 450,000 = £2,250,000

4 £2 ((a)(iv)) × 450,000 = £900,000

5 Per (a)(v)

6 Given in task data (do not change with volume)

Task 2.2

Memo

To: Robert Maxton, managing director of Omicron division
From: Management accountant
Date: 20 December 20X2
Subject: **Differences between budgeted and actual profit – year ended 30 November 20X2**

A little over a year ago you imposed a budget on the senior management in your company. The original actual results show a profit in excess of even your imposed budget.

(a) **Situations when an imposed budget might be suitable**

There are times when it might be preferable to impose a budget rather than to prepare one with the participation of senior managers.

- If budgets need to be set quickly

- If management do not have the necessary budgeting skills
- If managers are likely to include budgetary slack in their budget (overestimate costs and/or underestimate income)
- If there is a lack of goal congruence (ie if management's goals do not coincide with organisational goals)

(b) **Reasons why original actual operating profit was greater than the revised budget's operating profit**

(1) Actual production was greater than sales volume and so there was closing stock and, as the actual results were prepared on an absorption costing basis, some of the actual fixed overheads incurred were carried forward in the closing stock value to be written off against profit in future periods. There was no closing stock in the revised budget and hence all fixed costs were set against profit.

(2) Actual depreciation charged was less than planned.

(3) Actual maintenance costs were less than planned.

(4) The electricity supplier eliminated the fixed charge and so overall electricity costs fell.

(c) **Why original and flexible budget statement actual operating profits differ**

The original actual results were prepared on an absorption costing basis, the revised results on a marginal costing basis.

As production was greater than sales, some units were held in closing stock. When absorption costing is used, the units in closing stock are valued at full cost (ie including absorbed fixed overhead) and so the fixed overhead included in the units in closing stock is not charged against the current period's profit but against the profit when the units are sold. With marginal costing, however, units in closing stock are valued at marginal cost only. Fixed costs are charged in their entirety in the period in which they are incurred.

There was therefore a higher charge for fixed overheads when marginal costing was used in the flexible budget statement and hence the profit was less.

Answers to AAT
Specimen Exams

AAT SPECIMEN EXAM PAPER – 2003 STANDARDS

NVQ/SVQ in ACCOUNTING, LEVEL 4

UNIT 8

CONTRIBUTING to the MANAGEMENT of PERFORMANCE and the ENHANCEMENT of VALUE (PEV)

SUGGESTED ANSWERS

These answers have been prepared by BPP Publishing Ltd.

UNIT 8 (PEV) Pilot paper : mapping against Standards

Performance Criteria / Range Statement		Task 1.1	Task 1.2	Task 2.1	Task 2.2
8.1 Collect, analyse cost information					
A	Identify relevant information	✓	✓		
B	Monitor and analyse trends	✓			
C	Compare trends and identify implications				
D	Compare standard and actual costs and analyse variances	✓			
E	Analyse accounting policies on reported costs	✓	✓		
F	Consult staff re trends and variances		✓		
G	Reports summarising data, presentation and trends	✓			
8.1 Range Statement					
Information					
Methods of summarising data			✓		
Methods of presenting information in reports		✓	✓		
Variance analysis		✓			
Build-up of costs		✓			
8.2 Monitor performance/ recommendations					
A	Analyse routine cost reports, implications				✓
B	Prepare/ monitor performance indicators, improvements			✓	✓
C	Consult specialists, identify reduction of costs, value				✓
D	Exception reports	✓			
E	Make recommendations		✓		✓
8.2 Range statement					
Performance indicators				✓	
Recommendations					✓

SECTION 1

Task 1.1

> **Tutorial note**. Your calculations ((a)(i)) will show you that the number of compact discs issued to production was greater than the number actually manufactured. You therefore need to base the standard cost of actual production ((a)(ix)) on a production level of 96,000 – not on the number of compact discs issued to production. The easiest way to calculate this is to use the standard cost of producing 800 compact discs, and multiply this by 96,000/800.
>
> For (b)(vi) you needed to calculate a standard absorption rate per compact disc. This can be found from the absorption rate per labour hour ÷ number of compact discs produced in an hour.
>
> Always check that the sum of the capacity and efficiency variances equals the volume variance.
>
> Don't forget that you should include either the fixed overhead volume variance *or* the capacity and efficiency variances in the reconciliation statement, but not both. The assessor mentioned this in his report.

(a)   (i)   **Actual number of blank compact discs issued to production**

Actual cost of blank compact discs issued to production = actual price paid per blank compact disc × actual number of blank compact discs issued to production

∴ £20,790 = £0.21 × number issued

∴ Number issued = £20,790/£0.21 = 99,000

(ii)   **Budgeted machine hours of the department**

For every eight labour hours worked, one machine hour is worked.

Budgeted labour hours = 880

∴ Budgeted machine hours = 880/8 = 110

(iii)   **Standard number of compact discs produced per labour hour**

800 compact discs are produced in eight labour hours

∴ 800/8 = 100 compact discs are produced in one labour hour

(iv)   **Standard labour hours produced**

96,000 compact discs were manufactured.

Standard number of compact discs produced per labour hour (from (iii)) = 100

∴ 96,000/100 = 960 standard labour hours were produced.

(v)   **Budgeted fixed overheads of the pressing department**

Budgeted total factory fixed costs = £33,000

Budgeted total factory labour hours = 1,320

Budgeted labour hours in the pressing department = 880 hrs

Overheads are apportioned on the basis of budgeted labour hours and so budgeted fixed overheads of the department = £33,000 × 880/1,320 = £22,000.

(vi)   **Actual fixed overheads of the pressing department**

Actual total fixed costs = £34,500

Overheads are again apportioned on the basis of budgeted labour hours (see (v) above) and so actual fixed overheads of the department = £34,500 × 880/1,320 = £23,000

(vii)   **Standard fixed overhead rate per labour hour**

Standard fixed overhead rate per machine hour = £200

Eight labour hours are worked for every machine hour

∴ Standard fixed overhead rate per labour hour = £200/8 = £25

(viii) **Actual cost of actual production, including fixed overheads**

	£
Blank compact discs	20,790
Labour	7,252
Fixed overheads (from (vi))	23,000
	51,042

(ix)   **Standard cost of actual production, including fixed overheads**

Standard cost of 800 compact discs = £416

∴ Standard cost of 96,000 CDs = (96,000/800) × £416 = £49,920

(b)   (i)   **Material price variance**

	£
99,000 (from (a)(i)) compact discs should have cost (× £0.20)	19,800
but did cost	20,790
	990 (A)

(ii)   **Material usage variance**

96,000 CDs manufactured should use (× 1)	96,000 CDs
bud did use (from (a)(i))	99,000 CDs
Variance in compact discs	3,000 CDs (A)
× standard cost per compact disc	× £0.20
	£600 (A)

(iii) **Labour rate variance**

	£
980 hours should have cost (× £7)	6,860
but did cost	7,252
	392 (A)

(iv) Labour efficiency variance

96,000 compact discs should have taken (÷ 100 (from (a)(iii)))	960 hrs
but did take	980 hrs
Variance in hours	20 hrs (A)
× standard rate per hour	× £7
	£140 (A)

(v) Fixed overhead expenditure variance

	£
Budgeted expenditure (from (a)(v))	22,000
Actual expenditure (from (a)(vi))	23,000
	1,000 (A)

(vi) Fixed overhead volume variance

Budgeted output (880 hrs × 100 (from (a)(iii)))	88,000
Actual output	96,000
Variance in compact discs	8,000 (F)
× standard absorption rate per CD	
(= £25 (from (a)(vii))/100 (from (a)(iii)))	× £0.25
	£2,000 (F)

(vii) Fixed overhead capacity variance

Budgeted hours	880 hrs
Actual hours	980 hrs
Variance in hours	100 hrs (F)
× standard absorption rate per hr (from (a)(vii))	× £25
	£2,500 (F)

(viii) Fixed overhead efficiency variance

This is the same as the labour efficiency variance in hrs	20 hrs (A)
× standard absorption rate per hr (from (a)(vii))	× £25
	£500 (A)

(c)   **Statement of reconciliation**
       Pressing department
       Week ended 14 November 2003

	(F) £	(A) £	£	
Standard absorption cost of actual production (from (a)(ix))			49,920	
Variances				
Material price		990		
Material usage		600		
Labour rate		392		
Labour efficiency		140		
Fixed overhead expenditure		1,000		
Fixed overhead capacity	2,500			
Fixed overhead efficiency		500		
	2,500	3,622	1,122	(A)
Actual absorption cost of actual production (from (a)(viii))			51,042	

Task 1.2

> **Tutorial note**. You may have been unable to see the link between the information provided in the data and task (c). You needed to refer back to the information in the data to task 1.1 and to your calculations for task 1.1 too.

Memo

To: Jennifer Oldham, managing director
From: Assistant management accountant
Date: 10 December 2003
Subject: Variances

(a)   **Investigating variances**

You suggested that, having established one possible reason for the material usage variance (scrapping of compact discs) and given the very low cost of blank compact discs, it might not be worth investigating other reasons for the occurrence of this variance.

Before a decision is made on whether or not to investigate a variance, there are a number of factors which should be considered, however.

(i)   **Materiality**

Because a standard cost is really only an average expected cost, small variations between actual and standard are bound to occur and are unlikely to be significant. A variance might therefore only be investigated if it is above a minimum absolute amount or above a minimum percentage amount.

(ii)   **Controllability**

The causes of some variances are outside the control of the manager to whom the variance is reported. If there is a general worldwide price increase in the price of blank compact discs, there is nothing that can be done by the management of Disc Makers Ltd to control this. Uncontrollable variances call for a change in the standard rather than an investigation into the past.

(iii) **Variance trend**

Although small variations in a single period are unlikely to be significant, small variations that occur consistently may need more attention.

(iv) **Cost**

If the cost of investigation into the cause of the variance is likely to be greater than any benefits obtained, investigation is not worthwhile.

(b) **Subdivision of the materials usage variance**

Given that one cause of the materials usage variance is known (scrapping), we can split the variance into that part due to discs being scrapped and that part due to other reasons.

96,000 fault-free compact discs were produced.

For every 100 of these, two additional compact discs were scrapped.

∴ The number of CDs scrapped was (96,000/100) × 2 = 1,920

	£	
∴ Part of variance due to discs being scrapped		
= 1,920 × standard cost per compact disc		
= 1,920 × £0.20 =	384	(A)
Total variance	600	(A)
Variance due to other reasons	216	(A)

(c) **Demand for pressing and finishing**

The standard costs used for quotation purposes include fixed overheads apportioned between the pressing and finishing departments on the basis of budgeted labour hours. This results in £22,000 being apportioned to the pressing department and £11,000 to the finishing department. The **pressing department** therefore **bears 2/3 of budgeted fixed overheads**. Use of such an apportionment basis **implies fixed overheads** in a department are **incurred in line with labour hours** worked in the department.

This is not necessarily the case. The pressing department uses a far higher proportion of the budgeted fixed overheads than the finishing department and in fact uses over 93% of the overheads.

This indicates that the **fixed overhead included in the standard costs** is **too low for the pressing department** and **too high for the finishing department.**

Because these standard costs are used as the basis for quoting prices to customers, the **prices quoted** for pressing are **too low** and those for finishing are **too high**.

Your company's prices for pressing are therefore probably lower than your competitors – hence the high demand – but those for finishing are probably higher – hence the low demand.

I suggest that an investigation into the application of activity based costing (ABC) should be carried out. ABC attempts to apportion overheads more realistically using cost drivers (the activities that cause costs to increase).

I trust the information and analysis I have provided proves useful. If you have any further comments please do not hesitate to contact me.

SECTION 2

Task 2.1

> **Tutorial note.** In part (i) you could have worked out the unit selling price and unit variable cost to determine contribution per unit.
>
> The assessor has explained how the capacity ratio should be calculated. Take note and learn it. It may appear unexplained in the exam you attempt.
>
> Remember the importance of showing your workings. If your answer is incorrect you will not be awarded credit for a valid process if the marker is unable to see where your figures have come from.

(a) **Sales (or net profit) margin**

= (net operating profit/turnover) × 100%
= (324,000/6,480,000) × 100% = 5%

(b) **Return on capital employed**

= (net operating profit/net assets) × 100%
= (324,000/1,620,000) × 100% = 20%

(c) **Asset turnover**

= turnover/net assets
= 6,480,000/1,620,000 = 4 times

(d) **Average age of stock in months**

= (closing stock/net purchases) × 12
= (120,000/1,080,000) × 12 = $1\frac{1}{3}$ months

(e) **Average age of creditors in months**

= (creditors/net purchases) × 12
= (180,000/1,080,000) × 12 = 2 months

(f) **Added value per production employee**

= (turnover – cost of bought-in materials and services*)/number of production employees
= £(6,480,000 – 1,080,000 – 108,000)/140 = £37,800

* material X24 and other material and bought-in services

(g) **Wages per production employee**

= £1,296,000/140 = £9,257

(h) **Capacity ratio**

= (actual production/maximum production) × 100%
= (10,800/12,000) × 100% = 90%

(i) **Contribution per Uno**

= (turnover – variable cost of sales)/no. of units sold
= £(6,480,000 – 2,484,000)/10,800 = £370

Task 2.2

> **Tutorial note.** In (a) you didn't need to allocate the costs to the two categories of quality cost, you simply had to calculate a total. You didn't need to mention the opportunity cost arising from lost contribution as this is an implicit cost and the cost of quality in the task data only included explicit costs.
>
> In (b), because the volume would change, the easiest approach is to start from revised unit contribution rather than original profit. (Remember what we said in the text about efficient calculations!)
>
> In (c), the fact that no closing stocks are held means that the cash balance would increase as the stocks do not have to be purchased. The decrease in creditors reduces the cash balance, however, because the purchases have to be paid for in the month received.
>
> Note the two ways to calculate the revised capital employed ((d)). The second is certainly more straightforward. Part (e) should have caused no problems at all!

(a) **Cost of quality**

Cost of quality = total of all costs incurred in preventing faults + costs involved in correcting faults once they have occurred

∴ Cost of quality is calculated as follows.

	£
Inspection cost	69,600
Cost of returns	48,000
Cost of customer support	194,400
Cost of remedial work	120,000
	432,000

(b) **Revised operating profit if supplier's conditions accepted**

	£	£
Revised unit contribution = £(370 − 10) = £360		
Revised volume = 12,000 units		
Revised total contribution = £360 × 12,000 =		4,320,000
Revised fixed costs:		
existing	3,672,000	
less cost of quality saved	(432,000)	
		3,240,000
Revised operating profit		1,080,000

(c) **Increase in cash balance before reducing the loan amount**

	£
Increase in profit (all cash transactions) (£(1,080,000 − 324,000))	756,000
+ decrease in stocks (no longer purchased)	120,000
− decrease in creditors (purchases now have to be paid for)	(180,000)
	696,000

(d)   **Revised capital employed if no stocks or creditors and surplus cash used to reduce loan**

	£'000
Revised shareholders' funds (£(800,000 + 756,000 (increase in profit from (c))	1,556
Revised loan balance (£(820,000 – 696,000 (increase in cash))	124
	1,680

Alternatively	£'000
Net fixed assets	1,600
Cash	80
	1,680

(e)   **Revised return on capital employed**

Revised ROCE   = (revised operating profit/revised capital employed) × 100%
                = (£1,080,000 (from (b))/£1,680,000 (from (d))) × 100%
                = 64.3%

AAT SPECIMEN EXAM PAPER – 2003 STANDARDS

NVQ/SVQ in ACCOUNTING, LEVEL 4

UNIT 9

CONTRIBUTING to the PLANNING and CONTROL of RESOURCES (PCR)

SUGGESTED ANSWERS

These answers have been prepared by BPP Publishing Ltd.

UNIT 9 (PCR) Pilot paper : mapping against Standards

Performance Criteria / Range Statement	Task 1.1	Task 1.2	Task 2.1	Task 2.2
9.1 Prepare forecasts of income/expenditure				
A Identify relevant data for projections	✓	✓	✓	
B Communicate with individuals		✓		✓
C Prepare forecasts, clear format, assumptions etc	✓	✓		
D Review/revise validity of forecasts in light of changes		✓		✓
9.1 Range Statement				
Data	✓	✓	✓	
Forecasts	✓	✓	✓	✓
Projections		✓	✓	
9.2 Prepare draft budget proposals				
A Present clear draft budget proposals	✓			
B Verify consistency, relevant data and assumptions	✓	✓		✓
C Break down budgets into periods	✓	✓		
D Communicate with budget holders		✓		✓
9.2 Range statement				
Types of budget	✓			✓
Data	✓	✓		✓
9.3 Monitor performance against budgets				
A Check and reconcile budget figures		✓	✓	
B Code/allocate to responsibility centres	✓			
C Identify variances/prepare relevant reports			✓	✓
D Discuss significant variances/help managers take action				✓
9.3 Range statement				
Types of budget	✓	✓	✓	
Responsibility centres	✓			
Variances			✓	

SECTION 1

> **Tutorial note.** As usual, clear presentation is vital! When a very, very similar version of these tasks was set under the old version of the standards, the assessor commented that for the material purchases budget, some candidates provided a single row of figures, hidden within these being, presumably, the several stages making up the material purchases budget. Apart from the presentational issues, unless there are no mistakes in the answer, the result is unlikely to be recognised by the assessor and credit will be lost. Always use a logical presentation which reflects the sequence of steps involved in deriving the budget.
>
> Note that the assessor has included one of his favourite features – the need to adjust the labour budget to take account of a rate of efficiency of less than 100%. You must be able to cope with this sort of complication.
>
> Did you notice that shortfalls of material could only be met from a surplus in the immediately preceding period – not any period?

Task 1.1

(a) **Production budget for Deltas**

	Period 1 Units	Period 2 Units	Period 3 Units	Period 4 Units	Period 5 Units
Number required/demand	5,700	5,700	6,840	6,460	6,080
Add closing stock*	855	1,026	969	912	
	6,555	6,726	7,809	7,372	
Less opening stock	1,330	855	1,026	969	
Required production	5,225	5,871	6,783	6,403	

* Number of days per period = 4 weeks × 5 days = 20 days
∴ Closing stock each period = 3/20 × demand for next period

(b) **Materials purchases budget (litres)**

	Period 1	Period 2	Period 3	Period 4
Production (units)	5,225	5,871	6,783	6,403
	Litres	Litres	Litres	Litres
Material required (production units × 6 litres)	31,350	35,226	40,698	38,418
Maximum material available from existing supplier	34,000	34,000	34,000	34,000
Initial (shortage)/excess of material	2,650	(1,226)	(6,698)	(4,418)
Rescheduled purchases	(1,226)	1,226	-	-
Final (shortage)/excess of material	1,424	-	(6,698)	(4,418)
Material purchases from existing supplier (i)	32,576*	34,000	34,000	34,000
Material purchases from outside supplier (ii)			6,698	4,418
Total material purchases	32,576	34,000	40,698	38,418

* 31,350 + 1,226 = 32,576

(c)   **Material purchases budget (£)**

	Period 1 £	Period 2 £	Period 3 £	Period 4 £
Material purchases from existing supplier ((b)(i) × £8)	260,608	272,000	272,000	272,000
Material purchases from outside supplier ((b)(ii) × £12)			80,376	53,016
Total cost of material purchases	260,608	272,000	352,376	325,016

> **Tutorial note.** We have assumed that material from the alternative source is purchased and paid for in the month it is required.

(d)   **Labour hours budget**

	Period 1	Period 2	Period 3	Period 4
Production (units)	5,225	5,871	6,783	6,403
	Hours	Hours	Hours	Hours
Standard hours required (production units × 2 hours)	10,450	11,742	13,566	12,806
Adjust for 95% efficiency (5/95 × standard hours)	550	618	714	674
Total labour hours required	11,000	12,360	14,280	13,480
Basic hours available (78 employees × 4 weeks × 40 hours)	12,480	12,480	12,480	12,480
Overtime hours required	Nil	Nil	1,800	1,000

(e)   **Cost of labour budget**

	Period 1 £	Period 2 £	Period 3 £	Period 4 £
Basic wage (£160 × 78 employees × 4 weeks)	49,920	49,920	49,920	49,920
Overtime payments (overtime hours × £6 per hour)			10,800	6,000
Total cost of labour	49,920	49,920	60,720	55,920

Task 1.2

> **Tutorial note.** The most obvious opportunities for short-term cost savings arise from advancing production to the earlier periods when the material and labour restrictions cause fewer problems. The quickest way to calculate the resulting cost savings is to take an incremental approach. This simply involves calculating the cost difference in one step, rather than calculating the total cost before your proposals, and the total cost after your proposals and then determining the difference. Both approaches should produce the same answer but if you used the latter approach, check through our answer below and hopefully you will agree that it is much quicker.

Memo

To: Nicola Brown, managing director
From: Management accountant
Subject: **Potential cost savings in the manufacture of Deltas**
Date: 7 December 2003

This memo discusses and evaluates potential cost savings in the manufacture of Deltas, in both the short term and longer term.

(a) **A proposal for immediate cost savings**

If some of the production of Deltas is brought forward to periods 1 and 2, this would reduce both the requirement for overtime in periods 3 and 4 and the amount of material purchased from the external supplier.

(b) **Material cost savings**

The potential supply of material from the existing supplier is 34,000 litres, but in period 1 the budgeted purchases are only 32,576 litres. Additional purchases of (34,000 – 32,576) 1,424 litres could therefore be made from the existing supplier at the lower price (instead of from the external supplier).

Saving in material cost = 1,424 litres × difference in price per litre = 1,424 litres × £(12 – 8) = £5,696

> **Tutorial note.** Alternatively the 1,424 litres could be purchased in advance. The extra purchases in period 1 could then be used in period 2 and any resulting surplus in period 2 could then be used in period 3, so reducing the purchases at the higher price.

Labour cost saving

Unused basic labour hours in periods 1 and 2 are as follows.

	Period 1 Hours	*Period 2* Hours
Basic hours available	12,480	12,480
Hours utilised in budget	11,000	12,360
Unused basic labour hours	1,480	120

Labour cost saving = (1,480 + 120) hours × £6 overtime = £9,600

Although material must be purchased at the higher price in periods 1 and 2 as a result, the higher price would have been paid anyway during periods 3 and 4.

However these calculations **ignore the cost of storing the unused material and the Deltas produced in advance, and they assume that neither are perishable**.

(c) (i) **Minimum material requirement each period** = 5,700 Deltas × 6 litres = 34,200 litres

Since the existing supplier is able to supply only 34,000 litres per period, the need to obtain material supplies from the alternative source is a **longer-term problem**.

(ii) **Minimum labour requirement** = 5,700 Deltas × 2 hours = 11,400 hours

Adjustment for efficiency (× 5/95) = 600 hours

∴ Total labour hours required each period = 11,400 + 600 = 12,000 hours

The basic labour hours available each period are 12,480 (78 employees × 4 weeks × 40 hours).

Therefore the need for overtime payments is a **short-term problem** which is not forecast to continue.

(d)   **Potential longer-term cost savings**

   (i)   Seek alternative sources of material supply. A cheaper source than the £12 per litre supply might be found.

   (ii) Negotiate with the existing supplier to see whether ways can be found to alleviate their output constraint.

   (iii) Negotiate with World Products plc to see whether the minimum stock requirement can be reduced. This would require Berry Ltd to adopt rapidly adjustable, flexible working arrangements in order to cope with fluctuations in demand.

SECTION 2

Task 2.1

> **Tutorial note.** You could have used what the assessor calls the incremental approach for (i) to (iii): the difference in cost or revenue between the two budgets ÷ difference in volumes = cost or price per unit. For example, material cost per unit = £(176,000 − 160,000) ÷ (22,000 − 20,000).
>
> In (b), the production fixed costs are those charged to the cost of production.
>
> We have included detailed commentary within (c) as you may have found this part tricky. You may have been unsure about whether to include cost of production and closing stock on your marginal costing profit statement but given that you then had to prepare a flexible budget, simply showing cost of sales is sufficient.

(a)   (i)   **Budgeted selling price per unit**

         Sales volume × selling price per unit = turnover

         ∴ Using original budget data, budgeted selling price per unit = £700,000/20,000 = £35

     (ii) **Budgeted material cost per unit**

         Volume × material cost per unit = total material cost

         ∴ Using original budget data, budgeted material cost per unit = £160,000/20,000 = £8

     (iii) **Budgeted labour cost per unit**

         Volume × labour cost per unit = total labour cost

         ∴ Using original budget data, budgeted labour cost per unit = £300,000/20,000 = £15

(iv) **Budgeted variable (or marginal) cost of general expenses per unit**

The difference between the two total costs must be the variable cost of the difference in output volumes.

			£
Total budget cost of	22,000	units =	114,000
Total budget cost of	20,000	units =	110,000
Variable cost of	2,000	units =	4,000

∴ Variable cost per unit = £4,000/2,000 = £2

(v) **Budgeted fixed cost of general expenses**

	£
Total cost for 20,000 units =	110,000
Variable cost of 20,000 units (from (iv)) = £2 × 20,000	40,000
Fixed cost	70,000

(b) **Actual production fixed costs** = £75,000 (ie those included in the cost of production)

(c) **Actual results for year to 30 November 2003 – marginal costing basis**

	£'000
Turnover	782
Material (23/25 × £225,000)	207
Labour (23/25 × £350,000)	322
Variable general expenses (£(125,000 – 71,000))	54
Cost of sales	583
Contribution	199
Fixed costs:	
Production overhead	75
General expenses	71
	146
Profit	53

Commentary

- Cost of sales figures are shown (ie cost of production minus cost of closing stock) and hence there is no need to show closing stock.

- The cost of sales figures for material and labour are based on volumes sold and so are 23/25 of the costs of production.

- Variable general expenses vary with the units sold and so are included in full (ie not reduced by 23/25).

(d)   **Flexible budget statement for year to 30 November 2003**

	Flexible budget	Actual results	Variances	
Volume (units)	23,000	23,000	-	
	£'000	£'000	£'000	
Turnover (23,000 × £35*)	805	782	23	(A)
Material (23,000 × £8*)	184	207	23	(A)
Labour (23,000 × £15*)	345	322	23	(F)
Variable general expenses (23,000 × £2*)	46	54	8	(A)
Cost of sales	575	583	8	(A)
Contribution	230	199	31	(A)
Fixed costs				
Production overhead	74	75	1	(A)
General expenses	70	71	1	(A)
	144	146	2	(A)
Operating profit	86	53	33	(A)

* These variable costs and revenue per unit were found in part (a).

Task 2.2

Memo

To: Nicola Brown, managing director
From: Management accountant
Date: 14 December 2003
Subject: Budgets and forecasting

This memo covers the issues raised in our recent discussion.

(a)   **Differences between flexible budget and revised budget**

The **revised budget** represents a **plan** which Berry Ltd management were committed to achieving and attempted to achieve. This plan was based on sales and production volumes of 22,000 units.

The **flexible budget** is not a plan or target but rather a **control device**. It represents what costs and revenues should have been given the actual sales volume of 23,000 units (and production volume of 25,000 units). In other words, it is a budget for the actual volume of sales. Comparisons made between budgeted and actual figures therefore produce more meaningful differences (variances) as both budget and actual results are based on the same sales volumes.

Given that the **flexible budget** is based on a **different volume of sales to that used to draw up the revised budget, turnover** has been **changed. Variable or marginal costs**, which are costs that vary in line with changes in activity level (such as labour), have also been **amended**. Production overhead is a **fixed cost** which means that it does not vary with changes in activity level. It is therefore the **same** in both budgets. General expenses include both fixed and variable costs.

BPP
PROFESSIONAL EDUCATION

(b)   **Differences between flexible budget statement actual results and the actual results given in the task data**

The **original actual results** were prepared using **absorption costing**. Each unit of production is allocated a share of the overheads. This means that the overheads are only charged to the profit and loss account when units are sold. If a unit is produced but then held in closing stock, the cost of the unit (and hence the overhead included in that unit) is not charged against profit. Some of the fixed overhead is therefore not charged in the current period but carried forward in closing stock values to be charged against profit when the unit is sold.

On the other hand the **actual results in the flexible budget** statement are prepared on a **marginal costing** basis. Using this approach, fixed costs are assumed to vary with time rather than with volume. They are therefore charged against the profit and loss account in their entirety in the period in which they are incurred.

The **production overhead** incurred during the period is therefore **charged in full** against **marginal costing** profit whereas a **proportion** of it is **carried forward** in closing stock values to be charged against profit in a subsequent period when **absorption costing** is used.

It is this difference in treatment which causes the different results in the two statements.

(c)   **Forecasting techniques that Berry Ltd could currently use**

(i)   **Sales personnel** could be asked to provide forecasts . The sales team should have up-to-date first hand knowledge of current sales patterns and will have a 'feel for the market'.

(ii)   **Survey/market research methods** could be used.

(iii)   **Secondary sources of data** for the industry and/or for other industries could be investigated, although the data will have been collected for another purpose and so its limitations will not be known.

(iv)   **Customers** could be consulted about their anticipated requirements. This can be particularly useful if there are just a small number of customers.

(v)   Demand could be considered in terms of the **product life cycle**. This gives some indication of likely sales volumes given the stage of the product's sales history.

(vi)   By following what is happening to a **leading indicator**, a variable which anticipates the trend of another variable, information about likely demand for Zetas may be provided.

(d)   **Forecasting techniques Berry Ltd is currently unable to use**

Because the Zeta has only been in production for twelve months, there is insufficient past sales data available upon which to base forecasts. Techniques such as linear regression analysis and time series analysis, which involve extrapolating a trend based on past data, could therefore provide misleading results.

Lecturers' Resource Pack Activities

BPP
PROFESSIONAL EDUCATION

Note to Students

The answers to these activities and assessments are provided to your lecturers, who will distribute them in class.

If you are not on a classroom based course, a copy of the answers can be obtained from BPP Customer Services on 020 8740 2211 or e-mail publishing@bpp.com.

Note to Lecturers

The answers to these activities and assessments are included in the Lecturers' Resource Pack, provided free to colleges.

If your college has not received the Lecturers' Resource Pack, please contact BPP Customer Services on 020 8740 2211 or e-mail publishing@bpp.com.

BPP PROFESSIONAL EDUCATION

	Page	Done

LECTURERS' RESOURCE PACK ACTIVITIES

Chapters 1 and 2 Introduction/Behaviour, recording and reporting of costs

Chapter 3 Collecting data

Data collection is also covered in activity 6.

Chapter 4 Analysing data

Index numbers are also covered in activity 17.

Chapter 5 Forecasting

Forecasting is also covered in activity 13.

Chapters 6 and 7 Variances

Chapters 8 and 9 Budgets

Chapters 10 and 11 Budgetary control and further aspects of budgeting

Spreadsheets are also covered in activity 14.

		Page	Done

BPP
PROFESSIONAL EDUCATION

Chapters 1 and 2 Introduction/Behaviour, recording and reporting of costs

1 Durban Products Ltd

Durban Products Ltd makes and sells two products, the A and the B. The following information is available.

	Period 1 £	Period 2 £
Production (units)		
A	2,500	1,900
B	1,750	1,250
Sales (units)		
A	2,300	1,700
B	1,600	1,250

Financial data	A £	B £
Unit selling price	90	75
Unit variable costs		
Direct materials	15	12
Direct labour (£6/hr)	18	12
Variable production overheads	12	8

Fixed costs for the company in total were £110,000 in period 1 and £82,000 in period 2. Fixed costs are recovered on direct labour hours.

Tasks

(a) (i)   Calculate the profit for period 1 using marginal costing principles.
      (ii) Calculate the profit for period 2 using marginal costing principles.

(b) (i)   Calculate the profit reported for period 1 using absorption costing principles.
      (ii) Calculate the profit reported for period 2 using absorption costing principles.

Chapter 3 Collecting data

2 Retail store (35 mins)

A large retail store wishes to determine customers' attitude to the services it provides by a survey, with the aid of a questionnaire, to a representative sample of customers who hold credit accounts with the store.

Task

Discuss the advantages and disadvantages of the survey being undertaken by:
(a)   personal interview within the store;
(b)   questionnaires sent out by post;
(c)   telephone interviews to the customer's residence.

3 Collecting information (35 mins)

The following four situations describe how information was collected for four surveys.

Task

In each situation identify the sampling method used and discuss how each survey could have been better undertaken.

(a)   To determine public opinion towards the UK replacing the pound as currency with the euro, a national newspaper printed a voting form in one edition, requesting readers to complete and send it back to the newspaper's office.

(b)   To determine the reaction to an increase in its fares, a bus company placed interviewers in a city's Central Bus Station and instructed each to canvas the opinions of 50 travellers.

(c)   To determine the potential popularity of a new brand of coffee, every customer entering a café was given a free drink and their impression recorded.

(d)   To determine the reaction to new car parking regulations at a college, 10% of the lecturers were interviewed and their comments recorded.

Data collection is also covered in activity 6.

Chapter 4 Analysing data

4 Applications of indices

(a)   XY Ltd pays its workforce £16 per hour based on an index of labour costs of 220 in 20X1. The index now stands at 460.

Task

Calculate the hourly rate the workforce should receive based on the increase in the index.

(b)   What are the disadvantages of using an average earnings index to assess the reasonableness of a wage rate being paid?

> Index numbers are also covered in activity 17.

Chapter 5 Forecasting

5 Tanger Partnership

You are employed by Tanger Partnership, a firm of consultants specialising in assisting charities and similar organisations to work more efficiently. It is the end of the calendar year and you are currently working on an assignment with Nirmal Ghosh, one of the partners, to review the operations of Mount Simeon House (a stately home in the West of England). The main source of income for Mount Simeon House is from admitting visitors to the house and gardens.

As a first step in the investigation, Nirmal has asked you to prepare a forecast of the income from visitor admissions for the next year. You have therefore collected the following information to assist you in this task.

Mount Simeon House is open throughout the year and ticket prices are normally increased at the beginning of the second quarter of the year.

Jenny Smallcorn, the administrator at Mount Simeon House, has prepared the following table of admissions.

		Admissions 000's
Year 1		54.0
Year 2		61.0
Year 3		74.0
Year 4		81.0
Year 5	Quarter 1	16.5
	Quarter 2	25.3
	Quarter 3	28.6
	Quarter 4 (estimate)	17.6

Jenny's observation over the last five years has been that the seasonal variation in admissions fits the following pattern.

	Quarter 1	Quarter 2	Quarter 3	Quarter 4
Seasonal variations as a percentage of trend	−25%	+15%	+30%	−20%

Ticket prices at present (quarter 4 of year 5) are £5 per person. It is proposed to increase ticket prices by 10% at the beginning of quarter 2 in year 6.

Tasks

(a) Prepare a three-year moving average of admissions over years 1 to 5, to give moving annual averages for years 2, 3 and 4.

(b) Forecast the admissions in year 6.

(c) Convert your year 6 admissions into quarterly figures and forecast the revenue for each quarter.

6 Alan Dunn (35 mins)

The managing director of Edge Ltd, Alan Dunn, has only recently been appointed. He is keen to develop the company and has already agreed to two new products being developed. These will be launched in eighteen months' time. While talking to you about the budget he mentions that the quality of sales forecasting will need to improve if the company is to grow rapidly. Currently, the budgeted sales figure is found by initially adding 5% to the previous year's sales volume and then revising the figure following discussions with the marketing director. He believes this approach is increasingly inadequate and now requires a more systematic approach.

A few days later Alan Dunn sends you a memo. In that memo, he identifies three possible strategies for increasing sales volume. They are:

- more sales to existing customers;
- the development of new markets;
- the development of new products.

He asks for your help in forecasting likely sales volume from these sources.

Task

Write a brief memo to Alan Dunn. Your memo should:

(a)   identify FOUR ways of forecasting future sales volume;

(b)   show how each of your four ways of forecasting can be applied to ONE of the sales strategies identified by Alan Dunn and justify your choice;

(c)   give TWO reasons why forecasting methods might not prove to be accurate.

Forecasting is also covered in activity 13.

Chapters 6 and 7 Variances

7 XYZ Ltd

XYZ Ltd is planning to make 120,000 units per period of a new product. The following standards have been set.

		Per unit
Direct material A		1.2 kgs at £11 per kg
Direct material B		4.7 kgs at £6 per kg
Direct labour:	Operation 1	42 minutes
	Operation 2	37 minutes
	Operation 3	11 minutes

Overheads are absorbed at the rate of £30 per labour hour. All direct operatives are paid at the rate of £8 per hour.

Actual results for the period were as follows.

Production 126,000 units
Direct labour cost £1.7m for 215,000 clock hours
Material A cost £1.65m for 150,000 kgs
Material B cost £3.6m for 590,000 kgs

Tasks
(a) Calculate the standard cost for one unit.
(b) Calculate the labour rate and efficiency variances.
(c) Calculate the material price and usage variances.

8 Component RYX

A manufacturing company has provided you with the following date which relates to component RYX, for the period which has just ended.

	Budget	Actual
Number of labour hours	8,400	7,980
Production units	1,200	1,100
Overhead cost (all fixed)	£22,260	£25,536

Overheads are absorbed at a rate per standard labour hour.

Tasks

(a) Calculate the fixed production overhead cost variance and the following subsidiary variances.

    (i)   Expenditure
    (ii)   Efficiency
    (iii) Capacity

(b) Provide a summary statement of these four variances.

9 Omega (70 mins)

You are employed as part of the management accounting team in a large industrial company which operates a four-weekly system of management reporting. Your division makes a single product, the Omega, and, because of the nature of the production process, there is no work in progress at any time.

The group management accountant has completed the calculation of the material and labour standard costing variances for the current period to 1 April but has not had the time to complete any other variances. Details of the variances already calculated are reproduced in the working papers below, along with other standard costing data.

Standard costing and budget data – four weeks ended 1 April			
	Quantity	Unit price	Cost per unit
Material (kgs)	7	£25.00	£175
Labour (hours)	40	£7.50	£300
Fixed overheads (hours)	40	£12.50	£500
			£975
	Units	Standard unit cost	Standard cost of production
Budgeted production for the four weeks	4,100	£975	£3,997,500

Working papers

Actual production and expenditure for the four weeks ended 1 April

Units produced	3,850
Cost of 30,000 kgs of materials consumed	£795,000
Cost of 159,000 labour hours worked	£1,225,000
Expenditure on fixed overheads	£2,195,000

Material and labour variances

Material price variance	£45,000 (A)
Material usage variance	£76,250 (A)
Labour rate variance	£32,500 (A)
Labour efficiency variance	£37,500 (A)

Tasks

You have been requested to do the following.

(a)   Calculate the following variances.

    (i)   The fixed overhead expenditure variance
    (ii)   The fixed overhead volume variance
    (iii)   The fixed overhead capacity variance
    (iv)   The fixed overhead efficiency variance

(b)   Prepare a report for presentation to the production director reconciling the standard cost of production for the period with the actual cost of production.

(c)   The production director, who has only recently been appointed, is unfamiliar with fixed overhead variances. Because of this, the group management accountant has asked you to prepare a *brief* memo to the production director.

Your memo should do the following.

(i)   Outline the similarities and differences between fixed overhead variances and other cost variances such as the material and labour variances.

(ii)   Explain what is meant by the fixed overhead expenditure, volume, capacity and efficiency variances, and show, by way of examples, how these can be of help to the production director in the planning and controlling of the division.

10 Splitting variances (20 mins)

(a)   The standard cost per kg of material L is £15.60, based on its expected average price over the next twelve months. A time series analysis of the cost of material L over the last four years has been performed. This indicates that the following seasonal variations in price can be expected.

Quarter 1	+£1.70
Quarter 2	+£3.50
Quarter 3	−£0.20
Quarter 4	−£2.90

Task

Given the fact that 5,000 kg of material L were used in quarter 3, at a total cost of £79,200, calculate the material price variance and analyse it into the part due to the seasonality of the price and the part due to other influences.

(b)   When W Ltd set labour rate standards, the relevant wage rate index was 300 but was expected to rise to 309 by the time the standard was in use. A standard rate per hour of £14.42 was therefore set to take account of this.

By the time the standard was in use, employees had been awarded a 4% pay increase.

In the period in question, £201,250 had been paid for 12,500 hours of work.

Task

Analyse the total labour rate variance for the period into the part due to the actual pay rise and the part due to other factors.

11 Holden plc (100 mins)   6/01

(a)   Holden plc manufactures several chemicals at its main factory. One chemical, X40, has proven so popular that Holden has recently opened a new factory in another town to meet the increased demand.

The X40 is produced in tins and its standard cost is as follows.

Standard cost card for X40			
Expense	Units	Unit cost £	Cost per tin £
Material	7 litres	8.00	56.00
Labour	4 hours	5.00	20.00
Fixed overheads	4 hours	6.00	24.00
Standard cost per tin			100.00

The new factory's actual results for the first four weeks of operations are shown below.

Operating results of new factory
4 weeks ended 1 June 20X1

Production (tins)		16,000
		£
Material	113,600 litres	920,160
Labour	68,640 hours	336,336
Fixed overheads		410,000
Cost of production		1,666,496

Other information relating to the new factory

- The X40 is the only product made.
- Budgeted fixed overheads total £5,040,000 per year.
- Fixed overheads are charged to production on the basis of labour hours.
- There are 50 operating weeks in the year.
- Production is budgeted to take place evenly throughout the 50 operating weeks.

You are employed in the central accounts department of Holden. One of your responsibilities is to prepare and monitor standard costing variances at the new factory.

Tasks

(i)   Calculate the following information relating to the new factory.

    (1)   Actual price of material per litre
    (2)   Actual labour rate per hour
    (3)   Actual labour hours per tin
    (4)   Budgeted production of tins for the year
    (5)   Budgeted production of tins for the four weeks ended 1 June 20X1
    (6)   Budgeted fixed overheads for the four weeks ended 1 June 20X1

    (ii)   Calculate the following variances for X40 production at the new factory.

          (1)   Material price variance
          (2)   Material usage variance
          (3)   Labour rate variance
          (4)   Labour efficiency variance
          (5)   Fixed overhead expenditure variance
          (6)   Fixed overhead volume variance
          (7)   Fixed overhead capacity variance
          (8)   Fixed overhead efficiency variance

    (iii)   Prepare a statement reconciling the standard cost of actual production to the actual cost of actual production for the four weeks ended 1 June 20X1.

(b)   At a meeting called to discuss the performance of the new factory, the general manager gives you the following information.

- The material and labour standard costs were based on the standards at the main factory.

- The cost of material per litre at the new factory will always be 1.25% more than at the main factory due to additional transport costs.

- Production workers are currently taking 10% longer to make a tin of X40 than they will when fully trained.

- The standard fixed overhead was based on estimated costs at the new factory alone.

- The machinery at the new factory is more modern than the machinery at the main factory.

Tasks

Write a memo to the general manager. Your memo should do the following.

    (i)   Identify a revised standard price of material per litre for the new factory.

    (ii)   Estimate the labour hours per tin of X40 after the production workers are fully trained.

    (iii)   Subdivide the labour efficiency variance into two parts.

          (1)   That part due to the production workers not being fully trained
          (2)   That part due to other reasons

    (iv)   Suggest TWO possible explanations for the labour efficiency variance due to other reasons.

Chapters 8 and 9 Budgets

12 Bertram plc (55 mins)

Bertram plc manufactures Product B using three different raw materials. The product details are as follows.

Selling price per unit is £250.

Material A	3 kgs	material price £3.50 per kg
Material B	2 kgs	material price £5.00 per kg
Material C	4 kgs	material price £4.50 per kg
Direct labour	8 hours	labour rate £8.00 per hour

The company is considering its budgets for next year and has made the following estimates of sales demand for Product B for July to October 20X9.

July	August	September	October
400 units	300 units	600 units	450 units

It is company policy to hold stocks of finished goods at the end of each month equal to 50% of the following month's sales demand, and it is expected that the stock at the start of the budget period will meet this policy.

At the end of the production process the products are tested: it is usual for 10% of those tested to be faulty. It is not possible to rectify these faulty units.

Raw material stocks are expected to be as follows on 1 July 20X9.

Material A	1,000 kgs
Material B	400 kgs
Material C	600 kgs

Stocks are to be increased by 20% in July 20X9, and then remain at their new level for the foreseeable future.

Labour is paid at an hourly rate based on attendance. In addition to the unit direct labour hours shown above, 20% of **attendance time** is spent on tasks which support production activity.

Tasks

(a) Prepare the following budgets for the quarter from July 20X9 to September 20X9 inclusive.

    (i)   Sales budget in quantity and value

    (ii)   Production budget in units

    (iii)   Raw material usage budget in kgs

    (iv)   Raw material purchases budget in kgs and value

    (v)   Labour requirements budget in hours and value

(b) Explain the term 'principal' budget factor' and why its identification is an important part of the budget preparation process.

13 Wilmslow Ltd (85 mins)   6/99

(a) Wilmslow Ltd makes two products, the Alpha and the Beta. Both products use the same material and labour but in different amounts. The company divides its year into four quarters, each of 12 weeks. Each week consists of five days and each day comprises seven hours.

You are employed as the management accountant to Wilmslow Ltd and you originally prepared a budget for quarter 3, the 12 weeks to 17 September 20X5. The basic data for that budget is reproduced below.

Original budgetary data: quarter 3 – 12 weeks to 17 September 20X5		
Product	Alpha	Beta
Estimated demand	1,800 units	2,100 units
Material per unit	8 kilograms	12 kilograms
Labour per unit	3 hours	6 hours

Since the budget was prepared, three developments have taken place.

- The company has begun to use linear regression and seasonal variations to forecast sales demand. Because of this, the estimated demand for quarter 3 has been revised to 2,000 Alphas and 2,400 Betas.

- As a result of the revised sales forecasting, you have developed more precise estimates of sales and closing stock levels.

  The sales volume of both the Alpha and Beta in quarter 4 (the 12 weeks ending 10 December 20X5) will be 20% more than in the revised budget for quarter 3 as a result of seasonal variations.

  The closing stock of finished Alphas at the end of quarter 3 should represent five days sales for quarter 4.

  The closing stock of finished Betas at the end of quarter 3 should represent ten days sales for quarter 4.

  Production in quarter 4 of both Alpha and Beta is planned to be 20% more than in the revised budget for quarter 3. The closing stock of materials at the end of quarter 3 should be sufficient for **20 days production** in quarter 4.

- New equipment has been installed. The workforce is not familiar with the equipment. Because of this, for quarter 3, they will only be working at 80% of the efficiency assumed in the original budgetary data.

Other data from your original budget which has not changed is reproduced below.

- 50 production employees work a 35 hour week and are each paid £210 per week.
- Overtime is paid for at £9 per hour.
- The cost of material is £10 per kilogram.
- Opening stocks at the beginning of quarter 3 are as follows.

Finished Alphas	500 units
Finished Betas	600 units
Material	12,000 kilograms

- There will not be any work in progress at any time.

Task

The production director of Wilmslow Ltd wants to schedule production for quarter 3 (the 12 weeks ending 17 September 20X5) and asks you to use the revised information to prepare the following.

(i)   The revised production budget for Alphas and Betas
(ii)   The material purchases budget in kilograms
(iii)   A statement showing the cost of material purchases
(iv)   The labour budget in hours
(v)   A statement showing cost of labour

(b)   Margaret Brown is the financial director of Wilmslow Ltd. She is not convinced that the use of linear regression, even when adjusted for seasonal variations, is the best way of forecasting sales volumes for Wilmslow Ltd.

The quality of sales forecasting is an agenda item for the next meeting of the Board of Directors and she asks for your advice.

Task

Write a **brief** memo to Margaret Brown. Your memo should do the following.

(i)   Identify TWO limitations of the use of linear regression as a forecasting technique
(ii)   Suggest TWO other ways of sales forecasting

14 Wimpole Ltd (70 mins)   **12/01**

(a)   You are employed as the assistant management accountant at Wimpole Ltd where one of your duties is the preparation of budgets every four weeks. You report to Ann Jones, the senior management accountant.

Wimpole Ltd makes several products, two of which are the Alpha and the Beta. Budget data for the two products for the four weeks ending 1 February 20X2 is shown below.

Production and sales data	Alpha	Beta
Budgeted sales volume	2,000 units	3,000 units
Opening finished stocks	300 units	297 units
Closing finished stocks	500 units	595 units
Material per unit	10.00 metres	12.00 metres
Labour per unit	1.150 hours	1.380 hours

Note. Production takes place evenly over the four weeks.

Material data

Cost of material per metre	£17.00
Opening material stock	8,750 metres
Closing material stock	15,530 metres
Wastage rate of material	3% of material issued to production

Labour data

46 employees work a guaranteed 35-hour week. The guaranteed wage for each employee is £210.00 per week. Any overtime necessary is paid at a rate of £8.00 per hour.

Since collecting the original budget data, you have made a number of discoveries.

- The maximum amount of material available from the supplier for the four weeks ending 1 February 20X2 will be 61,580 metres.

- The wastage is material left over after lengths have been cut to make Alphas and Betas but before any labour cost has been incurred. The wastage has no scrap value.

- Betas are sold to a large furniture retailer under a long-term contract that cannot be broken. The budgeted sales volume of 3,000 Betas for the four weeks ending 1 February 20X2 must be provided under the contract.

- It is not possible to reduce the level of any of the opening or closing stocks.

Task

Prepare the following information for Ann Jones for the four weeks ended 1 February 20X2.

(i)   The production budget in units for Alpha and Beta assuming there was no shortage of materials

(ii)   A statement taking into account the shortage of material and showing the following.

    (1)   Metres of material available for production before any wastage

    (2)   Metres of material required for Beta production (including any wastage)

    (3)   Metres of material available for Alpha production

    (4)   Number of Alphas to be produced

    (5)   Labour hours to be worked

    (6)   Cost of labour budget

(iii)   The revised budgeted sales volumes for Alpha and Beta

(b)   Ann Jones is preparing the budgeted operating statement for a third product, the Delta, using a computer spreadsheet. Although she has entered selling price and cost data, these are uncertain and may be changed before the budget is agreed.

She asks you to complete the spreadsheet for the Delta using formulae that will allow a revised budgeted operating profit to be calculated automatically if price, cost and volume data change.

Task

Using the template shown below, enter formulae for the following in cells B6 to B10 of the spreadsheet.

(i)   Turnover
(ii)   Total variable cost
(iii)   Contribution
(iv)   Fixed costs
(v)   Operating profit

	A	B
1	Selling price per unit £	140
2	Variable cost per unit	£70
3	Fixed costs per four-week period	£40,000
4	Volume per period	1,000
5	Four weeks ending	1 February 20X2
6	Turnover	
7	Total variable cost	
8	Contribution	
9	Fixed costs	
10	Operating profit	

Chapters 10 and 11 Budgetary control and further aspects of budgeting

15 Cost behaviour and cost reporting (25 mins)

The information below relates to budget and actual production and sales of Extension Ltd during 20X7. It has been prepared using absorption costing.

	Budget	Actual
Volume	7,500	9,000
	£	£
Turnover	615,000	702,000
Variable costs	277,500	360,000
Fixed overheads	329,000	301,000
Operating profit	8,500	41,000

Additional information – actual costs

	Closing stocks	Cost of sales	Cost of production
Units	1,500	9,000	10,500
	£	£	£
Variable costs	60,000	360,000	420,000
Fixed overheads	66,000	301,000	235,000

Task

Prepare a flexible budget statement for 20X7 using marginal costing principles.

16 George Ltd (25 mins)

You work as the assistant to the management accountant for George Limited, a medium-sized manufacturing company.

The company's marketing assistant has approached you for help in understanding the company's planning and control systems. She has been talking with the distribution manager who has tried to explain how flexible budgets are used to control distribution costs within George Limited. She makes the following comment:

'I thought that budgets were supposed to provide a target to plan our activities and against which to monitor our costs. How can we possibly plan and control our costs if we simply change the budgets when activity levels alter?'

Task

Prepare a memorandum to the marketing assistant which explains the following.

(a)   Why fixed budgets are useful for planning but flexible budgets may be more useful to enable management to exercise effective control over distribution costs.

(b)   Two possible activity indicators which could be used as a basis for flexing the budget for distribution costs.

(c)   How a flexible budget cost allowance is calculated and used for control purposes. Use your own examples and figures where appropriate to illustrate your explanations.

17 Vecstar Ltd (70 mins)

(a)   Vecstar Ltd produces and sells a single product, the Alpha. The company uses an accounting software package which calculates variances by comparing the fixed budget for the year against actual expenditure. For accounting purposes, the company divides its year into 13, four-weekly periods. The report for the four weeks ended 29 May 20X8 is reproduced below.

Vecstar Ltd Performance Report for four weeks ended 29 May 20X8				
		Actual	*Budget*	*Variance*
Units produced:		60,000	48,000	12,000 F
		£	£	£
Variable costs:	Material	18,546	12,480	6,066 A
	Labour	7,200	5,760	1,440 A
Semi-variable costs:	Power	900	1,060	160 F
	Maintenance	1,600	1,680	80 F
Fixed costs:	Supervision	3,400	3,440	40 F
	Rent and insurance	2,050	1,820	230 A
	Depreciation	4,000	4,000	
Total		37,696	30,240	7,456 A
Key: A = adverse; F = favourable				

You are employed as an accounting technician by Green and Co, the auditors to Vecstar Ltd. On a recent visit to Vecstar, you suggested to James Close, the company's managing director, that the variances calculated by the software package are likely to be misleading and that a system of flexible budgeting would produce more meaningful management information.

James tells you that the following assumptions were made when preparing the budget.

•   The four-weekly cost of power was estimated at £100 and the additional cost of power per Alpha produced was estimated at 2p.

•   The fixed cost of maintenance was estimated at £1,200 per four weeks and 1p per Alpha produced.

•   The annual fixed overhead absorption rate is 20p per Alpha. This was derived by adding the budgeted fixed costs to the fixed element of the budgeted semi-variable costs and dividing by the normal annual production.

Tasks

(i)   Prepare a flexible budget statement for the four weeks to 29 May 20X8.

(ii)   Estimate the normal ANNUAL production of Alphas used to determine the fixed overhead absorption rate.

(b)   When you present James Close with the revised budget, he writes to tell you that he cannot understand why some budgeted costs have changed but others have remained the same as in the original fixed budget. In addition, he is concerned that the budgeted cost data becomes increasingly inaccurate, the closer the accounting period is to the year end. By way of example, he gives you the following general indices of production costs.

- Index when budget prepared   160.00
- Index at commencement of accounting year   162.40
- Average index for four weeks ended 26 June 20X8 (estimated)   165.12

Finally James is disappointed that the revised report no longer highlights the variations in the units produced between original budget and actual. For May 20X8, production increased by 25% from 48,000 to 60,000 units but this has been largely ignored.

Tasks

Prepare a letter to James Close. Your letter should:

(i)   **briefly** explain why in the flexible budget, some budgeted costs have remained the same while others have altered;

(ii)   estimate the **total cost** of producing 62,000 Alphas in the four weeks to 26 June using your answer in task (a) and the indices given above;

(iii)   give ONE possible reason why the index used may not be an appropriate one for Vecstar Ltd;

(iv)   suggest ONE way of expressing in a meaningful form for management the variation between original budgeted units and actual units produced.

18 Colour plc (105 mins)   12/98

(a)   Colour plc has two subsidiaries, Red Ltd and Green Ltd. Red Ltd makes only one product, a part only used by Green Ltd. Because Green is the only customer and there is no market price for the part, the part is sold to Green at cost.

Last year, Red prepared two provisional budgets because Green was not certain how many parts it would buy from Red in the current year. These two budgets are reproduced below.

Red Ltd provisional budgets - 12 months to 30 November 20X8		
Volume (units)	18,000	20,000
	£	£
Material	180,000	200,000
Labour	308,000	340,000
Power and maintenance	33,000	35,000
Rent, insurance and depreciation	98,000	98,000
Total cost	619,000	673,000

Shortly afterwards, Green told Red that it needed 20,000 parts over the year to 30 November 20X8. Red's budget for the year was then based on that level of production.

During the financial year, Green Ltd only bought 19,500 parts. Red's performance statement for the year to 30 November 20X8 is reproduced below.

Red Ltd performance statement - year to 30 November 20X8			
	Budget	Actual	Variance
Units (units)	20,000	19,500	
	£	£	£
Material	20,000	197,000	3,000 F
Labour	340,000	331,000	9,000 F
Power and maintenance	35,000	35,000	
Rent, insurance and depreciation	98,000	97,500	500 F
Total cost	37,696	30,240	12,500 F

Key: A = adverse; F = favourable

Tasks

(i)   Using the data in the provisional budgets, calculate the fixed and variable cost elements within each of the expenditure headings.

(ii)   Using the data in the performance statement and your solution to part (i), prepare a revised performance statement using flexible budgeting. Your statement should show both the revised budget and the variances.

(b)   Colour plc is about to introduce performance-related payments for senior managers in the three subsidiaries. The purpose is to motivate senior managers to improve performance.

For Red Ltd, the additional payments will be based on two factors.

•   Achieving or exceeding annual budgeted volumes of production set by the Board of Directors of Colour plc at the beginning of the year

•   Keeping unit costs below budget

Tony Brown, the managing director of Red Ltd, is about to call a meeting of his senior managers to discuss the implications of the proposals. He is not certain that performance-related pay will automatically lead to improved performance in the subsidiaries. Even if it does, he is not certain that performance-related pay will help *his* subsidiary improve performance.

Task

Write a memo to Tony Brown. Your memo should identify the following.

(i)   THREE general conditions necessary for performance-related pay to lead to improved performance

(ii)   TWO reasons why the particular performance scheme might not be appropriate for the senior management of Red Ltd

(iii)   ONE example where it would be possible for the managers of Red Ltd to misuse the proposed system by achieving performance-related pay without extra effort on their part

---

Spreadsheets are also covered in activity 14.

Chapters 12 and 13 Measurement of performance

19 Ratio analysis

You work as assistant management accountant for Addison Ltd, which has the following abridged accounts for the past two years.

Year ended 30 November

	20X8 £	20X7 £
Sales	1,380,000	1,250,000
Direct materials	440,000	375,000
Direct wages	372,000	312,500
Production overheads	201,000	187,500
Selling and distribution overheads	101,000	91,000
Administration overheads	90,000	80,000
	1,204,000	1,046,000
Net profit	176,000	204,000

The following additional data are available.

	20X8	20X7
Production staff	40	39
Selling and distribution staff	8	8
Administration staff	5	5
Capital employed	£2.2 m	£2 m

An analysis of costs gives the following breakdown between variable and fixed elements.

	20X8		20X7	
	Variable %	Fixed %	Variable %	Fixed %
Direct material	100	–	100	–
Direct wages	90	10	90	10
Production overhead	80	20	85	15
Selling and distribution overhead	70	30	65	35
Administration overhead	10	90	10	90

Tasks

(a) Calculate six ratios to compare the performance and profitability of the company in the two years.

(b) Comment on your calculations in (a).

20 Homely Ltd (50 mins)

Stately Hotels plc is considering an offer to buy a small privately owned chain of hotels, Homely Limited. In order to carry out an initial appraisal you have been provided with an abbreviated set of their accounts for 20X8.

Homely Limited - Profit and loss account for the year ended 31 December 20X8 (extract)

	£'000
Turnover	820
Operating costs	754
Operating profit	66
Interest	4
Profit before tax	62
Taxation	8
Profit after tax	44
Dividends	22
Retained profits	22

Homely Limited - Balance sheet as at 31 December 20X8 (extract)

	£'000
Fixed assets at net book value	230
Net current assets	70
Total assets	300
Long-term loans	50
	250
Shareholders' funds	250
Number of employees (full-time equivalents)	20
Numbers of rooms, each available for 365 nights	18
Number of room nights achieved in 20X8	5,900

Stately Hotels plc uses a number of key accounting ratios to monitor the performance of the group of hotels and of individual hotels in the chain. An extract from the target ratios for 20X8 is as follows.

Stately Hotels plc - Target ratios for 20X8 (extract)

- Return on capital employed, based on profit before interest and tax   26%

- Operating profit percentage   13%

- Asset turnover   2 times

- Working capital period $= \dfrac{\text{working capital}}{\text{operating costs}} \times 365$ 20 days

- % room occupancy $= \dfrac{\text{no of room nights let}}{\text{no of room nights available}} \times 100\%$ 85%

- Turnover per employee (full-time equivalent)   £30,000

Tasks

(a)   Calculate the six target ratios above based on Homely Limited's accounts and present them in a table which enables easy comparison with Stately Hotel's target ratios for 20X8.

(b)   Prepare a memorandum for the management accountant of Stately Hotels plc, giving your initial assessment of Homely Limited based on a comparison of these ratios with Stately Hotel's target ratios. Your memorandum should provide the following information for *each* of the six ratios.

  (i)   Comments on the performance of Homely Limited and suggestions about the management action which might be necessary to correct any apparent adverse performance

  (ii)   A discussion of any limitations in the use of the ratio for this performance comparison

21 'What if' analysis

Fenton Products Ltd has reported the following results for 20X1.

Turnover	£2,750,000
Operating profit	£276,000
Net assets	£4,100,000

Targets for the year were ROCE of 7.5% and asset turnover of 9%.

Tasks

(a)   If the company's balance sheet remains unchanged, calculate the operating profit that Fenton Products Ltd would need to earn to achieve the target ROCE.

(b)   If the company's balance sheet remains unchanged, calculate the revenue it would have earned if it had achieved the target asset turnover.

22 Diamond Ltd (50 mins)

(a)   Diamond Ltd is a retail jeweller operating 30 branches in similar localities. Common accounting policies operate throughout all branches, including a policy of using straight-line depreciation for fixed assets.

All branches use rented premises. These are accounted for under 'other costs' in the operating statement. Fixed assets are predominantly fixtures and fittings.

Each branch is individually responsible for ordering stock, the authorising of payments to creditors and the control of debtors. Cash management, however, is managed by Diamond's head office with any cash received by a branch being paid into a head office bank account twice daily.

You are employed in the head office of Diamond Ltd as a financial analyst monitoring the performance of all 30 branches. This involves calculating performance indicators for each branch and comparing each branch's performance with company standards. Financial data relating to Branch 24 is reproduced below.

Diamond Ltd - Branch 24 – Year ended 31 December 20X7					
Operating Statement					
	£'000	£'000		£'000	£'000
Turnover		720.0	Fixed assets		
Opening stock	80.0		Cost		225.0
Purchases	340.0		Accumulated		
Closing stock	(60.0)		depreciation		(90.0)
		360.0	Net book value		135.0
Gross profit		360.0	Working capital		
Wages and salaries	220.6		Stocks	60.0	
Depreciation	45.0		Debtors	96.0	
Other costs	36.8		Creditors	(51.0)	
		302.4			105.0
Operating profit		57.6	Net assets		240.0

Tasks

Prepare a statement showing the following performance indicators for Branch 24.

(i)   The return on capital employed

(ii)   The gross profit margin as a percentage

(iii) The asset turnover

(iv)   The sales (or net profit) margin as a percentage

(v)   The average age of debtors in months

(vi)   The average age of creditors in months

(vii) The average age of the closing stock in months

(b)   The financial director of Diamond Ltd is Charles Walden. He is concerned that Branch 24 is not performing as well as the other branches. All other branches are able to meet or exceed most of the performance standards laid down by the company.

Charles is particularly concerned that branches should achieve the standards for return on capital employed and the asset turnover. He also feels that managers should try to achieve the standards laid down for working capital management. The relevant standards are:

- return on capital employed   40%
- asset turnover   4 times per annum
- average age of debtors   0.5 months
- average age of creditors   3 months
- average age of closing stock   1 month

Charles Walden has recently attended a course on financial modelling and scenario planning. Charles explains that scenario planning shows the likely performance of a business under different assumed circumstances. It requires an understanding of the relationship between the different elements within the financial statements and how these change as the circumstances being modelled change. As an example, he tells you that if the volume of branch turnover was to increase then the cost of sales would also increase but that all other expenses would remain the same as they are fixed costs.

He believes scenario planning would be particularly helpful to the manager of Branch 24, Angela Newton. Charles has previously discussed the performance of the branch with Angela and emphasised the importance of improving the asset turnover and maintaining control of working capital. However, Angela raised the following objections:

- Turning over assets is not important, making profit should be the main objective;
- Branch 24 has been in existence for two years less than all the other branches.

Task

Charles Walden asks you to write a memo to Angela Newton. Your memo should do the following.

(i)   Show the return on capital employed that Branch 24 would have achieved had it been able to achieve the company's asset turnover during the year to 31 December 20X7 while maintaining prices and the existing capital employed.

(ii) Show the return on capital employed and the asset turnover for the year if Branch 24 had been able to achieve the company's standards for the average age of debtors, the average age of creditors and the average age of finished stock while maintaining its existing sales volume.

(iii) **Using the data in task (a) and your solution to task (b)(i),** address the issues raised by Angela Newton.

23 Denton Management Consultants (60 mins)   12/99

(a)   You are employed as a financial analyst with Denton Management Consultants and report to James Alexander, a local partner. Denton Management Consultants has recently been awarded the contract to implement accrual accounting in the St Nicolas Police Force and will shortly have to make a presentation to the Head of the Police Force. The presentation is concerned with showing how performance indicators are developed in 'for profit' organisations and how these can be adapted to help 'not for profit' organisations.

James Alexander has asked for your help in preparing a draft of the presentation that Denton Management Consultants will make to the Head of the Police Force. He suggests that a useful framework would be the balanced scorecard and examples of how this is used by private sector organisations.

The balanced scorecard views performance measurement in a 'for profit' organisation from four perspectives.

The financial perspective

This is concerned with satisfying shareholders and measures used include the return on capital employed and the sales margin.

The customer perspective

This attempts to measure how customers view the organisation and how they measure customer satisfaction. Examples include the speed of delivery and customer loyalty.

The internal perspective

This measures the quality of the organisation's output in terms of technical excellence and consumer needs. Examples include unit cost and total quality measurement.

The innovation and learning perspective

This emphasises the need for continual improvement of existing products and the ability to develop new products to meet customers' changing needs. In a 'for profit' organisation, this might be measured by the percentage of turnover attributable to new products.

To help you demonstrate how performance indicators are developed in 'for profit' organisations, he gives you the following financial data relating to a manufacturing client of Denton Management Consultants.

Profit and loss account 12 months ended 30 November 20X1		
	£'000	£'000
Turnover		240.0
Material	18.0	
Labour	26.0	
Production overheads	9.0	
Cost of production	53.0	
Opening finished stock	12.0	
Closing finished stock	(13.0)	
Cost of sales		52.0
Gross profit		188.0
Research and development	15.9	
Training	5.2	
Administration	118.9	
		140.0
Net profit		48.0

Extract from Balance sheet at 30 November 20X1				
	Opening balance £'000	Additions £'000	Deletions £'000	Closing balance £'000
Fixed assets				
Cost	200.0	40.0	10.0	230.0
Depreciation	80.0	8.0	8.0	80.0
Net book value				150.0
Net current assets				
Stock of finished goods			13.0	
Debtors			40.0	
Cash			6.0	
Creditors			(9.0)	
				50.0
Net assets				200.0

PROFESSIONAL EDUCATION

Task

James Alexander asks you to calculate the following performance indicators and, for each indicator, to identify ONE balanced scorecard perspective being measured.

(i) The return on capital employed

(ii) The sales margin (or net profit) percentage

(iii) The asset turnover

(iv) Research and development as a percentage of production

(v) Training as a percentage of labour costs

(vi) Average age of finished stock in months

(b) On receiving your calculations, James Alexander tells you that he has recently received details of the current performance measures used by the St Nicolas Police Force. Four indicators are used.

- The percentage of cash expenditure to allocated funds for the year
- The average police-hours spent per crime investigated
- The average police-hours spent per crime solved
- The clear-up rate (defined as number of crimes solved ÷ number of crimes investigated)

He also provides you with the data for the current year used in developing the current indicators, as follows.

Funds allocated for the year	£3,000,000
Cash expenditure during the year	£2,910,000
Number of reported crimes in the last year	8,000 crimes
Number of crimes investigated in the year	5,000 crimes
Number of crimes solved in the year	2,000 crimes
Number of police-hours spent on investigating and solving crimes	40,000 hours
Number of police hours spent on crime prevention	500 hours

Tasks

James Alexander asks you to prepare short notes for him. Your notes should do the following.

(i) Calculate the four indicators currently used by the St Nicolas Police Force.

(ii) Identify ONE limitation in the calculation of the clear-up rate.

(iii) Briefly suggest the following.

(1) ONE reason why the percentage of cash expenditure to allocated funds may be an inadequate measure of the financial perspective

(2) ONE reason why the clear-up rate might be an inadequate measure of the customer perspective other than because of the limitation identified in part (b)(ii)

(3) ONE reason why the hours spent per crime investigated might be an inadequate measure of the internal perspective

(4) ONE measure which might focus on the innovation and learning perspective

BPP
PROFESSIONAL EDUCATION

Chapter 14 and 15 Cost management

24 ABC

You are the assistant management accountant for a company which assembles and programs electronic equipment to suit individual customers' requirements.

Two jobs are currently in progress, order JM3 and order AM5.

Estimated direct costs

	Order JM3 £	Order AM5 £
Purchased equipment	9,750	8,490
Purchased software	3,500	3,510
Assembly labour	2,300	1,600
Additional programming	1,850	2,900
	17,400	16,500

Additional information

	Order JM3	Order AM5
Distance to customer (miles)	3	100
Sales visits needed	2	8
Extra design time (hours)	10	100
Sourcing required (items)	3	16
Testing (hours)	5	80
Customer training (hours)	10	150
Special packaging	None	£200
Delivery cost	£50	£800
Overtime needed	None	for all programming

Activity	Annual cost	Cost driver	Cost driver units pa
Sales	£50,000	Miles travelled	20,000
Design	£40,000	Design hours worked	2,000
Sourcing	£30,000	Items bought in	1,000
Testing	£30,000	Testing hours	2,000
Training	£30,000	Training hours	2,000

Overtime will add 50% to estimated programming cost.

Task

Calculate the estimated costs of each order.

25 Quality control system

Your company is considering the introduction of a quality control system. Write a short informal report to management which explains the costs and benefits of operating such a system.

BPP
PROFESSIONAL EDUCATION

Lecturers'
Assessments

UNIT 8 LECTURERS' ASSESSMENT

NVQ/SVQ4 in ACCOUNTING, LEVEL 4

UNIT 8

CONTRIBUTING to the MANAGEMENT of PERFORMANCE and the ENHANCEMENT of VALUE (PEV)

This examination paper is in TWO sections.

You have to show competence in BOTH sections.

You should therefore attempt and aim to complete EVERY task in BOTH sections.

You should spend about 100 minutes on Section 1 and 80 minutes on Section 2.

Include all essential workings within your answers, where appropriate.

SECTION 1

You should spend about 100 minutes on this section.

DATA

NGJ Ltd is a furniture manufacturer. It makes three products, the Basic, the Grand and the Super. You are the management accountant reporting to the product line manager for the Basic. Reproduced below is NGJ's unit standard material and labour cost data and budgeted production for the year to 31 May 20X0 together with details of the budgeted and actual factory fixed overheads for the year.

Unit standard material and labour cost data by product for the year to 31 May 20X0			
Product	Basic	Grand	Super
Material at £12 per metre	6 metres	8 metres	10 metres
Labour at £5.00 per hour	6 hours	1 hour	1 hour
Budgeted production	10,000 units	70,000 units	70,000 units

Total budgeted and actual factory fixed overheads for the year to 31 May 20X0		
	Budgeted £	Actual £
Rent and rates	100,000	100,000
Depreciation	200,000	200,000
Light, heat and power	60,000	70,000
Indirect labour	240,000	260,000
Total factory fixed overheads	600,000	630,000

Apportionment policy

As all products are made in the same factory, budgeted and actual total factory fixed overheads are apportioned to each product on the basis of budgeted total labour hours per product.

During the year 11,500 Basics were made. The actual amount of material used, labour hours worked and costs incurred were as follows.

Actual material and labour cost of producing 11,500 Basics for the year to 31 May 20X0		
	Units	Total cost
Material	69,230 metres	£872,298
Labour	70,150 hours	£343,735

Task 1.1

(a)   Calculate the following information.

(i)   The total budgeted labour hours of production for NGJ Ltd
(ii)   The standard factory fixed overhead rate per labour hour
(iii)   The budgeted and actual factory fixed overhead apportioned to Basic production
(iv)   The actual cost of material per metre and the actual labour hourly rate for Basic production
(v)   The total standard absorption cost of actual Basic production
(vi)   The actual absorption cost of actual Basic production

(b)   Calculate the following variances for Basic production.

(i)   The material price variance
(ii)   The material usage variance
(iii)   The labour rate variance
(iv)   The labour efficiency variance
(v)   The fixed overhead expenditure variance
(vi)   The fixed overhead volume variance
(vii)   The fixed overhead capacity variance
(viii) The fixed overhead efficiency variance

(c)   Prepare a statement reconciling the actual absorption cost of actual Basic production with the standard absorption cost of actual Basic production.

DATA

The product line manager for the Basic is of the opinion that the standard costs and variances do not fairly reflect the effort put in by staff. The manager made the following points.

(a)   Because of a shortage of materials for the Basic, the purchasing manager had entered into a contract for the year with a single supplier in order to guarantee supplies.

(b)   The actual price paid for the material per metre was 10% less than the market price throughout the year.

(c)   The Basic is a hand-made product made in a small, separate part of the factory and uses none of the expensive machines shared by the Grand and the Super.

(d)   Grand and Super production uses the same highly mechanised manufacturing facilities and only one of those products can be made at any one time. A change in production from one product to another involves halting production in order to set up the necessary tools and production line.

In response to a request from the Basic product line manager, a colleague has re-analysed the budgeted and actual factory fixed overheads by function. The revised analysis is reproduced below.

PROFESSIONAL EDUCATION

Functional analysis of factory fixed overheads for the year to 31 May 20X0		
	Budgeted	Actual
	£	£
Setting up of tools and production lines	202,000	228,000
Depreciation attributable to production	170,000	170,000
Stores	60,000	59,000
Maintenance	40,000	48,000
Light, heat and power directly attributable to production	48,000	45,000
Rent and rates directly attributable to production	80,000	80,000
Total factory fixed overheads	600,000	630,000

Task 1.2

Write a memo to the Basic product line manager. Your memo should do the following.

(a)   Identify the market price of the material used in the Basic.

(b)   Subdivide the material price variance into that part due to the contracted price being different from the market price and that due to other reasons.

(c)   Identify ONE benefit to NGJ Ltd, which is not reflected in the variances, arising from the purchasing manager's decision to enter into a contract for the supply of materials.

(d)   Briefly explain what is meant by activity-based costing.

(e)   Refer to the task data, where appropriate, to briefly discuss whether or not activity-based costing would have reduced the budgeted and actual fixed overheads of Basic production.

SECTION 2

You should spend about 80 minutes on this section.

DATA

LandAir and SeaAir are two small airlines operating flights to Waltonville. LandAir operates from an airport based at a town on the same island as Waltonville but SeaAir operates from an airport based on another island. In both cases, the flight to Waltonville is 150 air-miles. Each airline owns a single aircraft, an 80-seat commuter jet, and both airlines operate flights for 360 days per year.

You are employed as the management accountant at SeaAir and report to Carol Jones, SeaAir's chief executive. Recently, both airlines agreed to share each other's financial and operating data as a way of improving efficiency. The data for the year to 31 May 20X0 for both airlines is reproduced below. The performance indicators for LandAir are reproduced below.

Operating statement year ended 31 May 20X0	LandAir $'000	SeaAir $'000
Revenue	51,840	29,700
Fuel and aircraft maintenance	29,160	14,580
Take-off and landing fees at Waltonville	4,320	2,160
Aircraft parking at Waltonville	720	2,880
Depreciation of aircraft	500	400
Salaries of flight crew	380	380
Home airport costs	15,464	8,112
Net profit	1,296	1,188

Extract from balance sheet at 31 May 20X0

	LandAir $'000	SeaAir $'000
Fixed assets		
Aircraft	10,000	10,000
Accumulated depreciation	2,500	4,000
Net book value	7,500	6,000
Net current assets	3,300	5,880
	10,800	11,800

Other operating data		
Number of seats on aircraft	80	80
Return flights per day	12	6
Return fare	$200	$275
Air-miles per return flight	300	300

Performance indicators	*LandAir*
Return on capital employed	12.00%
Asset turnover per year	4.80
Sales (or net profit) margin	2.50%
Actual number of return flights per year	4,320
Actual number of return passengers per year	259,200
Average seat occupancy[1]	75.00%
Actual number of passenger-miles[2]	77,760,000
Cost per passenger mile	$0.65

Notes

1 Actual number of return passengers ÷ maximum possible number of return passengers from existing flights

2 Actual number of passengers carried × number of miles flown

Task 2.1

Carol Jones asks you to prepare the following performance indicators for SeaAir.

(a) Return on capital employed
(b) Asset turnover
(c) Sales (or net profit) margin
(d) Actual number of return flights per year
(e) Actual number of return passengers per year
(f) Average seat occupancy
(g) Actual number of passenger-miles
(h) Cost per passenger mile

Data

Carol Jones is concerned that the overall performance of SeaAir is below that of LandAir, despite both airlines operating to the same destination and over a similar distance. She finds it all the more difficult to understand as LandAir has to compete with road and rail transport. Carol Jones has recently attended a seminar on maintaining competitive advantage and is eager to apply the concepts to SeaAir. She explains that there are two ways to gain a competitive advantage.

- By being the lowest cost business
- By having a unique aspect to the product or service, allowing a higher price to be charged

This involves managers attempting to eliminate costs which do not enhance value, that is, costs for which customers are not prepared to pay either in the form of a higher price or increased demand.

She makes the following proposals for next year, the year ending 31 May 20X1.

- The number of return flights is increased to 9 per day.
- The estimated average seat occupancy will change to 55%.
- The price of a return fare will remain the same.

As a result of the proposals, there will be some changes in operating costs.

- Fuel and aircraft maintenance, and take-off and landing fees at Waltonville airport, will increase in proportion with the increase in flights.

- Aircraft parking at Waltonville will be halved.

- Aircraft depreciation will increase to $600,000 for the forthcoming year.

- Additional flight crew will cost an extra $58,000.

- There will be no other changes in costs.

Task 2.2

Carol Jones is interested in forecasting the performance of SeaAir for next year, the year to 31 May 20X1. Write a memo to Carol Jones. In your memo you should do the following.

(a) Calculate the forecast number of passengers next year for SeaAir.

(b) Calculate SeaAir's forecast net profit for next year.

(c) Show SeaAir's forecast return on capital employed for next year assuming no change in its net assets other than any additional depreciation.

(d) Identify ONE competitive advantage SeaAir has over LandAir.

(e) Identify ONE expense in SeaAir's operating statement which does not add value.

UNIT 9 LECTURERS' ASSESSMENT

NVQ/SVQ4 in ACCOUNTING, LEVEL 4

UNIT 9

CONTRIBUTING to the PLANNING and the CONTROL of RESOURCES (PCR)

This examination paper is in TWO sections.

You have to show competence in BOTH sections.

You should therefore attempt and aim to complete EVERY task in BOTH sections.

You should spend about 90 minutes on Section 1 and 90 minutes on Section 2.

Include all essential workings within your answers, where appropriate.

SECTION 1

You should spend about 90 minutes on this section.

DATA

You are employed as a management accountant in the head office of Alton Products plc. One of your tasks involves helping to prepare quarterly budgets for the divisional companies of Alton Products. Each quarter consists of 12 five-day weeks for both production and sales purposes.

One division, Safety Care, makes two chemicals, Delta and Omega. These are sold in standard boxes. Both products use the same material and labour but in different proportions. You have been provided with the following information relating to the two products for quarter 3, the 12 weeks ending 29 September 20X0.

	Delta	Omega
• Budgeted sales		
Quarter 3: 12 weeks to 29 September 2000	3,000 boxes	2,400 boxes
Quarter 4: 12 weeks to 22 December 2000	3,300 boxes	2,640 boxes
• Finished stocks for quarter 3		
Opening stock	630 boxes	502 boxes
Closing stock (days sales in quarter 4)	6 days	8 days
• Production inputs		
Material per box	12 kgs	15 kgs
Labour per box	3 hours	6 hours

• Material stocks and costs for quarter 3	
Opening stock (kgs)	13,560
Closing stock (kgs)	21,340
Budgeted purchase price per kg	£7.00

- Labour costs for quarter 3
  52 production employees work a 36-hour week and are each paid £180 per week.
  Any overtime is payable at £7.50 per hour
- Faulty production
  10% of production is found to be faulty on completion. Faulty production has to be scrapped and has no scrap value.

Task 1.1

The production director of Safety Care asks you to prepare the following for quarter 3.

(a) The number of boxes of Delta and Omega planned to be in closing stock
(b) The number of labour hours available for production before incurring overtime
(c) The production budget for Deltas and Omegas required to meet the budgeted sales
(d) The material purchases budget in kilograms and cost
(e) The labour budget in hours and cost

DATA

Garden Care is another division of Alton Products plc. The sales director of Garden Care, Hazel Brown, has noticed a distinct trend and pattern of seasonal variations for one of Garden Care's products since the product was introduced in the third quarter of 20W7. She provides you with the following sales volumes for the product.

Units sold by quarter				
Year	Quarter 1	Quarter 2	Quarter 3	Quarter 4
20W7			142	142
20W8	150	150	142	158
20W9	150	166	142	174
20X0	150	182*		
				*estimate

Task 1.2

Hazel Brown asks you to do the following.

(a)   Calculate the Centred Four-Point Moving Average Trend figures.

(b)   Calculate the seasonal variations on the assumption that the seasonal variations are additive.

(c)   Use your results in a) and b) to forecast the sales volume for quarter 2 of year 20X0.

(d)   Suggest TWO reasons why there might be a difference between the forecast figure calculated in c) and the result given in the data.

SECTION 2

You should spend about 90 minutes on this section.

DATA

Visiguard Ltd is another division of Alton Products plc. It makes a single product, the Raider. Just over a year ago, the chief executive of Alton Products, Mike Green, was concerned to find that Visiguard was budgeting to make only £20,000 profit in the year to 31 May 20X0. As a result, he imposed his own budget on the division. His revised budget made the following assumptions.

- Increased sales volume of the Raider
- Increased selling prices
- Suppliers' agreement to reduce the cost of the material used in the Raider by 10%

The only other changes to the original budget arose solely as a result of the increased volume in the revised budget.

The original budget and the revised budget imposed by Mike Green are reproduced below, together with the actual results for the year to 31 May 20X0.

Visiguard Limited: Budgeted and actual operating statements for one year ended 31 May 20X0			
	Original budget	*Revised budget*	*Actual results*
Sales and production volume	10,000	11,000	11,600
	£	£	£
Turnover	1,400,000	1,760,000	1,844,400
Variable materials	400,000	396,000	440,800
Production and administrative labour	580,000	630,000	677,600
Light, heat and power	160,000	164,000	136,400
Fixed overheads	240,000	240,000	259,600
Budgeted profit	20,000	330,000	330,000

Task 2.1

Using the information provided in the two budgets, calculate the following.

(a) The unit selling price of the Raider in the revised budget
(b) The material cost per Raider in the revised budget
(c) The variable cost of production and administrative labour per Raider
(d) The fixed cost of production and administrative labour
(e) The variable cost of light, heat and power per Raider
(f) The fixed cost of light, heat and power

DATA

On receiving the actual results for the year, Mike Green states that they prove that his revised budget motivated managers to produce better results.

Task 2.2

Write a memo to Mike Green. Your memo should do the following.

(a)   Use the information calculated in task 2.1 to prepare a flexible budget statement for Visiguard including any variances.

(b)   Identify TWO situations where an imposed budget might be preferable to one prepared with the participation of managers.

(c)   Briefly discuss whether or not his requirement that material costs be reduced would have motivated the managers of Visiguard.

(d)   Identify TWO ways in which profit could have increased without additional effort by the managers of Visiguard.

See overleaf for information on other
BPP products and how to order

To BPP Professional Education, Aldine Place, London W12 8AW
Tel: 020 8740 2211. Fax: 020 8740 1184
E-mail: Publishing@bpp.com Web:www.bpp.com

Mr/Mrs/Ms (Full name)
Daytime delivery address

Postcode
E-mail

Daytime Tel

TOTAL FOR PRODUCTS £

POSTAGE & PACKING

Texts/Kits	First	Each extra	
UK	£3.00	£3.00	£
Europe*	£6.00	£4.00	£
Rest of world	£20.00	£10.00	£
Passcards			
UK	£2.00	£1.00	£
Europe*	£3.00	£2.00	£
Rest of world	£8.00	£8.00	£
Tapes			
UK	£2.00	£1.00	£
Europe*	£3.00	£2.00	£
Rest of world	£8.00	£8.00	£

TOTAL FOR POSTAGE & PACKING £
(Max £12 Texts/Kits/Passcards - deliveries in UK)

Grand Total (Cheques to *BPP Professional Education*)
I enclose a cheque for (incl. Postage) £
Or charge to Access/Visa/Switch
Card Number

Expiry date   Start Date

Issue Number (Switch Only)

Signature

	5/03 Texts	5/03 Kits	Special offer	8/03 Passcards	Tapes
FOUNDATION (£14.95 except as indicated)				Foundation	
Units 1 & 2 Receipts and Payments	☐	☐			
Unit 3 Ledger Balances and Initial Trial Balance			Foundation Sage Bookeeping and Excel Spreadsheets CD-ROM free if ordering all Foundation Text and Kits, including Units 21 and 22/23	£6.95 ☐	£10.00 ☐
Unit 4 Supplying Information for Mgmt Control	☐				
Unit 21 Working with Computers (£9.95) (6/03)	☐				
Unit 22/23 Healthy Workplace/Personal Effectiveness (£9.95)	☐				
Sage and Excel for Foundation (CD-ROM £9.95)	☐		☐		
INTERMEDIATE (£9.95 except as indicated)					
Unit 5 Financial Records and Accounts	☐	☐		£5.95 ☐	£10.00 ☐
Unit 6/7 Costs and Reports (Combined Text £14.95)	☐				
Unit 6 Costs and Revenues		☐		£5.95 ☐	£10.00 ☐
Unit 7 Reports and Returns		☐		£5.95 ☐	
TECHNICIAN (£9.95 except as indicated)					
Unit 8/9 Managing Performance and Controlling Resources	☐	☐	Spreadsheets for Technicians CD-ROM free if take Unit 8/9 Text and Kit	£5.95 ☐	£10.00 ☐
Spreadsheets for Technician (CD-ROM)					
Unit 10 Core Managing Systems and People (£14.95)	☐				
			☐		
Unit 11 Option Financial Statements (A/c Practice)	☐	☐		£5.95 ☐	£10.00 ☐
Unit 12 Option Financial Statements (Central Govnmt)	☐	☐		£5.95 ☐	
Unit 15 Option Cash Management and Credit Control	☐	☐		£5.95 ☐	
Unit 17 Option Implementing Audit Procedures	☐	☐		£5.95 ☐	
Unit 18 Option Business Tax (FA03)(8/03 Text & Kit)	☐	☐		£5.95 ☐	
Unit 19 Option Personal Tax (FA 03)(8/03 Text & Kit)	☐	☐		£5.95 ☐	
TECHNICIAN 2002 (£9.95)					
Unit 18 Option Business Tax FA02 (8/02 Text & Kit)	☐	☐			
Unit 19 Option Personal Tax FA02 (8/02 Text & Kit)	☐	☐			
SUBTOTAL	£	£	£	£	£

We aim to deliver to all UK addresses inside 5 working days; a signature will be required. Orders to all EU addresses should be delivered within 6 working days. All other orders to overseas addresses should be delivered within 8 working days. * Europe includes the Republic of Ireland and the Channel Islands.

See overleaf for information on other
BPP products and how to order

AAT Order

To BPP Professional Education, Aldine Place, London W12 8AW

Tel: 020 8740 2211. Fax: 020 8740 1184

E-mail: Publishing@bpp.com Web:www.bpp.com

Mr/Mrs/Ms (Full name)

Daytime delivery address

Postcode

Daytime Tel   E-mail

OTHER MATERIAL FOR AAT STUDENTS	8/03 Texts	3/03 Text
FOUNDATION (£5.95)		
Basic Mathematics	☐	
INTERMEDIATE (£5.95)		
Basic Bookkeeping (for students exempt from Foundation)	☐	
FOR ALL STUDENTS (£5.95)		
Building Your Portfolio (old standards)	☐	
Building Your Portfolio (new standards)	☐	☐

£ ☐   £ ☐

TOTAL FOR PRODUCTS			£ ☐

POSTAGE & PACKING

Texts/Kits	First	Each extra	
UK	£3.00	£3.00	£ ☐
Europe*	£6.00	£4.00	£ ☐
Rest of world	£20.00	£10.00	£ ☐
Passcards			
UK	£2.00	£1.00	£ ☐
Europe*	£3.00	£2.00	£ ☐
Rest of world	£8.00	£8.00	£ ☐
Tapes			
UK	£2.00	£1.00	£ ☐
Europe*	£3.00	£2.00	£ ☐
Rest of world	£8.00	£8.00	£ ☐

TOTAL FOR POSTAGE & PACKING	£ ☐

(Max £12 Texts/Kits/Passcards - deliveries in UK)

Grand Total (Cheques to *BPP Professional Education*)

I enclose a cheque for (incl. Postage) **£** ☐

Or charge to Access/Visa/Switch

Card Number ☐☐☐☐☐☐☐☐☐☐☐☐☐

Expiry date _____ Start Date _____

Issue Number (Switch Only) _____

Signature _____

We aim to deliver to all UK addresses inside 5 working days; a signature will be required. Orders to all EU addresses should be delivered within 6 working days. All other orders to overseas addresses should be delivered within 8 working days. * Europe includes the Republic of Ireland and the Channel Islands.

Review Form & Free Prize Draw – Unit 8 and 9 Managing Performance and Controlling Resources (5/03)

All original review forms from the entire BPP range, completed with genuine comments, will be entered into one of two draws on 31 January 2004 and 31 July 2004. The names on the first four forms picked out on each occasion will be sent a cheque for £50.

Name: _____   Address: _____

_____

_____

How have you used this Assessment Kit?
(Tick one box only)

☐ Home study (book only)

☐ On a course: college _____

☐ With 'correspondence' package

☐ Other _____

Why did you decide to purchase this Assessment Kit? *(Tick one box only)*

☐ Have used BPP Texts in the past

☐ Recommendation by friend/colleague

☐ Recommendation by a lecturer at college

☐ Saw advertising

☐ Other _____

During the past six months do you recall seeing/receiving any of the following?
(Tick as many boxes as are relevant)

☐ Our advertisement in *Accounting Technician* magazine

☐ Our advertisement in *Pass*

☐ Our brochure with a letter through the post

Which (if any) aspects of our advertising do you find useful?
(Tick as many boxes as are relevant)

☐ Prices and publication dates of new editions

☐ Information on Assessment Kit content

☐ Facility to order books off-the-page

☐ None of the above

Have you used the companion Interactive Text for this subject?   ☐ Yes   ☐ No

Your ratings, comments and suggestions would be appreciated on the following areas

	Very useful	Useful	Not useful
Introduction	☐	☐	☐
Practice Activities	☐	☐	☐
Full skills based assessments	☐	☐	☐
Full exam based assessments	☐	☐	☐
Sample simulation	☐	☐	☐
Specimen exam	☐	☐	☐
Lecturers Resource Section	☐	☐	☐

	Excellent	Good	Adequate	Poor
Overall opinion of this Kit	☐	☐	☐	☐

Do you intend to continue using BPP Interactive Texts/Assessment Kits?   ☐ Yes   ☐ No

Please note any further comments and suggestions/errors on the reverse of this page.

The BPP author of this edition can be e-mailed at: alisonmchugh@bpp.com

Please return this form to: Janice Ross, BPP Professional Education, FREEPOST, London, W12 8BR

Review Form & Free Prize Draw (continued)

Please note any further comments and suggestions/errors below

Free Prize Draw Rules

1   Closing date for 31 January 2004 draw is 31 December 2003. Closing date for 31 July 2004 draw is 30 June 2004.

2   Restricted to entries with UK and Eire addresses only. BPP employees, their families and business associates are excluded.

3   No purchase necessary. Entry forms are available upon request from BPP Professional Education. No more than one entry per title, per person. Draw restricted to persons aged 16 and over.

4   Winners will be notified by post and receive their cheques not later than 6 weeks after the relevant draw date.

5   The decision of the promoter in all matters is final and binding. No correspondence will be entered into.